# English Phonetics and Phonology
## A practical course

**Fourth edition**

# English Phonetics and Phonology
## A practical course

**Fourth edition**

PETER ROACH

*Emeritus Professor of Phonetics*
*University of Reading*

CAMBRIDGE
UNIVERSITY PRESS

CAMBRIDGE UNIVERSITY PRESS
Cambridge, New York, Melbourne, Madrid, Cape Town, Singapore,
São Paulo, Delhi, Dubai, Tokyo, Mexico City

Cambridge University Press
The Edinburgh Building, Cambridge CB2 8RU, UK

www.cambridge.org
Information on this title: www.cambridge.org/9780521717403



First published 1983
Fourth edition 2009
3rd printing 2010

Printed in the United Kingdom at the University Press, Cambridge

*A catalogue record for this publication is available from the British Library*

*Library of Congress Cataloging in Publication data*
Roach, Peter (Peter John)
English phonetics and phonology : a practical course / Peter Roach. – 4th ed.
p. cm.
Includes bibliographical references and index.
ISBN 978-0-521-71740-3 (pbk.) – ISBN 978-0-521-88882-0
1. English language – Phonetics. 2. English language – Phonology. 3. English language – Study and teaching – Foreign speakers. I. Title.
PE1133.R55 2009
421′.5–dc22 2008052020

ISBN 978-0-521-71740-3 Paperback with Audio CDs (2)
ISBN 978-0-521-88882-0 Hardback with Audio CDs (2)

# Contents

# Preface

In previous editions I have used the Preface as a place to thank all the people who have helped me with the book. My debt to them, which in some cases dates back more than twenty-five years, remains, and I have put copies of the Prefaces to the first three editions on the new website of the book so that those acknowledgements are not lost and forgotten. In this new edition, I would like firstly to thank Professor Nobuo Yuzawa of the Takasaki City University of Economics for his wise suggestions and his meticulous and expert scrutiny of the text, which have been invaluable to me. Any errors that remain are entirely my fault.

At Cambridge University Press, I would like to thank Jane Walsh, Jeanette Alfoldi, Liz Driscoll, Anna Linthe, Clive Rumble and Brendan Wightman.

As in all previous editions, I want to thank my wife Helen for all her help and support.

# List of symbols

1 *Symbols for phonemes*

| | |
|---|---|
| ɪ as in 'pit' pɪt | iː as in 'key' kiː |
| e as in 'pet' pet | ɑː as in 'car' kɑː |
| æ as in 'pat' pæt | ɔː as in 'core' kɔː |
| ʌ as in 'putt' pʌt | uː as in 'coo' kuː |
| ɒ as in 'pot' pɒt | ɜː as in 'cur' kɜː |
| ʊ as in 'put' pʊt | |
| ə as in 'about', upper' əbaʊt, ʌpə | |
| eɪ as in 'bay' beɪ | əʊ as in 'go' gəʊ |
| aɪ as in 'buy' baɪ | aʊ as in 'cow' kaʊ |
| ɔɪ as in 'boy' bɔɪ | |
| ɪə as in 'peer' pɪə | |
| eə as in 'pear' peə | |
| ʊə as in 'poor' pʊə | |
| p as in 'pea' piː | b as in 'bee' biː |
| t as in 'toe' təʊ | d as in 'doe' dəʊ |
| k as in 'cap' kæp | g as in 'gap' gæp |
| f as in 'fat' fæt | v as in 'vat' væt |
| θ as in 'thing' θɪŋ | ð as in 'this' ðɪs |
| s as in 'sip' sɪp | z as in 'zip' zɪp |
| ʃ as in 'ship' ʃɪp | ʒ as in 'measure' meʒə |
| h as in 'hat' hæt | |
| m as in 'map' mæp | l as in 'led' led |
| n as in 'nap' næp | r as in 'red' red |
| ŋ as in 'hang' hæŋ | j as in 'yet' jet |
| | w as in 'wet' wet |
| tʃ as in 'chin' tʃɪn | dʒ as in 'gin' dʒɪn |

2 *Non-phonemic symbols*

i as in ‘react’, ‘happy’ riækt, hæpi

u as in ‘to each’ tu iːtʃ

ʔ (glottal stop)

ʰ aspiration, as in ‘pin’ pʰɪn

ˌ syllabic consonant, as in ‘button’ bʌtn̩

˘ shortened vowel, as in ‘miss’ mɪ̆s

. syllable division, as in ‘differ’ dɪf.ə

3 *Word stress*

ˈ primary stress, as in ‘open’ ˈəʊpən

ˌ secondary stress, as in ‘half time’ ˌhaːf ˈtaɪm

4 *Intonation*

| tone-unit boundary

‖ pause

| Tones: | | |
|---|---|---|
| | ↘ | fall |
| | ↗ | rise |
| | ∨ | fall–rise |
| | ∧ | rise–fall |
| | _ | level |

ˈ stressed syllable in head, high pitch, as in ˈplease ↘<u>do</u>

ˌ stressed syllable in head, low pitch, as in ˌplease ↘<u>do</u>

· stressed syllable in the tail, as in ↘<u>my</u> ·turn

↑ extra pitch height, as in ↑↘<u>my</u> ·turn

# THE INTERNATIONAL PHONETIC ALPHABET (revised to 2005)

CONSONANTS (PULMONIC)



| | Bilabial | Labiodental | Dental | Alveolar | Postalveolar | Retroflex | Palatal | Velar | Uvular | Pharyngeal | Glottal |
|---|---|---|---|---|---|---|---|---|---|---|---|
| Plosive | p b | | | t d | | ʈ ɖ | c ɟ | k ɡ | q ɢ | | ʔ |
| Nasal | m | ɱ | | n | | ɳ | ɲ | ŋ | ɴ | | |
| Trill | ʙ | | | r | | | | | ʀ | | |
| Tap or Flap | | ⱱ | | ɾ | | ɽ | | | | | |
| Fricative | ɸ β | f v | θ ð | s z | ʃ ʒ | ʂ ʐ | ç ʝ | x ɣ | χ ʁ | ħ ʕ | h ɦ |
| Lateral fricative | | | | ɬ ɮ | | | | | | | |
| Approximant | | ʋ | | ɹ | | ɻ | j | ɰ | | | |
| Lateral approximant | | | | l | | ɭ | ʎ | ʟ | | | |

Where symbols appear in pairs, the one to the right represents a voiced consonant. Shaded areas denote articulations judged impossible.

CONSONANTS (NON-PULMONIC)

| Clicks | | Voiced implosives | | Ejectives | |
|---|---|---|---|---|---|
| ʘ | Bilabial | ɓ | Bilabial | ʼ | Examples: |
| ǀ | Dental | ɗ | Dental/alveolar | pʼ | Bilabial |
| ǃ | (Post)alveolar | ʄ | Palatal | tʼ | Dental/alveolar |
| ǂ | Palatoalveolar | ɠ | Velar | kʼ | Velar |
| ǁ | Alveolar lateral | ʛ | Uvular | sʼ | Alveolar fricative |

VOWELS

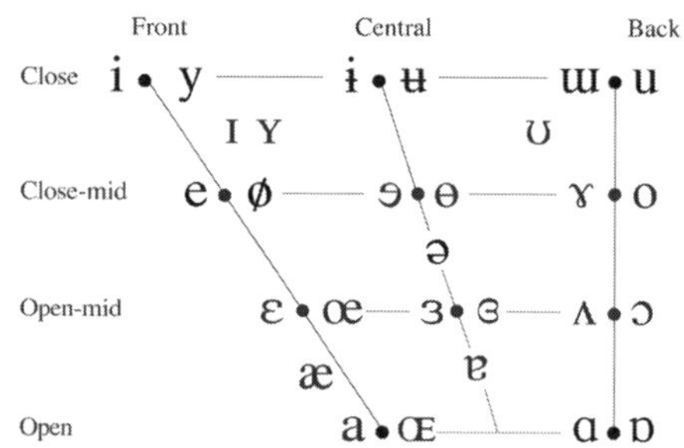


Where symbols appear in pairs, the one to the right represents a rounded vowel.

OTHER SYMBOLS

- ʍ Voiceless labial-velar fricative
- w Voiced labial-velar approximant
- ɥ Voiced labial-palatal approximant
- ʜ Voiceless epiglottal fricative
- ʢ Voiced epiglottal fricative
- ʡ Epiglottal plosive
- ɕ ʑ Alveolo-palatal fricatives
- ɺ Voiced alveolar lateral flap
- ɧ Simultaneous ʃ and x

Affricates and double articulations can be represented by two symbols joined by a tie bar if necessary. k͡p t͡s

SUPRASEGMENTALS

- ˈ Primary stress
- ˌ Secondary stress ˌfoʊnəˈtɪʃən
- ː Long eː
- ˑ Half-long eˑ
- ˘ Extra-short ĕ
- | Minor (foot) group
- ‖ Major (intonation) group
- . Syllable break ɹi.ækt
- ‿ Linking (absence of a break)

DIACRITICS Diacritics may be placed above a symbol with a descender, e.g. ŋ̊

| | | | | | | | | |
|---|---|---|---|---|---|---|---|---|
| ̥ | Voiceless | n̥ d̥ | ̤ | Breathy voiced | b̤ a̤ | ̪ | Dental | t̪ d̪ |
| ̬ | Voiced | s̬ t̬ | ̰ | Creaky voiced | b̰ a̰ | ̺ | Apical | t̺ d̺ |
| ʰ | Aspirated | tʰ dʰ | ̼ | Linguolabial | t̼ d̼ | ̻ | Laminal | t̻ d̻ |
| ̹ | More rounded | ɔ̹ | ʷ | Labialized | tʷ dʷ | ̃ | Nasalized | ẽ |
| ̜ | Less rounded | ɔ̜ | ʲ | Palatalized | tʲ dʲ | ⁿ | Nasal release | dⁿ |
| ̟ | Advanced | u̟ | ˠ | Velarized | tˠ dˠ | ˡ | Lateral release | dˡ |
| ̠ | Retracted | e̠ | ˤ | Pharyngealized | tˤ dˤ | ̚ | No audible release | d̚ |
| ̈ | Centralized | ë | ̴ | Velarized or pharyngealized | ɫ | | | |
| ̽ | Mid-centralized | e̽ | ̝ | Raised | e̝ (ɹ̝ = voiced alveolar fricative) | | | |
| ̩ | Syllabic | n̩ | ̞ | Lowered | e̞ (β̞ = voiced bilabial approximant) | | | |
| ̯ | Non-syllabic | e̯ | ̘ | Advanced Tongue Root | e̘ | | | |
| ˞ | Rhoticity | ɚ a˞ | ̙ | Retracted Tongue Root | e̙ | | | |

TONES AND WORD ACCENTS

| LEVEL | | | CONTOUR | | |
|---|---|---|---|---|---|
| e̋ or | ˥ | Extra high | ě or | ˩˥ | Rising |
| é | ˦ | High | ê | ˥˩ | Falling |
| ē | ˧ | Mid | e᷄ | ˦˥ | High rising |
| è | ˨ | Low | e᷅ | ˩˨ | Low rising |
| ȅ | ˩ | Extra low | e᷈ | ˧˦˧ | Rising-falling |
| ↓ | | Downstep | ↗ | | Global rise |
| ↑ | | Upstep | ↘ | | Global fall |

# 1 Introduction

You probably want to know what the purpose of this course is, and what you can expect to learn from it. An important purpose of the course is to explain how English is pronounced in the accent normally chosen as the standard for people learning the English spoken in England. If this was the only thing the course did, a more suitable title would have been "English Pronunciation". However, at the comparatively advanced level at which this course is aimed, it is usual to present this information in the context of a general theory about speech sounds and how they are used in language; this theoretical context is called **phonetics and phonology**. Why is it necessary to learn this theoretical background? A similar question arises in connection with grammar: at lower levels of study one is concerned simply with setting out how to form grammatical sentences, but people who are going to work with the language at an advanced level as teachers or researchers need the deeper understanding provided by the study of grammatical theory and related areas of linguistics. The theoretical material in the present course is necessary for anyone who needs to understand the principles regulating the use of sounds in spoken English.

## 1.1 How the course is organised

You should keep in mind that this is a *course*. It is designed to be studied from beginning to end, with the relevant exercises being worked on for each chapter, and it is therefore quite different from a reference book. Most readers are expected to be either studying English at a university, or to be practising English language teachers. You may be working under the supervision of a teacher, or working through the course individually; you may be a native speaker of a language that is not English, or a native English-speaker.

Each chapter has additional sections:

- Notes on problems and further reading: this section gives you information on how to find out more about the subject matter of the chapter.
- Notes for teachers: this gives some ideas that might be helpful to teachers using the book to teach a class.
- Written exercises: these give you some practical work to do in the area covered by the chapter. Answers to the exercises are given on pages 200–9.
- Audio exercises: these are recorded on the CDs supplied with this book (also convertible to mp3 files), and there are places marked in the text when there is a relevant exercise.

- Additional exercises: you will find more written and audio exercises, with answers, on the book's website.

Only some of the exercises are suitable for native speakers of English. The exercises for Chapter 1 are mainly aimed at helping you to become familiar with the way the written and audio exercises work.

## 1.2 The *English Phonetics and Phonology* website

If you have access to the Internet, you can find more information on the website produced to go with this book. You can find it at www.cambridge.org/elt/peterroach. Everything on the website is additional material – there is nothing that is essential to using the book itself, so if you don't have access to the Internet you should not suffer a disadvantage.

The website contains the following things:

- Additional exercise material.
- Links to useful websites.
- A discussion site for exchanging opinions and questions about English phonetics and phonology in the context of the study of the book.
- Recordings of talks given by Peter Roach.
- Other material associated with the book.
- A Glossary giving brief explanations of the terms and concepts found in phonetics and phonology.

## 1.3 Phonemes and other aspects of pronunciation

The nature of phonetics and phonology will be explained as the course progresses, but one or two basic ideas need to be introduced at this stage. In any language we can identify a small number of regularly used sounds (vowels and consonants) that we call **phonemes**; for example, the vowels in the words 'pin' and 'pen' are different phonemes, and so are the consonants at the beginning of the words 'pet' and 'bet'. Because of the notoriously confusing nature of English spelling, it is particularly important to learn to think of English pronunciation in terms of phonemes rather than letters of the alphabet; one must be aware, for example, that the word 'enough' begins with the same vowel phoneme as that at the beginning of 'inept' and ends with the same consonant as 'stuff'. We often use special symbols to represent speech sounds; with the symbols chosen for this course, the word 'enough' would be written (**transcribed**) as ɪnʌf. The symbols are always printed in **blue type** in this book to distinguish them from letters of the alphabet. A list of the symbols is given on pp. x–xi, and the chart of the International Phonetic Association (IPA) on which the symbols are based is reproduced on p. xii.

The first part of the course is mainly concerned with identifying and describing the phonemes of English. Chapters 2 and 3 deal with vowels and Chapter 4 with some consonants. After this preliminary contact with the practical business of how some English sounds are pronounced, Chapter 5 looks at the phoneme and at the use of symbols in a theoretical way, while the corresponding Audio Unit revises the material of Chapters 2–4. After the phonemes of English have been introduced, the rest of the course goes on to look at larger units of speech such as the **syllable** and at aspects of speech such as **stress** (which could be roughly described as the relative strength of a syllable) and **intonation** (the use of the pitch of the voice to convey meaning). As an example of stress, consider the difference between the pronunciation of 'contract' as a noun ('they signed a contract') and 'contract' as a verb ('it started to contract'). In the former the stress is on the first syllable, while in the latter it is on the second syllable. A possible example of intonation would be the different pitch movements on the word 'well' said as an exclamation and as a question: in the first case the pitch will usually fall from high to low, while in the second it will rise from low to high.

You will have to learn a number of technical terms in studying the course: you will find that when they are introduced in order to be defined or explained, they are printed in **bold type**. This has already been done in this Introduction in the case of, for example, **phoneme**, **phonetics** and **phonology***. Another convention to remember is that when words used as examples are given in spelling form, they are enclosed in single quotation marks – see for example 'pin', 'pen', etc. Double quotation marks are used where quotation marks would normally be used – that is, for quoting something that someone has said or might say. Words are sometimes printed in *italics* to mark them as specially important in a particular context.

## 1.4 Accents and dialects

Languages have different **accents**: they are pronounced differently by people from different geographical places, from different social classes, of different ages and different educational backgrounds. The word *accent* is often confused with **dialect**. We use the word *dialect* to refer to a variety of a language which is different from others not just in pronunciation but also in such matters as vocabulary, grammar and word order. Differences of accent, on the other hand, are pronunciation differences only.

The accent that we concentrate on and use as our model is the one that is most often recommended for foreign learners studying British English. It has for a long time been identified by the name **Received Pronunciation** (usually abbreviated to its initials, **RP**), but this name is old-fashioned and misleading: the use of the word "received" to mean "accepted" or "approved" is nowadays very rare, and the word if used in that sense seems to imply that other accents would *not* be acceptable or approved of. Since it is most familiar as the accent used by most announcers and newsreaders on BBC and British independent television broadcasting channels, a preferable name is **BBC pronunciation**. This should not be taken to mean that the BBC itself imposes an "official" accent – individual broadcasters all have their own personal characteristics, and an increasing number of broadcasters with Scottish, Welsh and Irish accents are employed. However, the accent described here is typical of broadcasters with an English accent, and there is a useful degree of consistency in the broadcast speech of these speakers.

---

* You will find these words in the Glossary on the website.

This course is not written for people who wish to study American pronunciation, though we look briefly at American pronunciation in Chapter 20. The pronunciation of English in North America is different from most accents found in Britain. There are exceptions to this – you can find accents in parts of Britain that sound American, and accents in North America that sound English. But the pronunciation that you are likely to hear from most Americans does sound noticeably different from BBC pronunciation.

In talking about accents of English, the foreigner should be careful about the difference between **England** and **Britain**; there are many different accents in England, but the range becomes very much wider if the accents of Scotland, Wales and Northern Ireland (Scotland and Wales are included in Britain, and together with Northern Ireland form the **United Kingdom**) are taken into account. Within the accents of England, the distinction that is most frequently made by the majority of English people is between **northern** and **southern**. This is a very rough division, and there can be endless argument over where the boundaries lie, but most people on hearing a pronunciation typical of someone from Lancashire, Yorkshire or other counties further north would identify it as "Northern". This course deals almost entirely with BBC pronunciation. There is no implication that other accents are inferior or less pleasant-sounding; the reason is simply that BBC is the accent that has usually been chosen by British teachers to teach to foreign learners, it is the accent that has been most fully described, and it has been used as the basis for textbooks and pronunciation dictionaries.

A term which is widely found nowadays is **Estuary English**, and many people have been given the impression that this is a new (or newly-discovered) accent of English. In reality there is no such accent, and the term should be used with care. The idea originates from the sociolinguistic observation that some people in public life who would previously have been expected to speak with a BBC (or RP) accent now find it acceptable to speak with some characteristics of the accents of the London area (the estuary referred to is the Thames estuary), such as glottal stops, which would in earlier times have caused comment or disapproval.

If you are a native speaker of English and your accent is different from BBC you should try, as you work through the course, to note what your main differences are for purposes of comparison. I am certainly not suggesting that you should try to change your pronunciation. If you are a learner of English you are recommended to concentrate on BBC pronunciation initially, though as you work through the course and become familiar with this you will probably find it an interesting exercise to listen analytically to other accents of English, to see if you can identify the ways in which they differ from BBC and even to learn to pronounce some different accents yourself.

## Notes on problems and further reading

The recommendation to use the name *BBC pronunciation* rather than *RP* is not universally accepted. 'BBC pronunciation' is used in recent editions of the *Cambridge English Pronouncing Dictionary* (Jones, eds. Roach, Hartman and Setter, 2006), in Trudgill (1999) and in Ladefoged (2004); for discussion, see the Introduction to the *Longman Pronunciation Dictionary* (Wells, 2008), and to the *Cambridge English Pronouncing Dictionary* (Jones, eds. Roach *et al.*, 2006). In Jones's original *English Pronouncing Dictionary* of 1917 the term used was *Public School Pronunciation* (PSP). Where I quote other writers who have used the term *RP* in discussion of standard accents, I have left the term unchanged. Other writers have suggested the name *GB* (*General British*) as a term preferable to RP: I do not feel this is satisfactory, since the accent being described belongs to England, and citizens of other parts of Britain are understandably reluctant to accept that this accent is the standard for countries such as Scotland and Wales. The BBC has an excellent Pronunciation Research Unit to advise broadcasters on the pronunciation of difficult words and names, but most people are not aware that it has no power to make broadcasters use particular pronunciations: BBC broadcasters only use it on a voluntary basis.

I feel that if we had a completely free choice of model accent for British English it would be possible to find more suitable ones: Scottish and Irish accents, for example, have a more straightforward relationship between spelling and sounds than does the BBC accent; they have simpler vowel systems, and would therefore be easier for most foreign learners to acquire. However, it seems that the majority of English teachers would be reluctant to learn to speak in the classroom with a non-English accent, so this is not a practical possibility.

For introductory reading on the choice of English accent, see Brown (1990: 12–13); Abercrombie (1991: 48–53); Cruttenden (2008: Chapter 7); Collins and Mees (2008: 2–6); Roach (2004, 2005). We will return to the subject of accents of English in Chapter 20.

Much of what has been written on the subject of "Estuary English" has been in minor or ephemeral publications. However, I would recommend looking at Collins and Mees (2008: 5–6, 206–8, 268–272); Cruttenden (2008: 87).

A problem area that has received a lot of attention is the choice of symbols for representing English phonemes. In the past, many different conventions have been proposed and students have often been confused by finding that the symbols used in one book are different from the ones they have learned in another. The symbols used in this book are in most respects those devised by A. C. Gimson for his *Introduction to the Pronunciation of English*, the latest version of which is the revision by Cruttenden (Cruttenden, 2008). These symbols are now used in almost all modern works on English pronunciation published in Britain, and can therefore be looked on as a *de facto* standard. Although good arguments can be made for some alternative symbols, the advantages of having a common set of symbols for pronunciation teaching materials and pronunciation entries in dictionaries are so great that it would be very regrettable to go back to the confusing diversity of earlier years. The subject of symbolisation is returned to in Section 5.2 of Chapter 5.

## Notes for teachers

Pronunciation teaching has not always been popular with teachers and language-teaching theorists, and in the 1970s and 1980s it was fashionable to treat it as a rather outdated activity. It was claimed, for example, that it attempted to make learners try to sound like native speakers of Received Pronunciation, that it discouraged them through difficult and repetitive exercises and that it failed to give importance to communication. A good example of this attitude is to be found in Brown and Yule (1983: 26–7). The criticism was misguided, I believe, and it is encouraging to see that in recent years there has been a significant growth of interest in pronunciation teaching and many new publications on the subject. There are very active groups of pronunciation teachers who meet at TESOL and IATEFL conferences, and exchange ideas via Internet discussions.

No pronunciation course that I know has ever said that learners must try to speak with a perfect RP accent. To claim this mixes up **models** with **goals**: the *model* chosen is BBC (RP), but the *goal* is normally to develop the learner's pronunciation sufficiently to permit effective communication with native speakers. Pronunciation exercises can be difficult, of course, but if we eliminate everything difficult from language teaching and learning, we may end up doing very little beyond getting students to play simple communication games. It is, incidentally, quite incorrect to suggest that the classic works on pronunciation and phonetics teaching concentrated on mechanically perfecting vowels and consonants: Jones (1956, first published 1909), for example, writes " 'Good' speech may be defined as a way of speaking which is clearly intelligible to all ordinary people. 'Bad' speech is a way of talking which is difficult for most people to understand ... A person may speak with sounds very different from those of his hearers and yet be clearly intelligible to all of them, as for instance when a Scotsman or an American addresses an English audience with clear articulation. Their speech cannot be described as other than 'good' " (pp. 4–5).

Much has been written recently about **English as an International Language**, with a view to defining what is used in common by the millions of people around the world who use English (Crystal, 2003; Jenkins, 2000). This is a different goal from that of this book, which concentrates on a specific accent. The discussion of the subject in Cruttenden (2008: Chapter 13) is recommended as a survey of the main issues, and the concept of an International English pronunciation is discussed there.

There are many different and well-tried methods of teaching and testing pronunciation, some of which are used in this book. I do not feel that it is suitable in this book to go into a detailed analysis of classroom methods, but there are several excellent treatments of the subject; see, for example, Dalton and Seidlhofer (1995); Celce-Murcia *et al.* (1996) and Hewings (2004).

## Written exercises

The exercises for this chapter are simple ones aimed at making you familiar with the style of exercises that you will work on in the rest of the course. The answers to the exercises are given on page 200.

1 Give three different names that have been used for the accent usually used for teaching the pronunciation of British English.

2 What is the difference between *accent* and *dialect*?
3 Which word is used to refer to the relative strength of a syllable?
4 How many sounds (phonemes) do you think there are in the following words?
a) love b) half c) wrist d) shrink e) ought

Now look at the answers on page 200.

# 2 The production of speech sounds

## 2.1 Articulators above the larynx

All the sounds we make when we speak are the result of muscles contracting. The muscles in the chest that we use for breathing produce the flow of air that is needed for almost all speech sounds; muscles in the **larynx** produce many different modifications in the flow of air from the chest to the mouth. After passing through the larynx, the air goes through what we call the **vocal tract**, which ends at the mouth and nostrils; we call the part comprising the mouth the **oral cavity** and the part that leads to the nostrils the **nasal cavity**. Here the air from the lungs escapes into the atmosphere. We have a large and complex set of muscles that can produce changes in the shape of the vocal tract, and in order to learn how the sounds of speech are produced it is necessary to become familiar with the different parts of the vocal tract. These different parts are called **articulators**, and the study of them is called **articulatory phonetics**.

Fig. 1 is a diagram that is used frequently in the study of phonetics. It represents the human head, seen from the side, displayed as though it had been cut in half. You will need to look at it carefully as the articulators are described, and you will find it useful to have a mirror and a good light placed so that you can look at the inside of your mouth.

i) The **pharynx** is a tube which begins just above the larynx. It is about 7 cm long in women and about 8 cm in men, and at its top end it is divided into two, one

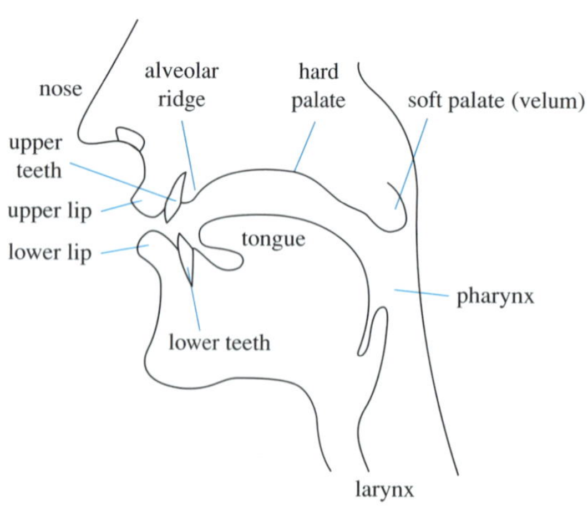


Fig. 1 The articulators

part being the back of the oral cavity and the other being the beginning of the way through the nasal cavity. If you look in your mirror with your mouth open, you can see the back of the pharynx.

ii) The **soft palate** or **velum** is seen in the diagram in a position that allows air to pass through the nose and through the mouth. Yours is probably in that position now, but often in speech it is raised so that air cannot escape through the nose. The other important thing about the soft palate is that it is one of the articulators that can be touched by the tongue. When we make the sounds k, g the tongue is in contact with the lower side of the soft palate, and we call these **velar** consonants.

iii) The **hard palate** is often called the "roof of the mouth". You can feel its smooth curved surface with your tongue. A consonant made with the tongue close to the hard palate is called **palatal.** The sound j in 'yes' is palatal.

iv) The **alveolar ridge** is between the top front teeth and the hard palate. You can feel its shape with your tongue. Its surface is really much rougher than it feels, and is covered with little ridges. You can only see these if you have a mirror small enough to go inside your mouth, such as those used by dentists. Sounds made with the tongue touching here (such as t, d, n) are called **alveolar.**

v) The **tongue** is a very important articulator and it can be moved into many different places and different shapes. It is usual to divide the tongue into different parts, though there are no clear dividing lines within its structure. Fig. 2 shows the tongue on a larger scale with these parts shown: **tip**, **blade**, **front**, **back** and **root**. (This use of the word "front" often seems rather strange at first.)

vi) The **teeth** (upper and lower) are usually shown in diagrams like Fig. 1 only at the front of the mouth, immediately behind the lips. This is for the sake of a simple diagram, and you should remember that most speakers have teeth to the sides of their mouths, back almost to the soft palate. The tongue is in contact with the upper side teeth for most speech sounds. Sounds made with the tongue touching the front teeth, such as English θ, ð, are called **dental.**

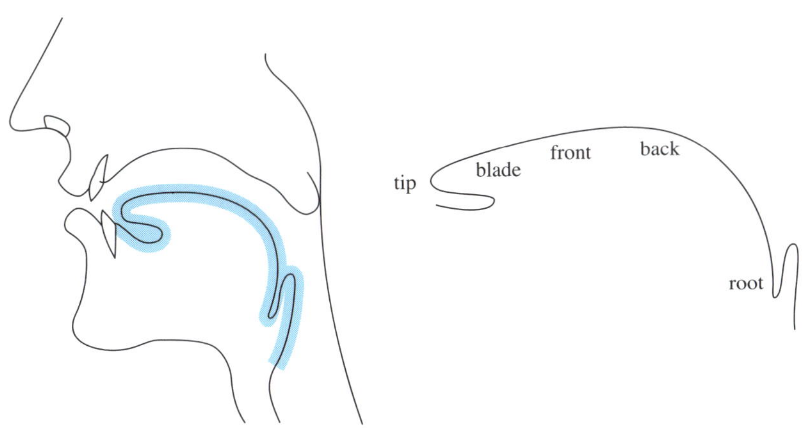


Fig. 2 Subdivisions of the tongue

vii) The **lips** are important in speech. They can be pressed together (when we produce the sounds p, b), brought into contact with the teeth (as in f, v), or rounded to produce the lip-shape for vowels like uː. Sounds in which the lips are in contact with each other are called **bilabial**, while those with lip-to-teeth contact are called **labiodental**.

The seven articulators described above are the main ones used in speech, but there are a few other things to remember. Firstly, the larynx (which will be studied in Chapter 4) could also be described as an articulator – a very complex and independent one. Secondly, the **jaws** are sometimes called articulators; certainly we move the lower jaw a lot in speaking. But the jaws are not articulators in the same way as the others, because they cannot themselves make contact with other articulators. Finally, although there is practically nothing active that we can do with the **nose** and the nasal cavity when speaking, they are a very important part of our equipment for making sounds (which is sometimes called our **vocal apparatus**), particularly nasal consonants such as m, n. Again, we cannot really describe the nose and the nasal cavity as articulators in the same sense as (i) to (vii) above.

## 2.2 Vowel and consonant

The words **vowel** and **consonant** are very familiar ones, but when we study the sounds of speech scientifically we find that it is not easy to define exactly what they mean. The most common view is that vowels are sounds in which there is no obstruction to the flow of air as it passes from the larynx to the lips. A doctor who wants to look at the back of a patient's mouth often asks them to say "ah"; making this vowel sound is the best way of presenting an unobstructed view. But if we make a sound like s, d it can be clearly felt that we are making it difficult or impossible for the air to pass through the mouth. Most people would have no doubt that sounds like s, d should be called consonants. However, there are many cases where the decision is not so easy to make. One problem is that some English sounds that we think of as consonants, such as the sounds at the beginning of the words 'hay' and 'way', do not really obstruct the flow of air more than some vowels do. Another problem is that different languages have different ways of dividing their sounds into vowels and consonants; for example, the usual sound produced at the beginning of the word 'red' is felt to be a consonant by most English speakers, but in some other languages (e.g. Mandarin Chinese) the same sound is treated as one of the vowels.

If we say that the difference between vowels and consonants is a difference in the way that they are produced, there will inevitably be some cases of uncertainty or disagreement; this is a problem that cannot be avoided. It is possible to establish two distinct groups of sounds (vowels and consonants) in another way. Consider English words beginning with the sound h; what sounds can come next after this h? We find that most of the sounds we normally think of as vowels can follow (e.g. e in the word 'hen'), but practically none of the sounds we class as consonants, with the possible exception of j in a word such as 'huge' hjuːdʒ. Now think of English words beginning with the two sounds bɪ; we find many cases where a consonant can follow (e.g. d in the word 'bid', or l in the word 'bill'), but practically no cases where a vowel may follow. What we are doing here is looking at the different contexts and positions in which particular sounds can occur; this is the study of the **distribution** of the sounds, and is of great importance in phonology. Study of the sounds found at the beginning and end of English words has shown that two groups of sounds with quite different patterns of distribution can be identified, and these two groups are those of vowel and consonant. If we look at the vowel–consonant distinction in this way, we must say that the most important difference between vowel and consonant is not the way that they are made, but their different distributions. It is important to remember that the distribution of vowels and consonants is different for each language.

We begin the study of English sounds in this course by looking at vowels, and it is necessary to say something about vowels in general before turning to the vowels of English. We need to know in what ways vowels differ from each other. The first matter to consider is the shape and position of the tongue. It is usual to simplify the very complex possibilities by describing just two things: firstly, the vertical distance between the upper surface of the tongue and the palate and, secondly, the part of the tongue, between front and back, which is raised highest. Let us look at some examples:

i) Make a vowel like the iː in the English word 'see' and look in a mirror; if you tilt your head back slightly you will be able to see that the tongue is held up close to the roof of the mouth. Now make an æ vowel (as in the word 'cat') and notice how the distance between the surface of the tongue and the roof of the mouth is now much greater. The difference between iː and æ is a difference of tongue height, and we would describe iː as a relatively **close** vowel and æ as a relatively **open** vowel. Tongue height can be changed by moving the tongue up or down, or moving the lower jaw up or down. Usually we use some combination of the two sorts of movement, but when drawing side-of-the-head diagrams such as Fig. 1 and Fig. 2 it is usually found simpler to illustrate tongue shapes for vowels as if tongue height were altered by tongue movement alone, without any accompanying jaw movement. So we would illustrate the tongue height difference between iː and æ as in Fig. 3.

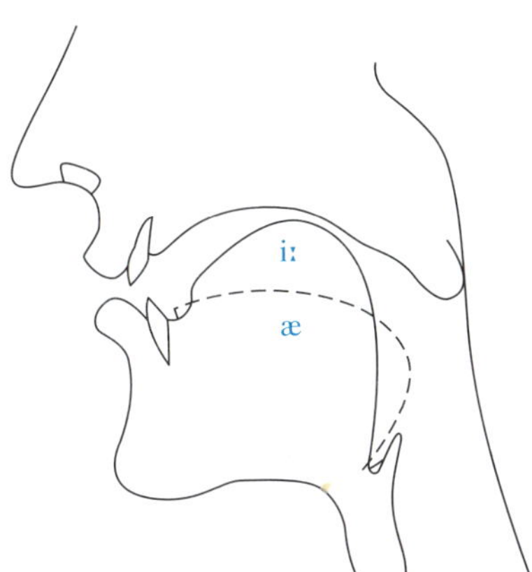


Fig. 3 Tongue positions for iː and æ

ii) In making the two vowels described above, it is the front part of the tongue that is raised. We could therefore describe iː and æ as comparatively **front** vowels. By changing the shape of the tongue we can produce vowels in which a different part of the tongue is the highest point. A vowel in which the back of the tongue is the highest point is called a **back** vowel. If you make the vowel in the word 'calm', which we write phonetically as ɑː, you can see that the back of the tongue is raised. Compare this with æ in front of a mirror; æ is a front vowel and ɑː is a back vowel. The vowel in 'too' (uː) is also a comparatively back vowel, but compared with ɑː it is close.

So now we have seen how four vowels differ from each other; we can show this in a simple diagram.

| | Front | Back |
|---|---|---|
| Close | iː | uː |
| Open | æ | ɑː |

However, this diagram is rather inaccurate. Phoneticians need a very accurate way of classifying vowels, and have developed a set of vowels which are arranged in a close–open, front–back diagram similar to the one above but which are not the vowels of any particular language. These **cardinal vowels** are a standard reference system, and people being trained in phonetics at an advanced level have to learn to make them accurately and recognise them correctly. If you learn the cardinal vowels, you are not learning to make English sounds, but you are learning about the range of vowels that the human vocal apparatus can make, and also learning a useful way of describing, classifying and comparing vowels. They are recorded on Track 12 of CD 2.

It has become traditional to locate cardinal vowels on a four-sided figure (a quadrilateral of the shape seen in Fig. 4 – the design used here is the one recommended by the **International Phonetic Association**). The exact shape is not really important – a square would do quite well – but we will use the traditional shape. The vowels in Fig. 4 are the so-called **primary** cardinal vowels; these are the vowels that are most familiar to the speakers of most European languages, and there are other cardinal vowels (**secondary** cardinal vowels) that sound less familiar. In this course cardinal vowels are printed within square brackets [ ] to distinguish them clearly from English vowel sounds.

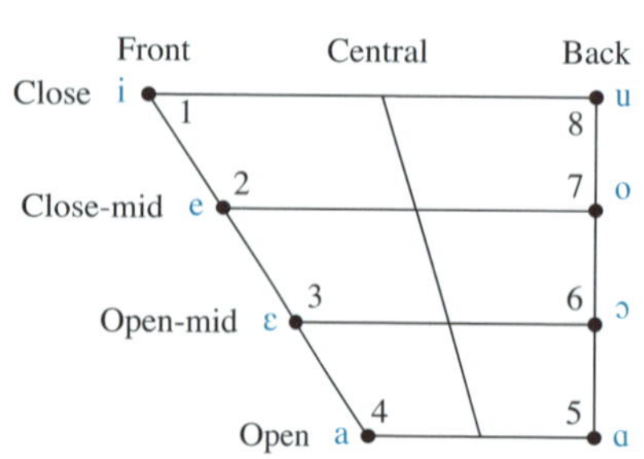


Fig. 4 Primary cardinal vowels

Cardinal vowel no. 1 has the symbol [i], and is defined as the vowel which is as close and as front as it is possible to make a vowel without obstructing the flow of air enough to produce friction noise; friction noise is the hissing sound that one hears in consonants like s or f. Cardinal vowel no. 5 has the symbol [ɑ] and is defined as the most open and back vowel that it is possible to make. Cardinal vowel no. 8 [u] is fully close and back and no. 4 [a] is fully open and front. After establishing these extreme points, it is possible to put in intermediate points (vowels no. 2, 3, 6 and 7). Many students when they hear these vowels find that they sound strange and exaggerated; you must remember that they are *extremes* of vowel quality. It is useful to think of the cardinal vowel framework like a map of an area or country that you are interested in. If the map is to be useful to you it must cover all the area; but if it covers the whole area of interest it must inevitably go a little way beyond that and include some places that you might never want to go to.

When you are familiar with these extreme vowels, you have (as mentioned above) learned a way of describing, classifying and comparing vowels. For example, we can say that the English vowel æ (the vowel in 'cat') is not as open as cardinal vowel no. 4 [a]. We have now looked at how we can classify vowels according to their tongue height and their frontness or backness. There is another important variable of vowel quality, and that is lip-position. Although the lips can have many different shapes and positions, we will at this stage consider only three possibilities. These are:

i) **Rounded**, where the corners of the lips are brought towards each other and the lips pushed forwards. This is most clearly seen in cardinal vowel no. 8 [u].
ii) **Spread**, with the corners of the lips moved away from each other, as for a smile. This is most clearly seen in cardinal vowel no. 1 [i].
iii) **Neutral**, where the lips are not noticeably rounded or spread. The noise most English people make when they are hesitating (written 'er') has neutral lip position.

Now, using the principles that have just been explained, we will examine some of the English vowels.

## 2.3 English short vowels

AU2 (CD 1), Exs 1–5

English has a large number of vowel sounds; the first ones to be examined are short vowels. The symbols for these short vowels are: ɪ, e, æ, ʌ, ɒ, ʊ. Short vowels are only *relatively* short; as we shall see later, vowels can have quite different lengths in different contexts.

Each vowel is described in relation to the cardinal vowels.

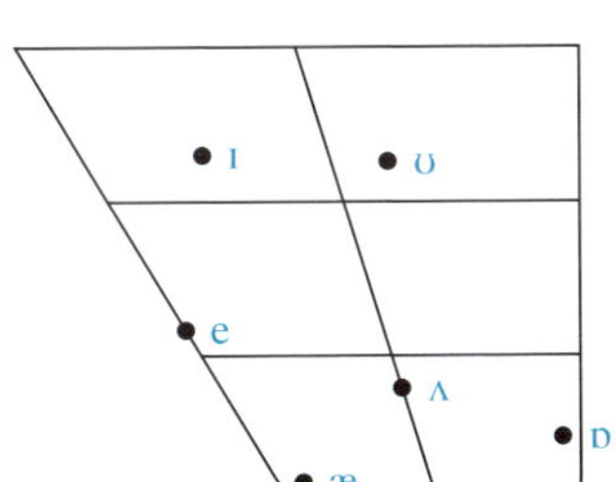


Fig. 5 English short vowels

- ɪ (example words: 'bit', 'pin', 'fish') The diagram shows that, though this vowel is in the close front area, compared with cardinal vowel no. 1 [i] it is more open, and nearer in to the centre. The lips are slightly spread.
- e (example words: 'bet', 'men', 'yes') This is a front vowel between cardinal vowel no. 2 [e] and no. 3 [ɛ]. The lips are slightly spread.
- æ (example words: 'bat', 'man', 'gas') This vowel is front, but not quite as open as cardinal vowel no. 4 [a]. The lips are slightly spread.
- ʌ (example words: 'cut', 'come', 'rush') This is a central vowel, and the diagram shows that it is more open than the open-mid tongue height. The lip position is neutral.
- ɒ (example words: 'pot', 'gone', 'cross') This vowel is not quite fully back, and between open-mid and open in tongue height. The lips are slightly rounded.
- ʊ (example words: 'put', 'pull', 'push') The nearest cardinal vowel is no. 8 [u], but it can be seen that ʊ is more open and nearer to central. The lips are rounded.

There is one other short vowel, for which the symbol is ə. This central vowel – which is called **schwa** – is a very familiar sound in English; it is heard in the first syllable of the words 'about', 'oppose', 'perhaps', for example. Since it is different from the other vowels in several important ways, we will study it separately in Chapter 9.

## Notes on problems and further reading

One of the most difficult aspects of phonetics at this stage is the large number of technical terms that have to be learned. Every phonetics textbook gives a description of the articulators. Useful introductions are Ladefoged (2006: Chapter 1), Ashby (2005), and Ashby and Maidment (2005: Chapter 3).

An important discussion of the vowel–consonant distinction is by Pike (1943: 66–79). He suggested that since the two approaches to the distinction produce such different results we should use new terms: sounds which do not obstruct the airflow (traditionally called "vowels") should be called **vocoids**, and sounds which *do* obstruct the airflow (traditionally called "consonants") should be called **contoids**. This leaves the terms "vowel" and "consonant" for use in labelling phonological elements according to their distribution and their role in syllable structure; see Section 5.8 of Laver (1994). While vowels are usually vocoids and consonants are usually contoids, this is not always the case; for example, j in 'yet' and w in 'wet' are (phonetically) vocoids but function (phonologically) as consonants. A study of the distributional differences between vowels and consonants in English is described in O'Connor and Trim (1953); a briefer treatment is in Cruttenden (2008: Sections 4.2 and 5.6). The classification of vowels has a large literature: I would recommend Jones (1975: Chapter 8); Ladefoged (2006) gives a brief introduction in Chapter 1, and much more detail in Chapter 9; see also Abercrombie (1967: 55–60 and Chapter 10). The *Handbook of the International Phonetic Association* (1999: Section 2.6) explains the IPA's principles of vowel classification. The distinction between primary and secondary cardinal vowels is a rather dubious one which appears to be based to some extent on a division between those vowels which are familiar and those which are unfamiliar to speakers of most European languages. It is possible to classify vowels quite unambiguously without resorting to this notion by specifying their front/back, close/open and lip positions.

## Written exercises

1 On the diagram provided, various articulators are indicated by labelled arrows (a–e). Give the names for the articulators.

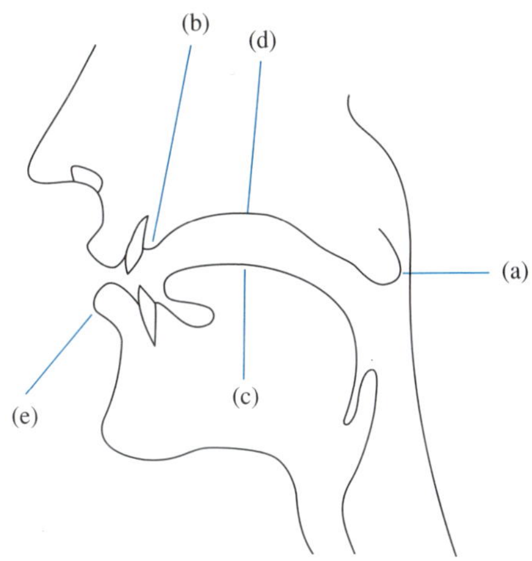


2 Using the descriptive labels introduced for vowel classification, say what the following cardinal vowels are:

a) [u] b) [e] c) [a] d) [i] e) [o]

3 Draw a vowel quadrilateral and indicate on it the correct places for the following English vowels:

a) æ b) ʌ c) ɪ d) e

4 Write the symbols for the vowels in the following words:

a) bread b) rough c) foot d) hymn
e) pull f) cough g) mat h) friend

# 3 Long vowels, diphthongs and triphthongs

## 3.1 English long vowels

In Chapter 2 the short vowels were introduced. In this chapter we look at other types of English vowel sound. The first to be introduced here are the five long vowels; these are the vowels which tend to be longer than the short vowels in similar contexts. It is necessary to say "in similar contexts" because, as we shall see later, the length of all English vowel sounds varies very much according to their context (such as the type of sound that follows them) and the presence or absence of stress. To remind you that these vowels tend to be long, the symbols consist of one vowel symbol plus a length mark made of two dots ː. Thus we have iː, ɜː, ɑː, ɔː, uː. We will now look at each of these long vowels individually.

The five long vowels are different from the six short vowels described in Chapter 2, not only in length but also in quality. If we compare some similar pairs of long and short vowels, for example ɪ with iː, or ʊ with uː, or æ with ɑː, we can see distinct differences in quality (resulting from differences in tongue shape and position, and lip position) as well as in length. For this reason, all the long vowels have symbols which are different from those of short vowels; you can see that the long and short vowel symbols would still all be different from each other even if we omitted the length mark, so it is important to remember that the length mark is used not because it is essential but because it helps learners to remember the length difference. Perhaps the only case where a long and a short vowel are closely similar in quality is that of ə and ɜː, but ə is a special case – as we shall see later.

AU3 (CD 1), Exs 1–5

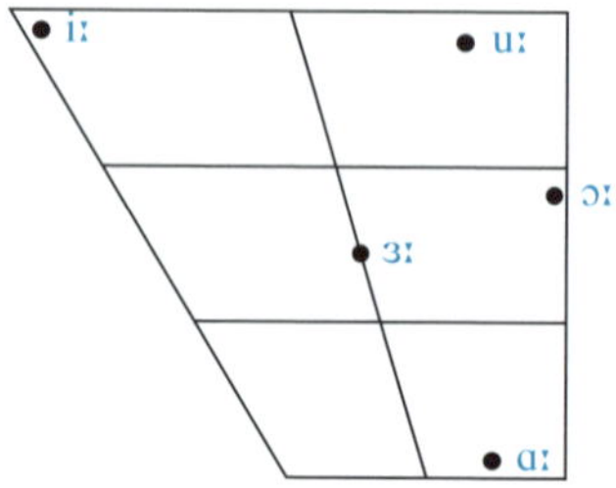


Fig. 6 English long vowels

iː (example words: 'beat', 'mean', 'peace') This vowel is nearer to cardinal vowel no. 1 [i] (i.e. it is closer and more front) than is the short vowel of 'bid', 'pin', 'fish' described in Chapter 2. Although the tongue shape is not much different from cardinal vowel no. 1, the lips are only slightly spread and this results in a rather different vowel quality.

ɜː (example words: 'bird', 'fern', 'purse') This is a mid-central vowel which is used in most English accents as a hesitation sound (written 'er'), but which many learners find difficult to copy. The lip position is neutral.

ɑː (example words: 'card', 'half', 'pass') This is an open vowel in the region of cardinal vowel no. 5 [ɑ], but not as back as this. The lip position is neutral.

ɔː (example words: 'board', 'torn', 'horse') The tongue height for this vowel is between cardinal vowel no. 6 [ɔ] and no. 7 [o], and closer to the latter. This vowel is almost fully back and has quite strong lip-rounding.

uː (example words: 'food', 'soon', 'loose') The nearest cardinal vowel to this is no. 8 [u], but BBC uː is much less back and less close, while the lips are only moderately rounded.

## 3.2 Diphthongs

AU3 (CD 1), Exs 6 & 7

BBC pronunciation has a large number of diphthongs – sounds which consist of a movement or glide from one vowel to another. A vowel which remains constant and does not glide is called a **pure vowel**.

In terms of length, diphthongs are similar to the long vowels described above. Perhaps the most important thing to remember about all the diphthongs is that the first part is much longer and stronger than the second part; for example, most of the diphthong aɪ (as in the words 'eye', 'I') consists of the a vowel, and only in about the last quarter of the diphthong does the glide to ɪ become noticeable. As the glide to ɪ happens, the loudness of the sound decreases. As a result, the ɪ part is shorter and quieter. Foreign learners should, therefore, always remember that the last part of English diphthongs must not be made too strongly.

The total number of diphthongs is eight (though ʊə is increasingly rare). The easiest way to remember them is in terms of three groups divided as in this diagram (Fig. 7):

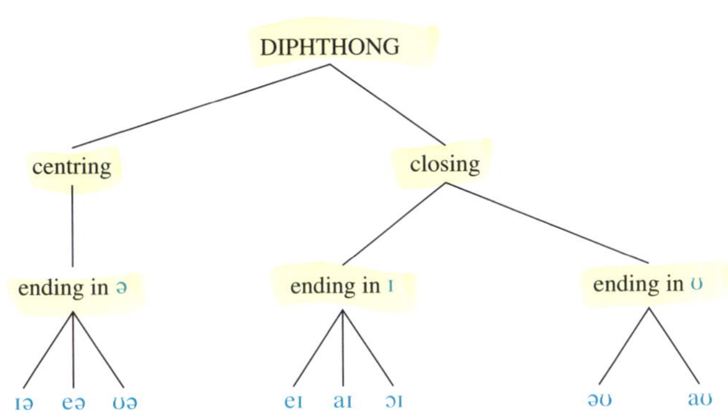


Fig. 7 Diphthongs

The centring diphthongs glide towards the ə (schwa) vowel, as the symbols indicate.

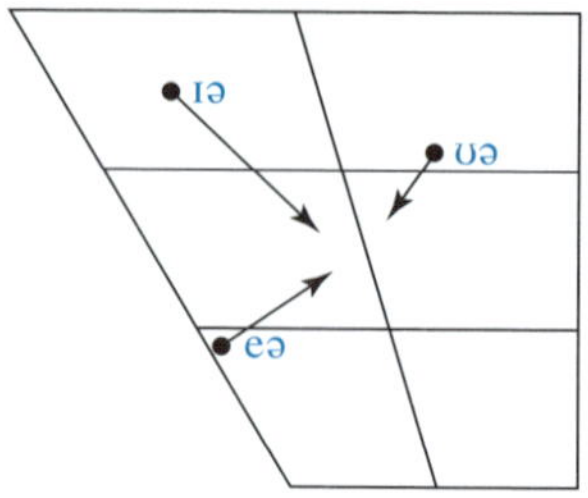


Fig. 8 Centring diphthongs

ɪə (example words: 'beard', 'weird', 'fierce') The starting point is a little closer than ɪ in 'bit', 'bin'.

eə (example words: 'aired', 'cairn', 'scarce') This diphthong begins with a vowel sound that is more open than the e of 'get', 'men'.

ʊə (example words: 'moored', 'tour', 'lure') For speakers who have this diphthong, this has a starting point similar to ʊ in 'put', 'pull'. Many speakers pronounce ɔː instead.

The closing diphthongs have the characteristic that they all end with a glide towards a closer vowel. Because the second part of the diphthong is weak, they often do not reach a position that could be called close. The important thing is that a glide from a relatively more open towards a relatively closer vowel is produced.

Three of the diphthongs glide towards ɪ, as described below:

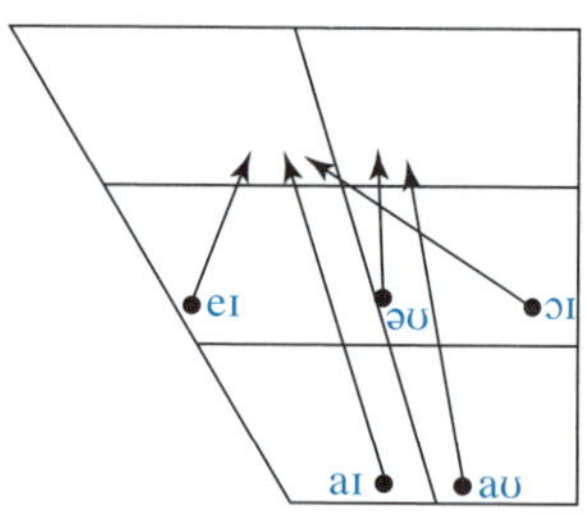


Fig. 9 Closing diphthongs

eɪ (example words: 'paid', 'pain', 'face') The starting point is the same as the e of 'get', 'men'.

aɪ (example words: 'tide', 'time', 'nice') This diphthong begins with an open vowel which is between front and back; it is quite similar to the ʌ of the words 'cut', 'bun'.

ɔɪ (example words: 'void', 'loin', 'voice') The first part of this diphthong is slightly more open than ɔː in 'ought', 'born'.

Two diphthongs glide towards ʊ, so that as the tongue moves closer to the roof of the mouth there is at the same time a rounding movement of the lips. This movement is not a large one, again because the second part of the diphthong is weak.

əʊ (example words: 'load', 'home', 'most') The vowel position for the beginning of this is the same as for the "schwa" vowel ə, as found in the first syllable of the word 'about'. The lips may be slightly rounded in anticipation of the glide towards ʊ, for which there is quite noticeable lip-rounding.

aʊ (example words: 'loud', 'gown', 'house') This diphthong begins with a vowel similar to aɪ. Since this is an open vowel, a glide to ʊ would necessitate a large movement, and the tongue often does not reach the ʊ position. There is only slight lip-rounding.

## 3.3 Triphthongs

The most complex English sounds of the vowel type are the **triphthongs**. They can be rather difficult to pronounce, and very difficult to recognise. A triphthong is a glide from one vowel to another and then to a third, all produced rapidly and without interruption. For example, a careful pronunciation of the word 'hour' begins with a vowel quality similar to ɑː, goes on to a glide towards the back close rounded area (for which we use the symbol ʊ), then ends with a mid-central vowel (schwa, ə). We use the symbol aʊə to represent the pronunciation of 'hour', but this is not always an accurate representation of the pronunciation.

The triphthongs can be looked on as being composed of the five closing diphthongs described in the last section, with ə added on the end. Thus we get:

| | |
|---|---|
| eɪ + ə = eɪə | əʊ + ə = əʊə |
| aɪ + ə = aɪə | aʊ + ə = aʊə |
| ɔɪ + ə = ɔɪə | |

The principal cause of difficulty for the foreign learner is that in present-day English the extent of the vowel movement is very small, except in very careful pronunciation. Because of this, the middle of the three vowel qualities of the triphthong (i.e. the ɪ or ʊ part) can hardly be heard and the resulting sound is difficult to distinguish from some of the diphthongs and long vowels. To add to the difficulty, there is also the problem of whether a triphthong is felt to contain one or two syllables. Words such as 'fire' faɪə or 'hour' aʊə are probably felt by most English speakers (with BBC pronunciation) to consist of only one syllable, whereas 'player' pleɪə or 'slower' sləʊə are more likely to be heard as two syllables.

We will not go through a detailed description of each triphthong. This is partly because there is so much variation in the amount of vowel movement according to how slow and careful the pronunciation is, and also because the "careful" pronunciation can be found by looking at the description of the corresponding diphthong and adding ə to the end. However, to help identify these triphthongs, some example words are given here:

| | |
|---|---|
| eɪə 'layer', 'player' | əʊə 'lower', 'mower' |
| aɪə 'liar', 'fire' | aʊə 'power', 'hour' |
| ɔɪə 'loyal', 'royal' | |

## Notes on problems and further reading

For more information about vowels, see Ashby (2005, Chapter 4), Ladefoged (2004, Chapter 3). Long vowels and diphthongs can be seen as a group of vowel sounds that are consistently longer *in a given context* than the short vowels described in the previous chapter. Some writers give the label *tense* to long vowels and diphthongs and *lax* to the short vowels. Giegerich (1992) explains how this concept applies to three different accents of English: SSE (Standard Scottish English), RP (BBC pronunciation) and GA (General American). The accents are described in 3.1 and 3.2; the idea of pairs of vowels differing in tenseness and laxness follows in 3.3. Jakobson and Halle (1964) explain the historical background to the distinction, which plays an important role in the treatment of the English vowel system by Chomsky and Halle (1968).

As mentioned in the notes on Chapter 1, the choice of symbols has in the past tended to vary from book to book, and this is particularly noticeable in the case of length marks for long vowels (this issue comes up again in Section 5.2 of Chapter 5); you could read Cruttenden (2008: Section 8.5). As an example of a contemporary difference in symbol choice, see Kreidler (2004, 4.3).

The phonemes iː, uː are usually classed as long vowels; it is worth noting that most English speakers pronounce them with something of a diphthongal glide, so that a possible alternative transcription could be ɪi, ʊu, respectively. This is not normally proposed, however.

It seems that triphthongs in BBC pronunciation are in a rather unstable state, resulting in the loss of some distinctions: in the case of some speakers, for example, it is not easy to hear a difference between 'tyre' taɪə, 'tower' taʊə, 'tar' tɑː. BBC newsreaders often pronounce 'Ireland' as ɑːlənd. Gimson (1964) suggested that this shows a change in progress in the phonemic system of RP.

## Notes for teachers

I mention above that iː, uː are often pronounced as slightly diphthongal: although this glide is often noticeable, I have never found it helpful to try to teach foreign learners to pronounce iː, uː in this way. Foreign learners who wish to get close to the BBC model should be careful not to pronounce the "r" that is often found in the spelling corresponding to ɑː, ɔː, ɜː ('ar', 'or', 'er').

Most of the essential pronunciation features of the diphthongs are described in Chapter 3. One of the most common pronunciation characteristics that result in a learner of English being judged to have a foreign accent is the production of pure vowels where a diphthong should be pronounced (e.g. [e] for eɪ, [o] for əʊ).

Two additional points are worth making. The diphthong ʊə is included, but this is not used as much as the others – many English speakers use ɔː in words like 'moor', 'mourn', 'tour'. However, I feel that it is important for foreign learners to be aware of this diphthong because of the distinctiveness of words in pairs like 'moor' and 'more', 'poor' and 'paw' for many speakers. The other diphthong that requires comment is əʊ. English speakers seem to be specially sensitive to the quality of this diphthong, particularly to the first part. It often happens that foreign learners, having understood that the first part of the diphthong is not a back vowel, exaggerate this by using a vowel that is too front, producing a diphthong like eʊ. Unfortunately, this gives the impression of someone trying to copy a "posh" or upper-class accent: eʊ for əʊ is noticeable in the speech of the Royal Family.

## Written exercises

1 On the vowel diagram provided, indicate the glides for the diphthongs in the following words:

a) fright c) clear
b) home d) cow

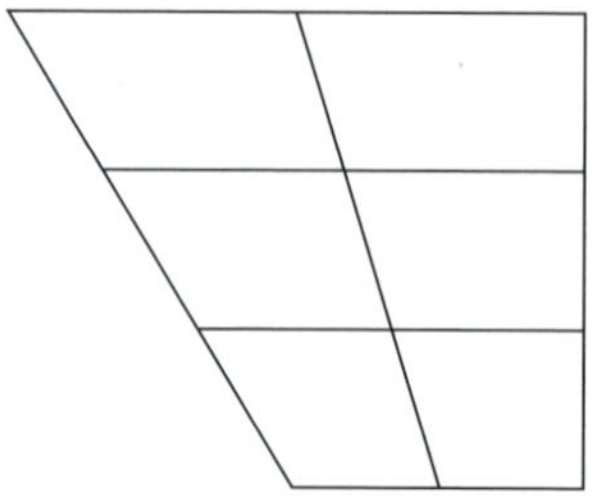

2 Write the symbols for the long vowels in the following words:

| | | |
|---|---|---|
| a) broad | d) learn | g) err |
| b) ward | e) cool | h) seal |
| c) calf | f) team | i) curl |

3 Write the symbols for the diphthongs in the following words:

| | | |
|---|---|---|
| a) tone | d) way | g) hair |
| b) style | e) beer | h) why |
| c) out | f) coil | i) prey |

# 4 Voicing and consonants

## 4.1 The larynx

We begin this chapter by studying the **larynx**. The larynx has several very important functions in speech, but before we can look at these functions we must examine its anatomy and physiology – that is, how it is constructed and how it works.

The larynx is in the neck; it has several parts, shown in Fig. 10. Its main structure is made of **cartilage**, a material that is similar to bone but less hard. If you press down on your nose, the hard part that you can feel is cartilage. The larynx's structure is made of two large cartilages. These are hollow and are attached to the top of the **trachea**; when we breathe, the air passes through the trachea and the larynx. The front of the larynx comes to a point and you can feel this point at the front of your neck – particularly if you are a man and/or slim. This point is commonly called the **Adam's Apple**.

Inside the "box" made by these two cartilages are the **vocal folds**, which are two thick flaps of muscle rather like a pair of lips; an older name for these is **vocal cords**. Looking down the throat is difficult to do, and requires special optical equipment, but Fig. 11 shows in diagram form the most important parts. At the front the vocal folds are joined together and fixed to the inside of the **thyroid cartilage**. At the back they are attached to a pair of

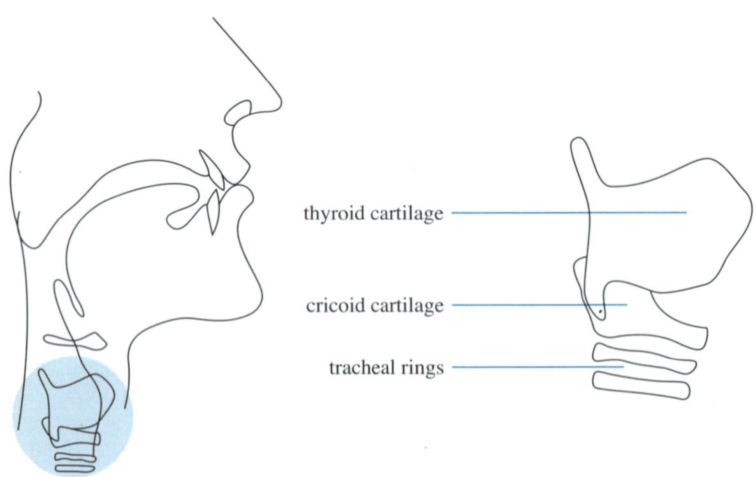


Fig. 10 The larynx

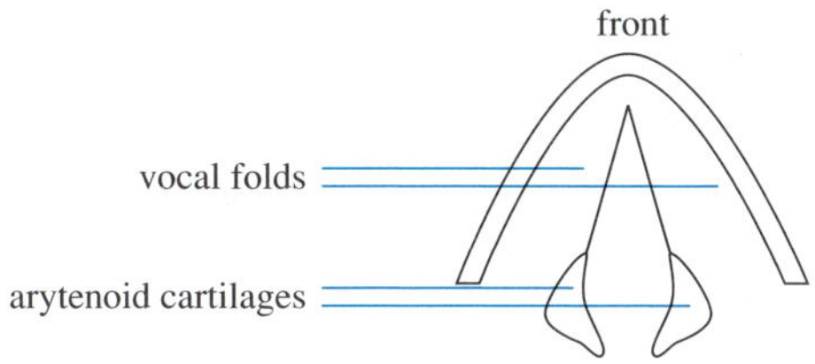


Fig. 11 The inside of the larynx seen from above

small cartilages called the **arytenoid cartilages** so that if the arytenoid cartilages move, the vocal folds move too.

The arytenoid cartilages are attached to the top of the **cricoid cartilage**, but they can move so as to move the vocal folds apart or together (Fig. 12). We use the word **glottis** to refer to the opening between the vocal folds. If the vocal folds are apart we say that the glottis is open; if they are pressed together we say that the glottis is closed. This seems quite simple, but in fact we can produce a very complex range of changes in the vocal folds and their positions.

These changes are often important in speech. Let us first look at four easily recognisable states of the vocal folds; it would be useful to practise moving your vocal folds into these different positions.

i) Wide apart: The vocal folds are wide apart for normal breathing and usually during voiceless consonants like p, f, s (Fig. 13a). Your vocal folds are probably apart now.

ii) Narrow glottis: If air is passed through the glottis when it is narrowed as in Fig. 13b, the result is a fricative sound for which the symbol is h. The sound is not very different from a whispered vowel. It is called a **voiceless glottal fricative.** (Fricatives are discussed in more detail in Chapter 6.) Practise saying hahahaha – alternating between this state of the vocal folds and that described in (iii) below.

iii) Position for vocal fold vibration: When the edges of the vocal folds are touching each other, or nearly touching, air passing through the glottis will usually cause vibration (Fig. 13c). Air is pressed up from the lungs and this air pushes the vocal folds apart so that a little air escapes. As the air flows quickly past the edges of

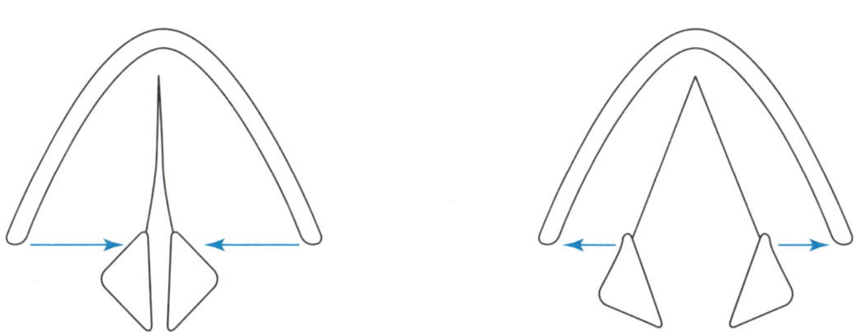

Fig. 12 Arytenoid cartilages causing closing and opening of the glottis

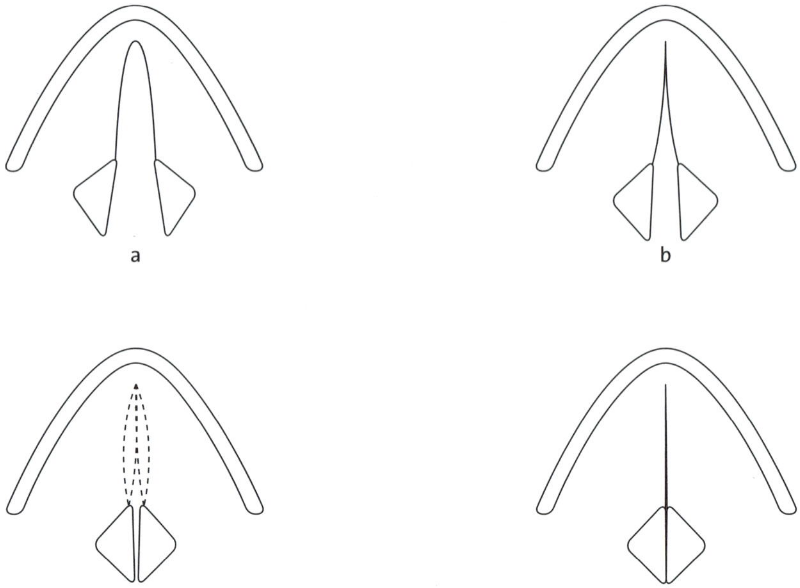


Fig. 13 Four different states of the glottis

the vocal folds, the folds are brought together again. This opening and closing happens very rapidly and is repeated regularly, roughly between two and three hundred times per second in a woman's voice and about half that rate in an adult man's voice.

iv) Vocal folds tightly closed: The vocal folds can be firmly pressed together so that air cannot pass between them (Fig. 13d). When this happens in speech we call it a **glottal stop** or **glottal plosive**, for which we use the symbol ʔ. You can practise this by coughing gently; then practise the sequence aʔaʔaʔaʔaʔa.

## 4.2 Respiration and voicing

Section 4.1 referred several times to air passing between the vocal folds. The normal way for this airflow to be produced is for some of the air in the lungs to be pushed out; when air is made to move out of the lungs we say that there is an **egressive pulmonic airstream**. All speech sounds are made with some movement of air, and the egressive pulmonic is by far the most commonly found air movement in the languages of the world. There are other ways of making air move in the vocal tract, but they are not usually relevant in the study of English pronunciation, so we will not discuss them here.

How is air moved into and out of the lungs? Knowing about this is important, since it will make it easier to understand many aspects of speech, particularly the nature of stress and intonation. The lungs are like sponges that can fill with air, and they are contained within the rib cage (Fig. 14). If the rib cage is lifted upwards and outwards there

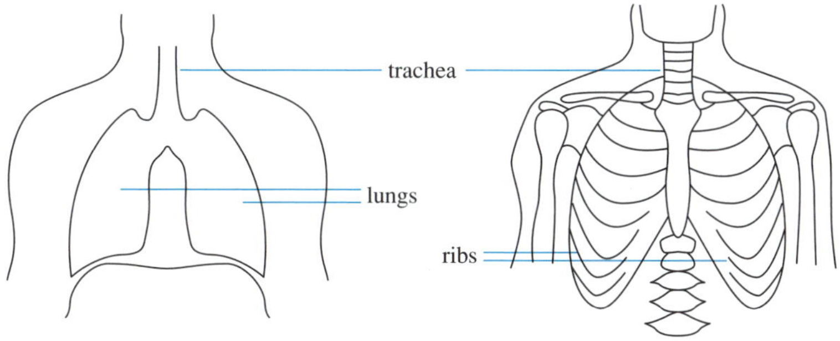


Fig. 14 The lungs and the rib cage

is more space in the chest for the lungs and they expand, with the result that they take in more air. If we allow the rib cage to return to its rest position quite slowly, some of the air is expelled and can be used for producing speech sounds. If we wish to make the egressive pulmonic airstream continue without breathing in again – for example, when saying a long sentence and not wanting to be interrupted – we can make the rib cage press down on the lungs so that more air is expelled.

In talking about making air flow into and out of the lungs, the process has been described as though the air were free to pass with no obstruction. But, as we saw in Chapter 2, to make speech sounds we must obstruct the airflow in some way – breathing by itself makes very little sound. We obstruct the airflow by making one or more obstructions or **strictures** in the vocal tract, and one place where we can make a stricture is in the larynx, by bringing the vocal folds close to each other as described in the previous section. Remember that there will be no vocal fold vibration unless the vocal folds are in the correct position and the air below the vocal folds is under enough pressure to be forced through the glottis.

If the vocal folds vibrate we will hear the sound that we call **voicing** or **phonation**. There are many different sorts of voicing that we can produce – think of the differences in the quality of your voice between singing, shouting and speaking quietly, or think of the different voices you might use reading a story to young children in which you have to read out what is said by characters such as giants, fairies, mice or ducks; many of the differences are made with the larynx. We can make changes in the vocal folds themselves – they can, for example, be made longer or shorter, more tense or more relaxed or be more or less strongly pressed together. The pressure of the air below the vocal folds (the **subglottal pressure**) can also be varied. Three main differences are found:

i) Variations in **intensity**: We produce voicing with high intensity for shouting, for example, and with low intensity for speaking quietly.
ii) Variations in **frequency**: If the vocal folds vibrate rapidly, the voicing is at high frequency; if there are fewer vibrations per second, the frequency is lower.
iii) Variations in **quality**: We can produce different-sounding voice qualities, such as those we might call *harsh*, *breathy*, *murmured* or *creaky*.

## 4.3 Plosives

A **plosive** is a consonant articulation with the following characteristics:

a) One articulator is moved against another, or two articulators are moved against each other, so as to form a stricture that allows no air to escape from the vocal tract. The stricture is, then, total.
b) After this stricture has been formed and air has been compressed behind it, it is **released** – that is, air is allowed to escape.
c) If the air behind the stricture is still under pressure when the plosive is released, it is probable that the escape of air will produce noise loud enough to be heard. This noise is called **plosion.**
d) There may be voicing during part or all of the plosive articulation.

To give a complete description of a plosive consonant we must describe what happens at each of the following four phases in its production:

i) The first phase is when the articulator or articulators move to form the stricture for the plosive. We call this the **closing phase.**
ii) The second phase is when the compressed air is stopped from escaping. We call this the **compression phase.**
iii) The third phase is when the articulators used to form the stricture are moved so as to allow air to escape. This is the **release phase**.
iv) The fourth phase is what happens immediately after (iii), so we will call it the **post-release phase.**

## 4.4 English plosives

English has six plosive consonants: p, t, k, b, d, g. The glottal plosive ʔ occurs frequently but it is of less importance, since it is usually just an alternative pronunciation of p, t, k in certain contexts. The plosives have different places of articulation. The plosives p, b are bilabial since the lips are pressed together (Fig. 15); t, d are alveolar since the tongue blade is pressed against the alveolar ridge (Fig. 16). Normally the tongue does not touch the front teeth as it does in the dental plosives found in many languages. The plosives k, g are velar; the back of the tongue is pressed against the area where the hard palate ends and the soft palate begins (Fig. 17).

The plosives p, t, k are always voiceless; b, d, g are sometimes fully voiced, sometimes partly voiced and sometimes voiceless. We will consider what b, d, g should be called in Section 4.5 below.

All six plosives can occur at the beginning of a word (**initial position**), between other sounds (**medial position**) and at the end of a word (**final position**). To begin with we will look at plosives preceding vowels (which can be abbreviated as CV, where C stands for a consonant and V stands for a vowel), between vowels (VCV) and following vowels (VC). We will look at more complex environments in later chapters.

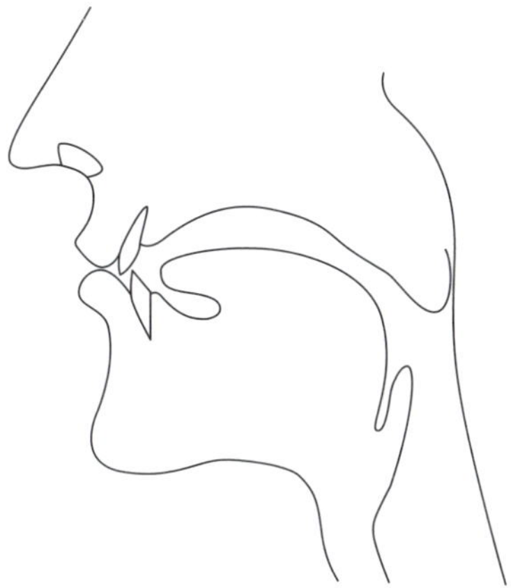

Fig. 15 Bilabial articulation

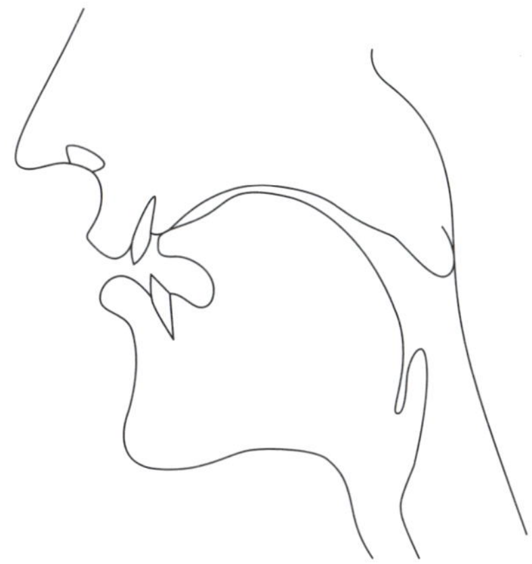

Fig. 16 Alveolar articulation

AU4 (CD 1), Ex 1

i) Initial position (CV): The closing phase for p, t, k and b, d, g takes place silently. During the compression phase there is no voicing in p, t, k; in b, d, g there is normally very little voicing – it begins only just before the release. If the speaker pronounces an initial b, d, g very slowly and carefully there may be voicing during the entire compression phase (the plosive is then fully voiced), while in rapid speech there may be no voicing at all.

The release of p, t, k is followed by audible plosion – that is, a burst of noise. There is then, in the post-release phase, a period during which air escapes through the vocal folds, making a sound like h. This is called **aspiration**. Then the vocal folds come together and voicing begins. The release of b, d, g is followed by weak plosion, and this happens at about the same time as, or shortly after, the beginning of voicing. The most noticeable and important difference, then, between initial p, t, k and b, d, g is the aspiration of the voiceless plosives p, t, k. The different phases of the plosive all happen very

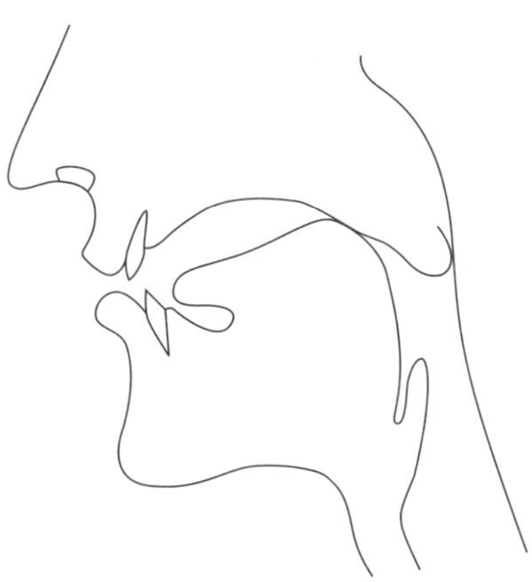

Fig. 17 Velar articulation

rapidly, but the ear distinguishes clearly between p, t, k and b, d, g. If English speakers hear a fully voiced initial plosive, they will hear it as one of b, d, g but will notice that it does not sound quite natural. If they hear a voiceless unaspirated plosive they will also hear that as one of b, d, g, because it is aspiration, not voicing which distinguishes initial p, t, k from b, d, g. Only when they hear a voiceless aspirated plosive will they hear it as one of p, t, k; experiments have shown that we perceive aspiration when there is a delay between the sound of plosion and the beginning (or **onset**) of voicing.

In initial position, b, d, g cannot be preceded by any consonant, but p, t, k may be preceded by s. When one of p, t, k is preceded by s it is unaspirated. From what was said above it should be clear that the unaspirated p, t, k of the initial combinations sp, st, sk have the sound quality that makes English speakers perceive a plosive as one of b, d, g; if a recording of a word beginning with one of sp, st, sk is heard with the s removed, an initial b, d or g is perceived by English speakers.

ii) Medial position (VCV): The pronunciation of p, t, k and b, d, g in medial position depends to some extent on whether the syllables preceding and following the plosive are stressed. In general we can say that a medial plosive may have the characteristics either of final or of initial plosives.

AU4 (CD 1), Exs 2 & 3

iii) Final position (VC): Final b, d, g normally have little voicing; if there is voicing, it is at the beginning of the compression phase; p, t, k are always voiceless. The plosion following the release of p, t, k and b, d, g is very weak and often not audible. The difference between p, t, k and b, d, g is primarily the fact that vowels preceding p, t, k are much shorter. The shortening effect of p, t, k is most noticeable when the vowel is one of the long vowels or diphthongs. This effect is sometimes known as **pre-fortis clipping**.

## 4.5 Fortis and lenis

Are b, d, g voiced plosives? The description of them makes it clear that it is not very accurate to call them "voiced"; in initial and final position they are scarcely voiced at all, and any voicing they may have seems to have no perceptual importance. Some phoneticians say that p, t, k are produced with more force than b, d, g, and that it would therefore be better to give the two sets of plosives (and some other consonants) names that indicate that fact; so the voiceless plosives p, t, k are sometimes called **fortis** (meaning 'strong') and b, d, g are then called **lenis** (meaning 'weak'). It may well be true that p, t, k are produced with more force, though nobody has really proved it – force of articulation is very difficult to define and measure. On the other hand, the terms fortis and lenis are difficult to remember. Despite this, we shall follow the practice of many books and use these terms.

The plosive phonemes of English can be presented in the form of a table as shown here:

| | PLACE OF ARTICULATION | | |
|---|---|---|---|
| | Bilabial | Alveolar | Velar |
| Fortis ("voiceless") | p | t | k |
| Lenis ("voiced") | b | d | g |

Tables like this can be produced for all the different consonants. Each major type of consonant (such as plosives like p, t, k, fricatives like s, z, and nasals like m, n) obstructs the airflow in a different way, and these are classed as different **manners of articulation**.

## Notes on problems and further reading

**4.1, 4.2** For more information about the larynx and about respiration in relation to speech, see Raphael *et al.*, (2006); Laver (1994: Chapters 6 and 7); Ashby and Maidment (2005: Chapter 2).

**4.3** The outline of the stages in the production of plosives is based on Cruttenden (2008: 158). In classifying consonants it is possible to go to a very high level of complexity if one wishes to account for all the possibilities; see, for example, Pike (1943: 85–156).

**4.4** It has been pointed out that the transcription sb, sd, sg could be used quite appropriately instead of sp, st, sk in syllable-initial position; see Davidsen-Nielsen (1969). The vowel length difference before final voiceless consonants is apparently found in many (possibly all) languages, but in English this difference – which is very slight in most languages – has become exaggerated so that it has become the most important factor in distinguishing between final p, t, k and b, d, g; see Chen (1970). Some phonetics books wrongly state that b, d, g lengthen preceding vowels, rather than that p, t, k shorten them. The conclusive evidence on this point is that if we take the pair 'right' raɪt and 'ride' raɪd, and then compare 'rye' raɪ, the length of the aɪ diphthong when no consonant follows is practically the same as in 'ride'; the aɪ in 'right' is much shorter than the aɪ in 'ride' and 'rye'.

**4.5** The *fortis/lenis* distinction is a very complicated matter. It is necessary to consider how one could measure "force of articulation"; many different laboratory techniques have been tried to see if the articulators are moved more energetically for fortis consonants, but all have proved inconclusive. The only difference that seems reasonably reliable is that fortis consonants have higher air pressure in the vocal tract, but Lisker (1970) has argued convincingly that this is not conclusive evidence for a "force of articulation" difference. It is possible to ask phonetically untrained speakers whether they feel that more energy is used in pronouncing p, t, k than in b, d, g, but there are many difficulties in doing this. A useful review of the "force of articulation" question is in Catford (1977: 199–208). I feel the best conclusion is that any term one uses to deal with this distinction (whether *fortis/lenis* or *voiceless/voiced*) is to be looked on as a **cover term** – a term which has no simple physical meaning but which may stand for a large and complex set of phonetic characteristics.

## Written exercises

1 Write brief descriptions of the actions of the articulators and the respiratory system in the words given below. Your description should start and finish with the position for normal breathing. Here is a description of the pronunciation of the word 'bee' biː as an example:

> Starting from the position for normal breathing, the lips are closed and the lungs are compressed to create air pressure in the vocal tract. The tongue moves to the position for a close front vowel, with the front of the tongue raised close to the hard palate. The vocal folds are brought close together and voicing begins; the lips then open, releasing the compressed air. Voicing continues for the duration of an iː vowel. Then the lung pressure is lowered, voicing ceases and the articulators return to the normal breathing position.

Words to describe: (a) goat; (b) ape.

2 Transcribe the following words:

| | | |
|---|---|---|
| a) bake | d) bought | g) bored |
| b) goat | e) tick | h) guard |
| c) doubt | f) bough | i) pea |

# 5 Phonemes and symbols

## 5.1 The phoneme

In Chapters 2–4 we have been studying some of the sounds of English. It is now necessary to consider some fundamental theoretical questions. What do we mean when we use the word "sound"? How do we establish what are the sounds of English, and how do we decide how many there are of them?

When we speak, we produce a continuous stream of sounds. In studying speech we divide this stream into small pieces that we call **segments**. The word 'man' is pronounced with a first segment m, a second segment æ and a third segment n. It is not always easy to decide on the number of segments. To give a simple example, in the word 'mine' the first segment is m and the last is n, as in the word 'man' discussed above. But should we regard the aɪ in the middle as one segment or two? We will return to this question.

As well as the question of how we divide speech up into segments, there is the question of how many different sounds (or segment types) there are in English. Chapters 2 and 3 introduced the set of vowels found in English. Each of these can be pronounced in many slightly different ways, so that the total range of sounds actually produced by speakers is practically infinite. Yet we feel quite confident in saying that the number of English vowels is not greater than twenty. Why is this? The answer is that if we put one of those twenty in the place of one of the others, we can change the meaning of a word. For example, if we substitute æ for e in the word 'bed' we get a different word: 'bad'. But in the case of two slightly different ways of pronouncing what we regard as "the same sound", we usually find that, if we substitute one for the other, a change in the meaning of a word does not result. If we substitute a more open vowel, for example cardinal vowel no. 4 [a] for the æ in the word 'bad', the word is still heard as 'bad'.

The principles involved here may be easier to understand if we look at a similar situation related to the letters of the alphabet that we use in writing English. The letter of the alphabet in writing is a unit which corresponds fairly well to the unit of speech we have been talking about earlier in this chapter – the segment. In the alphabet we have five letters that are called vowels: 'a', 'e', 'i', 'o', 'u'. If we choose the right context we can show how substituting one letter for another will change meaning. Thus with a letter 'p' before and a letter 't' after the vowel letter, we get the five words spelt 'pat', 'pet', 'pit', 'pot', 'put', each of which has a different meaning. We can do the same with *sounds*. If we look at the short vowels ɪ, e, æ, ʌ, ɒ, ʊ, for example, we can see how substituting one for another in between the plosives p and t gives us six different words as follows (given in spelling on the left):

| | |
|---|---|
| 'pit' pɪt | 'putt' pʌt |
| 'pet' pet | 'pot' pɒt |
| 'pat' pæt | 'put' pʊt |

Let us return to the example of letters of the alphabet. If someone who knew nothing about the alphabet saw these four characters:

'A' 'a' 'ɑ' 'u'

they would not know that to users of the alphabet three of these characters all represent the same letter, while the fourth is a different letter. They would quickly discover, through noticing differences in meaning, that 'u' is a different letter from the first three. What would our illiterate observer discover about these three? They would eventually come to the conclusion about the written characters 'a' and 'ɑ' that the former occurs most often in printed and typed writing while the latter is more common in handwriting, but that if you substitute one for the other it will not cause a difference in meaning. If our observer then examined a lot of typed and printed material they would eventually conclude that a word that began with 'a' when it occurred in the middle of a sentence would begin with 'A', and *never* with 'a', at the beginning of a sentence. They would also find that names could begin with 'A' but *never* with 'a'; they would conclude that 'A' and 'a' were different ways of writing the same letter and that a context in which one of them could occur was always a context in which the other could not. As will be explained below, we find similar situations in speech sounds.

If you have not thought about such things before, you may find some difficulty in understanding the ideas that you have just read about. The principal difficulty lies in the fact that what is being talked about in our example of letters is at the same time something *abstract* (the alphabet, which you cannot see or touch) and something *real* and *concrete* (marks on paper). The alphabet is something that its users know; they also know that it has twenty-six letters. But when the alphabet is used to write with, these letters appear on the page in a practically infinite number of different shapes and sizes.

Now we will leave the discussion of letters and the alphabet; these have only been introduced in this chapter in order to help explain some important general principles. Let us go back to the sounds of speech and see how these principles can be explained. As was said earlier in this chapter, we can divide speech up into segments, and we can find great variety in the way these segments are made. But just as there is an abstract alphabet as the basis of our writing, so there is an abstract set of units as the basis of our speech. These units are called **phonemes**, and the complete set of these units is called the **phonemic system** of the language. The phonemes themselves are abstract, but there are many slightly different ways in which we make the sounds that represent these phonemes, just as there are many ways in which we may make a mark on a piece of paper to represent a particular (abstract) letter of the alphabet.

We find cases where it makes little difference which of two possible ways we choose to pronounce a sound. For example, the b at the beginning of a word such as 'bad' will usually be pronounced with practically no voicing. Sometimes, though, a speaker may produce the b with full voicing, perhaps in speaking very emphatically. If this is done, the sound is still identified as the phoneme b, even though we can hear that it is different in some way. We have in this example two different ways of making b – two different **realisations** of the phoneme. One can be substituted for the other without changing the meaning.

We also find cases in speech similar to the writing example of capital 'A' and little 'a' (one can only occur where the other cannot). For example, we find that the realisation of t in the word 'tea' is aspirated (as are all voiceless plosives when they occur before stressed vowels at the beginning of syllables). In the word 'eat', the realisation of t is unaspirated (as are all voiceless plosives when they occur at the end of a syllable and are not followed by a vowel). The aspirated and unaspirated realisations are both recognised as t by English speakers despite their differences. But the aspirated realisation will never be found in the place where the unaspirated realisation is appropriate, and vice versa. When we find this strict separation of places where particular realisations can occur, we say that the realisations are in **complementary distribution**. One more technical term needs to be introduced: when we talk about different realisations of phonemes, we sometimes call these realisations **allophones**. In the last example, we were studying the aspirated and unaspirated allophones of the phoneme t. Usually we do not indicate different allophones when we write symbols to represent sounds.

## 5.2 Symbols and transcription

You have now seen a number of symbols of several different sorts. Basically the symbols are for one of two purposes: either they are symbols for phonemes (**phonemic** symbols) or they are **phonetic** symbols (which is what the symbols were first introduced as).

We will look first at phonemic symbols. The most important point to remember is the rather obvious-seeming fact that the number of phonemic symbols must be exactly the same as the number of phonemes we decide exist in the language. It is rather like typing on a keyboard – there is a fixed number of keys that you can press. However, some of our phonemic symbols consist of two characters; for example, we usually treat tʃ (as in 'chip' tʃɪp) as one phoneme, so tʃ is a phonemic *symbol* consisting of two *characters* (t and ʃ).

One of the traditional exercises in pronunciation teaching by phonetic methods is that of **phonemic transcription**, where every speech sound must be identified as one of the phonemes and written with the appropriate symbol. There are two different kinds of transcription exercise: in one, **transcription from dictation**, the student must listen to a person, or a recording, and write down what they hear; in the other, **transcription from a written text**, the student is given a passage written in orthography and must use phonemic symbols to represent how she or he thinks it would be pronounced by a speaker of a particular accent. In a phonemic transcription, then, only the phonemic symbols may be used; this has the advantage that it is comparatively quick and easy to learn to use it. The disadvantage is that as you continue to learn more about phonetics you become able to hear a lot of sound differences that you were not aware of before, and students at this stage find it frustrating not to be able to write down more detailed information.

The phonemic system described here for the BBC accent contains forty-four phonemes. We can display the complete set of these phonemes by the usual classificatory methods used by most phoneticians; the vowels and diphthongs can be located in the vowel quadrilateral – as was done in Chapters 2 and 3 – and the consonants can be placed in a chart or table according to place of articulation, manner of articulation and voicing. Human beings can make many more sounds than these, and phoneticians use a much larger set of symbols when they are trying to represent sounds more accurately. The best-known set of symbols is that of the International Phonetic Association's alphabet (the letters IPA are used to refer to the Association and also to its alphabet). The vowel symbols of the cardinal vowel system (plus a few others) are usually included on the chart of this alphabet, which is reproduced at the beginning of the book (p. xii). It is important to note that in addition to the many symbols on the chart there are a lot of **diacritics** – marks which modify the symbol in some way; for example, the symbol for cardinal vowel no. 4 [a] may be modified by putting two dots above it. This **centralisation** diacritic then gives us the symbol [ä] for a vowel which is nearer to central than [a]. It would not be possible in this course to teach you to use all these symbols and diacritics, but someone who did know them all could write a transcription that was much more accurate in phonetic detail, and contained much more information than a phonemic transcription. Such a transcription would be called a **phonetic transcription**; a phonetic transcription containing a lot of information about the exact quality of the sounds would be called a **narrow** phonetic transcription, while one which only included a little more information than a phonemic transcription would be called a **broad** phonetic transcription. One further type of transcription is one which is basically phonemic, but contains additional symbolic information about allophones of particular symbols: this is often called an **allophonic** transcription. As an example of the use of allophonic transcription, in this course phonetic symbols are used occasionally when it is necessary to give an accurate label to an allophone of some English phoneme, but we do not do any phonetic transcription of continuous speech: that is a rather specialised exercise. A widely-used convention is to enclose symbols within brackets that show whether they are phonemic or phonetic: when symbols are used to represent precise phonetic values, rather than phonemes, they are often enclosed in square brackets [ ], as we have done already with cardinal vowels; in many phonetics books, phonemic symbols are enclosed within slant brackets / /. While this convention is useful when giving a few examples, there is so much transcription in this book that I feel it would be an unnecessary distraction to enclose each example in brackets. We will continue to use square brackets for cardinal vowel symbols, but elsewhere all symbols are printed in **blue**

**type**, and the context should make it clear whether the symbols are phonemic or phonetic in function.

It should now be clear that there is a fundamental difference between phonemic symbols and phonetic symbols. Since the phonemic symbols do not have to indicate precise phonetic quality, it is possible to choose among several possible symbols to represent a particular phoneme; this has had the unfortunate result that different books on English pronunciation have used different symbols, causing quite a lot of confusion to students. In this course we are using the symbols now most frequently used in British publishing. It would be too long a task to examine other writers' symbols in detail, but it is worth considering some of the reasons for the differences. One factor is the complication and expense of using special symbols which create problems in typing and printing; it could, for example, be argued that a is a symbol that is found in practically all typefaces whereas æ is unusual, and that the a symbol should be used for the vowel in 'cat' instead of æ. Some writers have concentrated on producing a set of phonemic symbols that need the minimum number of special or non-standard symbols. Others have thought it important that the symbols should be as close as possible to the symbols that a phonetician would choose to give a precise indication of sound quality. To use the same example again, referring to the vowel in 'cat', it could be argued that if the vowel is noticeably closer than cardinal vowel no. 4 [a], it is more suitable to use the symbol æ, which is usually used to represent a vowel between open-mid and open. There can be disagreements about the most important characteristics of a sound that a symbol should indicate: one example is the vowels of the words 'bit' and 'beat'. Some writers have claimed that the most important difference between them is that the former is short and the latter long, and transcribed the former with i and the latter with iː (the difference being entirely in the length mark); other writers have said that the length (or quantity) difference is less important than the quality difference, and transcribe the vowel of 'bit' with the symbol ɪ and that of 'beat' with i. Yet another point of view is that quality and quantity are *both* important and should *both* be indicated; this point of view results in a transcription using ɪ for 'bit' and iː, a symbol different from ɪ both in shape of symbol (suggesting quality difference) and in length mark (indicating quantity difference), for 'beat'. This is the approach taken in this course.

## 5.3 Phonology

Chapters 2–4 were mainly concerned with matters of **phonetics** – the comparatively straightforward business of describing the sounds that we use in speaking. When we talk about how phonemes function in language, and the relationships among the different phonemes – when, in other words, we study the *abstract* side of the sounds of language, we are studying a related but different subject that we call **phonology**. Only by studying both the phonetics and the phonology of English is it possible to acquire a full understanding of the use of sounds in English speech. Let us look briefly at some areas that come within the subject of phonology; these areas of study will be covered in more detail later in the course.

### Study of the phonemic system

It is sometimes helpful to think of the phonemic system as being similar to the set of cards used in a card game, or the set of pieces used in a game of chess. In chess, for example, the exact shape and colour of the pieces are not important to the game as long as they can be reliably distinguished. But the number of pieces, the moves they can make and their relationship to all the other pieces are very important; we would say that if any of these were to be changed, the game would no longer be what we call chess. Similarly, playing cards can be printed in many different styles and sizes, but while changing these things does not affect the game played with them, if we were to remove one card from the pack or add one card to it before the start of a game, nobody would accept that we were playing the game correctly. In a similar way, we have a more or less fixed set of "pieces" (phonemes) with which to play the game of speaking English. There may be many slightly different realisations of the various phonemes, but the most important thing for communication is that we should be able to make use of the full set of phonemes.

### Phoneme sequences and syllable structure

In every language we find that there are restrictions on the sequences of phonemes that are used. For example, no English word begins with the consonant sequence zbf and no word ends with the sequence æh. In phonology we try to analyse what the restrictions and regularities are in a particular language, and it is usually found helpful to do this by studying the **syllables** of the language.

### Suprasegmental phonology

Many significant sound contrasts are not the result of differences between phonemes. For example, **stress** is important: when the word 'import' is pronounced with the first syllable sounding stronger than the second, English speakers hear it as a noun, whereas when the second syllable is stronger the word is heard as a verb. **Intonation** is also important: if the word 'right' is said with the pitch of the voice rising, it is likely to be heard as a question or as an invitation to a speaker to continue, while falling pitch is more likely to be heard as confirmation or agreement. These examples show sound contrasts that extend over several segments (phonemes), and such contrasts are called **suprasegmental**. We will look at a number of other aspects of suprasegmental phonology later in the course.

## Notes on problems and further reading

This chapter is theoretical rather than practical. There is no shortage of material to read on the subject of the phoneme, but much of it is rather difficult and assumes a lot of background knowledge. For basic reading I would suggest Katamba (1989: Chapter 2), Cruttenden (2008: Chapter 5, Section 3) or Giegerich (1992: 29–33). There are many classic works: Jones (1976; first published 1950) is widely regarded as such, although it is often criticised nowadays for being superficial or even naive. Another classic work is Pike's *Phonemics* (1947), subtitled "A Technique for Reducing Languages to Writing":

this is essentially a practical handbook for people who need to analyse the phonemes of unknown languages, and contains many examples and exercises.

The subject of symbols is a large one: there is a good survey in Abercrombie (1967: Chapter 7). The IPA has tried as far as possible to keep to Roman-style symbols, although it is inevitable that these symbols have to be supplemented with **diacritics** (extra marks that add detail to symbols – to mark the vowel [e] as long, we can add the length diacritic ː to give [eː], or to mark it as centralised we can add the centralisation diacritic ¨ to give [ë]). The IPA's present practice on symbolisation is set out in the *Handbook of the International Phonetic Association* (IPA, 1999). There is a lot of information about symbol design and choice in Pullum and Ladusaw (1996). Some phoneticians working at the end of the nineteenth century tried to develop non-alphabetic sets of symbols whose shape would indicate all essential phonetic characteristics; these are described in Abercrombie (1967: Chapter 7).

We have seen that one must choose between, on the one hand, symbols that are very informative but slow to write and, on the other, symbols that are not very precise but are quick and convenient to use. Pike (1943) presents at the end of his book an "analphabetic notation" designed to permit the coding of sounds with great precision on the basis of their articulation; an indication of the complexity of the system is the fact that the full specification of the vowel [o] requires eighty-eight characters. On the opposite side, many American writers have avoided various IPA symbols as being too complex, and have tried to use as far as possible symbols and diacritics which are already in existence for various special alphabetic requirements of European languages and which are available on standard keyboards. For example, where the IPA has ʃ and ʒ, symbols not usually found outside phonetics, many Americans use š and ž, the mark above the symbols being widely used for Slavonic languages that do not use the Cyrillic alphabet. The widespread use of computer printers and word processing has revolutionised the use of symbols, and sets of phonetic fonts are widely available via the Internet. We are still some way, however, from having a universally agreed set of IPA symbol codes, and for much computer-based phonetic research it is necessary to make do with conventions which use existing keyboard characters.

## Note for teachers

It should be made clear to students that the treatment of the phoneme in this chapter is only an introduction. It is difficult to go into detailed examples since not many symbols have been introduced at this stage, so further consideration of phonological issues is left until later chapters.

## Written exercises

The words in the following list should be transcribed first phonemically, then (in square brackets) phonetically. In your phonetic transcription you should use the following diacritics:

- b, d, g pronounced without voicing are transcribed b̥, d̥, g̊
- p, t, k pronounced with aspiration are transcribed $p^h$, $t^h$, $k^h$

- iː, ɑː, ɔː, ɜː, uː when shortened by a following fortis consonant should be transcribed iˑ, ɑˑ, ɔˑ, ɜˑ, uˑ
- ɪ, e, æ, ʌ, ɒ, ʊ, ə when shortened by a following fortis consonant should be transcribed ɪ̆, ĕ, ǣ, ʌ̆, ɒ̆, ʊ̆, ə̆. Use the same mark for diphthongs, placing the diacritic on the first part of the diphthong.

*Example* spelling: 'peat'; phonemic: piːt phonetic: pʰiˑt

*Words for transcription*

| | | | | |
|---|---|---|---|---|
| a) speed | c) book | e) car | g) appeared | i) stalk |
| b) partake | d) goat | f) bad | h) toast | |

# 6 Fricatives and affricates

## 6.1 Production of fricatives and affricates

**Fricatives** are consonants with the characteristic that air escapes through a narrow passage and makes a hissing sound. Most languages have fricatives, the most commonly found being something like s. Fricatives are **continuant** consonants, which means that you can continue making them without interruption as long as you have enough air in your lungs. Plosives, which were described in Chapter 4, are not continuants. You can demonstrate the importance of the narrow passage for the air in the following ways:

i) Make a long, hissing s sound and gradually lower your tongue so that it is no longer close to the roof of the mouth. The hissing sound will stop as the air passage gets larger.
ii) Make a long f sound and, while you are producing this sound, use your fingers to pull the lower lip away from the upper teeth. Notice how the hissing sound of the air escaping between teeth and lip suddenly stops.

**Affricates** are rather complex consonants. They begin as plosives and end as fricatives. A familiar example is the affricate heard at the beginning and end of the word 'church'. It begins with an articulation practically the same as that for t, but instead of a rapid release with plosion and aspiration as we would find in the word 'tip', the tongue moves to the position for the fricative ʃ that we find at the beginning of the word 'ship'. So the plosive is followed immediately by fricative noise. Since phonetically this affricate is composed of t and ʃ we represent it as tʃ, so that the word 'church' is transcribed as tʃɜːtʃ.

However, the definition of an affricate must be more restricted than what has been given so far. We would not class all sequences of plosive plus fricative as affricates; for example, we find in the middle of the word 'breakfast' the plosive k followed by the fricative f. English speakers would generally not accept that kf forms a consonantal unit in the way that tʃ seems to. It is usually said that the plosive and the following fricative must be made with the same articulators – the plosive and fricative must be **homorganic**. The sounds k, f are not homorganic, but t, d and ʃ, ʒ, being made with the tongue blade against the alveolar ridge, *are* homorganic. This still leaves the possibility of quite a large number of affricates since, for example, t, d are homorganic not only with ʃ, ʒ but also with s, z, so ts, dz would also count as affricates. We could also consider tr, dr as affricates for the same reason. However, we normally only count tʃ, dʒ as affricate phonemes of English.

Although tʃ, dʒ can be said to be composed of a plosive and a fricative, it is usual to regard them as being single, independent phonemes of English. In this way, t is one phoneme, ʃ is another and tʃ yet another. We would say that the pronunciation of the word 'church' tʃɜːtʃ is composed of three phonemes, tʃ, ɜː and tʃ. We will look at this question of "two sounds = one phoneme" from the theoretical point of view in Chapter 13.

## 6.2 The fricatives of English

English has quite a complex system of fricative phonemes. They can be seen in the table below:

| | PLACE OF ARTICULATION | | | | |
|---|---|---|---|---|---|
| | Labiodental | Dental | Alveolar | Post-alveolar | Glottal |
| Fortis ("voiceless") | f | θ | s | ʃ | h |
| Lenis ("voiced") | v | ð | z | ʒ | |

With the exception of glottal, each place of articulation has a pair of phonemes, one fortis and one lenis. This is similar to what was seen with the plosives. The fortis fricatives are said to be articulated with greater force than the lenis, and their friction noise is louder. The lenis fricatives have very little or no voicing in initial and final positions, but may be voiced when they occur between voiced sounds. The fortis fricatives have the effect of shortening a preceding vowel in the same way as fortis plosives do (see Chapter 4, Section 4). Thus in a pair of words like 'ice' aɪs and 'eyes' aɪz, the aɪ diphthong in the first word is considerably shorter than aɪ in the second. Since there is only one fricative with glottal place of articulation, it would be rather misleading to call it fortis or lenis (which is why there is a line on the chart above dividing h from the other fricatives).

🎧 AU6 (CD 1), Exs 1–3

We will now look at the fricatives separately, according to their place of articulation.

f, v (example words: 'fan', 'van'; 'safer', 'saver'; 'half', 'halve')

These are **labiodental**: the lower lip is in contact with the upper teeth as shown in Fig. 18. The fricative noise is never very strong and is scarcely audible in the case of v.

θ, ð (example words: 'thumb', 'thus'; 'ether', 'father'; 'breath', 'breathe')

The **dental** fricatives are sometimes described as if the tongue were placed between the front teeth, and it is common for teachers to make their students do this when they are trying to teach them to make this sound. In fact, however, the tongue is normally placed

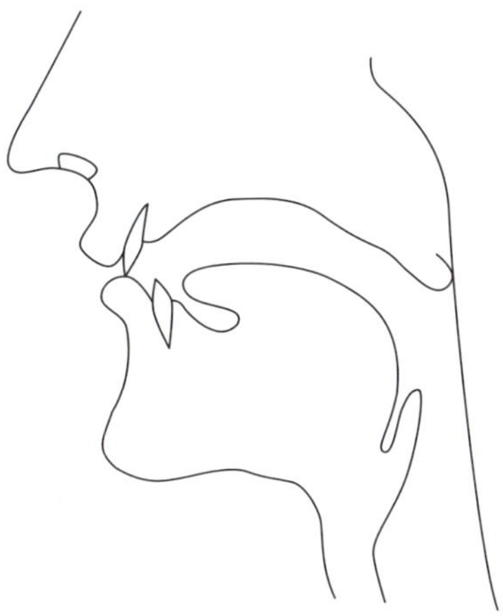

Fig. 18 Labiodental fricative

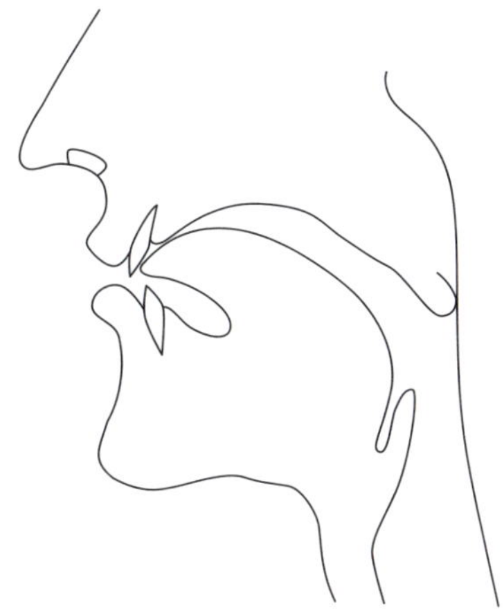

Fig. 19 Dental fricative

*behind* the teeth, as shown in Fig. 19, with the tip touching the inner side of the lower front teeth and the blade touching the inner side of the upper teeth. The air escapes through the gaps between the tongue and the teeth. As with f, v, the fricative noise is weak.

s, z (example words: 'sip', 'zip'; 'facing', 'phasing'; 'rice, 'rise')

These are alveolar fricatives, with the same place of articulation as t, d. The air escapes through a narrow passage along the centre of the tongue, and the sound produced is comparatively intense. The tongue position is shown in Fig. 16 in Chapter 4.

ʃ, ʒ (example words: 'ship' (initial ʒ is very rare in English); 'Russia', 'measure'; 'Irish', 'garage')

These fricatives are called **post-alveolar**, which can be taken to mean that the tongue is in contact with an area slightly further back than that for s, z (see Fig. 20). If you make s, then ʃ, you should be able to feel your tongue move backwards.

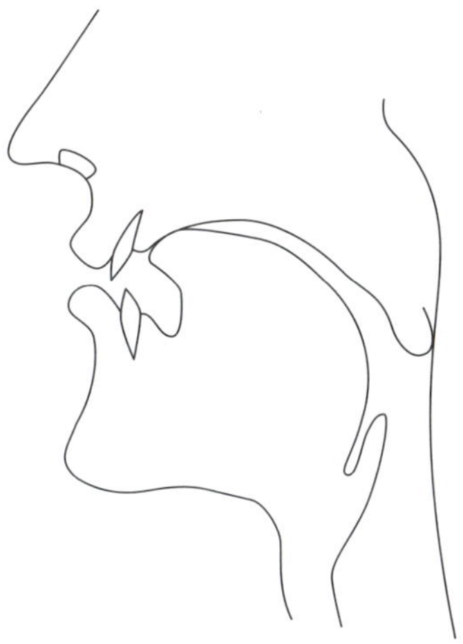

Fig. 20 Post-alveolar fricative

The air escapes through a passage along the centre of the tongue, as in s, z, but the passage is a little wider. Most BBC speakers have rounded lips for ʃ, ʒ, and this is an important difference between these consonants and s, z. The fricative ʃ is a common and widely distributed phoneme, but ʒ is not. All the other fricatives described so far (f, v, θ, ð, s, z, ʃ) can be found in initial, medial and final positions, as shown in the example words. In the case of ʒ, however, the distribution is much more limited. Very few English words begin with ʒ (most of them have come into the language comparatively recently from French) and not many end with this consonant. Only medially, in words such as 'measure' meʒə, 'usual' juːʒuəl is it found at all commonly.

h (example words: 'head', 'ahead', 'playhouse')

The place of articulation of this consonant is **glottal**. This means that the narrowing that produces the friction noise is between the vocal folds, as described in Chapter 4. If you breathe out silently, then produce h, you are moving your vocal folds from wide apart to close together. However, this is not producing speech. When we produce h in speaking English, many different things happen in different contexts. In the word 'hat', the h is followed by an æ vowel. The tongue, jaw and lip positions for the vowel are all produced simultaneously with the h consonant, so that the glottal fricative has an æ quality. The same is found for all vowels following h; the consonant always has the quality of the vowel it precedes, so that in theory if you could listen to a recording of h-sounds cut off from the beginnings of different vowels in words like 'hit', 'hat', 'hot', 'hut', etc., you should be able to identify which vowel would have followed the h. One way of stating the above facts is to say that *phonetically* h is a voiceless vowel with the quality of the voiced vowel that follows it.

Phonologically, h is a consonant. It is usually found before vowels. As well as being found in initial position it is found medially in words such as 'ahead' əhed, 'greenhouse' griːnhaʊs, 'boathook' bəʊthʊk. It is noticeable that when h occurs between voiced sounds (as in the words 'ahead', 'greenhouse'), it is pronounced with voicing – not the normal voicing of vowels but a weak, slightly fricative sound called **breathy voice**. It is not necessary for foreign learners to attempt to copy this voicing, although it is important to pronounce h where it should occur in BBC pronunciation. Many English speakers are surprisingly sensitive about this consonant; they tend to judge as sub-standard a pronunciation in which h is missing. In reality, however, practically all English speakers, however carefully they speak, omit the h in non-initial unstressed pronunciations of the words 'her', 'he', 'him', 'his' and the auxiliary 'have', 'has', 'had', although few are aware that they do this.

There are two rather uncommon sounds that need to be introduced; since they are said to have some association with h, they will be mentioned here. The first is the sound produced by some speakers in words which begin orthographically (i.e. in their spelling form) with 'wh'; most BBC speakers pronounce the initial sound in such words (e.g. 'which', 'why', 'whip', 'whale') as w (which is introduced in Chapter 7), but there are some (particularly when they are speaking clearly or emphatically) who pronounce the sound used by most American and Scottish speakers, a *voiceless* fricative with the same lip, tongue and jaw position as w. The phonetic symbol for this voiceless fricative is ʍ. We can find pairs of words showing the difference between this sound and the voiced sound w:

| | |
|---|---|
| 'witch' wɪtʃ | 'which' ʍɪtʃ |
| 'wail' weɪl | 'whale' ʍeɪl |
| 'Wye' waɪ | 'why' ʍaɪ |
| 'wear' weə | 'where' ʍeə |

The obvious conclusion to draw from this is that, since substituting one sound for the other causes a difference in meaning, the two sounds must be two different phonemes. It is therefore rather surprising to find that practically all writers on the subject of the phonemes of English decide that this answer is not correct, and that the sound ʍ in 'which', 'why', etc., is *not* a phoneme of English but is a realisation of a sequence of two phonemes, h and w. We do not need to worry much about this problem in describing the BBC accent. However, it should be noted that in the analysis of the many accents of English that do have a "voiceless w" there is not much more theoretical justification for treating the sound as h plus w than there is for treating p as h plus b. Whether the question of this sound is approached phonetically or phonologically, there is no h sound in the "voiceless w".

A very similar case is the sound found at the beginning of words such as 'huge', 'human', 'hue'. Phonetically this sound is a voiceless palatal fricative (for which the phonetic symbol is ç); there is no glottal fricative at the beginning of 'huge', etc. However, it is usual to treat this sound as h plus j (the latter is another consonant that is introduced in Chapter 7 – it is the sound at the beginning of 'yes', 'yet'). Again we can see that a phonemic analysis does not necessarily have to be exactly in line with phonetic facts. If we were to say that these two sounds ʍ, ç were phonemes of English, we would have two extra phonemes that do not occur very frequently. We will follow the usual practice of transcribing the sound at the beginning of 'huge', etc., as hj just because it is convenient and common practice.

## 6.3 **The affricates of English**

AU6 (CD 1), Exs 4 & 5

It was explained in Section 6.1 that tʃ, dʒ are the only two affricate phonemes in English. As with the plosives and most of the fricatives, we have a fortis/lenis pair, and the voicing characteristics are the same as for these other consonants. tʃ is slightly aspirated in the positions where p, t, k are aspirated, but not strongly enough for it to be necessary for foreign learners to give much attention to it. The place of articulation is the same as for ʃ, ʒ – that is, it is post-alveolar. This means that the t component of tʃ has a place of articulation rather further back in the mouth than the t plosive usually has. When tʃ is final in the syllable it has the effect of shortening a preceding vowel, as do other fortis consonants. tʃ, dʒ often have rounded lips.

## 6.4 Fortis consonants

All the consonants described so far, with the exception of h, belong to pairs distinguished by the difference between fortis and lenis. Since the remaining consonants to be described are not paired in this way, a few points that still have to be made about fortis consonants are included in this chapter.

The first point concerns the shortening of a preceding vowel by a syllable-final fortis consonant. As was said in Chapter 4, the effect is most noticeable in the case of long vowels and diphthongs, although it does also affect short vowels. What happens if something other than a vowel precedes a fortis consonant? This arises in syllables ending with l, m, n, ŋ, followed by a fortis consonant such as p, t, k as in 'belt' belt, 'bump' bʌmp, 'bent' bent, 'bank' bæŋk. The effect on those continuant consonants is the same as on a vowel: they are considerably shortened.

Fortis consonants are usually articulated with open glottis – that is, with the vocal folds separated. This is always the case with fricatives, where airflow is essential for successful production. However, with plosives an alternative possibility is to produce the consonant with completely *closed* glottis. This type of plosive articulation, known as **glottalisation**, is found widely in contemporary English pronunciation, though only in specific contexts. The glottal closure occurs immediately before p, t, k, tʃ. The most widespread glottalisation is that of tʃ at the end of a stressed syllable (I leave defining what "stressed syllable" means until Chapter 8). If we use the symbol ʔ to represent a glottal closure, the phonetic transcription for various words containing tʃ can be given as follows:

| | With glottalisation | Without glottalisation |
|---|---|---|
| 'nature' | neɪʔtʃə | neɪtʃə |
| 'catching' | kæʔtʃɪŋ | kætʃɪŋ |
| 'riches' | rɪʔtʃɪz | rɪtʃɪz |

There is similar glottalisation of p, t, k, although this is not so noticeable. It normally happens when the plosive is followed by another consonant or a pause; for example:

| | With glottalisation | Without glottalisation |
|---|---|---|
| 'actor' | æʔktə | æktə |
| 'petrol' | peʔtrəl | petrəl |
| 'mat' | mæʔt | mæt |
| 'football' | fʊʔtbɔːl | fʊtbɔːl |

Learners usually find these rules difficult to learn, from the practical point of view, and find it simpler to keep to the more conservative pronunciation which does not use glottalisation. However, it is worth pointing out the fact that this occurs – many learners notice the glottalisation and want to know what it is that they are hearing, and many of them find that they acquire the glottalised pronunciation in talking to native speakers.

## Notes on problems and further reading

The dental fricative ð is something of a problem: although there are not many English words in which this sound appears, those words are ones which occur very frequently – words like 'the', 'this, 'there', 'that'. This consonant often shows so little friction noise that on purely phonetic grounds it seems incorrect to class it as a fricative. It is more like a weak (lenis) dental plosive. This matter is discussed again in Chapter 14, Section 14.2.

On the phonological side, I have brought in a discussion of the phonemic analysis of two "marginal" fricatives ʍ, ç which present a problem (though not a particularly important or fundamental one): I feel that this is worth discussing in that it gives a good idea of the sort of problem that can arise in analysing the phonemic system of a language. The other problem area is the glottalisation described at the end of the chapter. There is now a growing awareness of how frequently this is to be found in contemporary English speech; however, it not easy to formulate rules stating the contexts in which this occurs. There is discussion in Brown (1990: 28–30), in Cruttenden (2008: Section 9.2.8), in Ladefoged (2006: 60–1) and in Wells (1982: Section 3.4.5).

## Notes for teachers

Whether learners should be taught to produce glottalisation of p, t, k, tʃ must depend on the level of the learner – I have often found advanced learners have been able to pick up this pronunciation, and I find the increase in naturalness in their accent very striking.

## Written exercises

1 Transcribe the following words phonemically:

| | |
|---|---|
| a) fishes | e) achieves |
| b) shaver | f) others |
| c) sixth | g) measure |
| d) these | h) ahead |

2 Following the style introduced in Exercise 1 for Chapter 4, describe the movements of the articulators in the first word of the above list.

# 7 Nasals and other consonants

So far we have studied two major groups of consonants – the plosives and fricatives – and also the affricates tʃ, dʒ; this gives a total of seventeen. There remain the **nasal** consonants – m, n, ŋ – and four others – l, r, w, j; these four are not easy to fit into groups. All of these seven consonants are continuants and usually have no friction noise, but in other ways they are very different from each other.

## 7.1 Nasals

The basic characteristic of a nasal consonant is that the air escapes through the nose. For this to happen, the soft palate must be lowered; in the case of all the other consonants and vowels of English, the soft palate is raised and air cannot pass through the nose. In nasal consonants, however, air does not pass through the mouth; it is prevented by a complete closure in the mouth at some point. If you produce a long sequence dndndndndn without moving your tongue from the position for alveolar closure, you will feel your soft palate moving up and down. The three types of closure are: bilabial (lips), alveolar (tongue blade against alveolar ridge) and velar (back of tongue against the palate). This set of places produces three nasal consonants – m, n, ŋ – which correspond to the three places of articulation for the pairs of plosives p b, t d, k g.

The consonants m, n are simple and straightforward with distributions quite similar to those of the plosives. There is in fact little to describe. However, ŋ is a different matter. It is a sound that gives considerable problems to foreign learners, and one that is so unusual in its phonological aspect that some people argue that it is not one of the phonemes of English at all. The place of articulation of ŋ is the same as that of k, g; it is a useful exercise to practise making a continuous ŋ sound. If you do this, it is very important not to produce a k or g at the end – pronounce the ŋ like m or n.

🎧 AU7 (CD 1), Exs 1 & 2

We will now look at some ways in which the distribution of ŋ is unusual.

i) In initial position we find m, n occurring freely, but ŋ never occurs in this position. With the possible exception of ʒ, this makes ŋ the only English consonant that does not occur initially.
ii) Medially, ŋ occurs quite frequently, but there is in the BBC accent a rather complex and quite interesting rule concerning the question of when ŋ may

be pronounced without a following plosive. When we find the letters 'nk' in the middle of a word in its orthographic form, a k will always be pronounced; however, some words with orthographic 'ng' in the middle will have a pronunciation containing ŋg and others will have ŋ without g. For example, in BBC pronunciation we find the following:

| A | B |
|---|---|
| 'finger' fɪŋgə | 'singer' sɪŋə |
| 'anger' æŋgə | 'hanger' hæŋə |

In the words of column A the ŋ is followed by g, while the words of column B have no g. What is the difference between A and B? The important difference is in the way the words are constructed – their **morphology**. The words of column B can be divided into two grammatical pieces: 'sing' + '-er', 'hang' + '-er'. These pieces are called **morphemes**, and we say that column B words are morphologically different from column A words, since these *cannot* be divided into two morphemes. 'Finger' and 'anger' consist of just one morpheme each.

We can summarise the position so far by saying that (within a word containing the letters 'ng' in the spelling) ŋ occurs without a following g if it occurs at the end of a morpheme; if it occurs in the middle of a morpheme it has a following g.

Let us now look at the ends of words *ending* orthographically with 'ng'. We find that these always end with ŋ; this ŋ is never followed by a g. Thus we find that the words 'sing' and 'hang' are pronounced as sɪŋ and hæŋ; to give a few more examples, 'song' is sɒŋ, 'bang' is bæŋ and 'long' is lɒŋ. We do not need a separate explanation for this: the rule given above, that no g is pronounced after ŋ at the end of a morpheme, works in these cases too, since the end of a word must also be the end of a morpheme. (If this point seems difficult, think of the comparable case of sentences and words: a sound or letter that comes at the end of a sentence must necessarily also come at the end of a word, so that the final k of the sentence 'This is a book' is also the final k of the word 'book'.)

Unfortunately, rules often have exceptions. The main exception to the above morpheme-based rule concerns the comparative and superlative suffixes '-er' and '-est'. According to the rule given above, the adjective 'long' will be pronounced lɒŋ, which is correct. It would also predict correctly that if we add another morpheme to 'long', such as the suffix '-ish', the pronunciation of ŋ would again be without a following g. However, it would additionally predict that the comparative and superlative forms 'longer' and 'longest' would be pronounced with no g following the ŋ, while in fact the correct pronunciation of the words is:

'longer' lɒŋgə 'longest' lɒŋgəst

As a result of this, the rule must be modified: it must state that comparative and superlative forms of adjectives are to be treated as single-morpheme words for the purposes of this rule. It is important to remember that English speakers in general (apart from those trained in phonetics) are quite ignorant of this rule, and yet if a foreigner uses the wrong pronunciation (i.e. pronounces ŋg where ŋ should occur, or ŋ where ŋg should be used), they notice that a mispronunciation has occurred.

iii) A third way in which the distribution of ŋ is unusual is the small number of vowels it is found to follow. It rarely occurs after a diphthong or long vowel, so only the short vowels ɪ, e, æ, ʌ, ɒ, ʊ, ə are regularly found preceding this consonant.

The velar nasal consonant ŋ is, in summary, phonetically simple (it is no more difficult to produce than m or n) but phonologically complex (it is, as we have seen, not easy to describe the contexts in which it occurs).

## 7.2 The consonant l

AU7 (CD 1), Ex 3

The l phoneme (as in 'long' lɒŋ, 'hill' hɪl) is a **lateral approximant**. This is a consonant in which the passage of air through the mouth does not go in the usual way along the centre of the tongue; instead, there is complete closure between the centre of the tongue and the part of the roof of the mouth where contact is to be made (the alveolar ridge in the case of l). Because of this complete closure along the centre, the only way for the air to escape is along the sides of the tongue. The lateral approximant is therefore somewhat different from other approximants, in which there is usually much less contact between the articulators. If you make a long l sound you may be able to feel that the sides of your tongue are pulled in and down while the centre is raised, but it is not easy to become consciously aware of this; what is more revealing (if you can do it) is to produce a long sequence of alternations between d and l without any intervening vowel. If you produce dldldldldl without moving the middle of the tongue, you will be able to feel the movement of the sides of the tongue that is necessary for the production of a lateral. It is also possible to see this movement in a mirror if you open your lips wide as you produce it. Finally, it is also helpful to see if you can feel the movement of air past the sides of the tongue; this is not really possible in a voiced sound (the obstruction caused by the vibrating vocal folds reduces the airflow), but if you try to make a very loud whispered l, you should be able to feel the air rushing along the sides of your tongue.

We find l initially, medially and finally, and its distribution is therefore not particularly limited. In BBC pronunciation, the consonant has one unusual characteristic: the realisation of l found before vowels sounds quite different from that found in other contexts. For example, the realisation of l in the word 'lea' liː is quite different from that in 'eel' iːl.The sound in 'eel' is what we call a "dark l"; it has a quality rather similar to an [u] vowel, with the back of the tongue raised. The phonetic symbol for this sound is ɫ. The sound in 'lea' is what is called a "clear l"; it resembles an [i] vowel, with the front of the tongue raised (we do not normally use a special phonetic symbol, different from l, to indicate this sound). The "dark l" is also found when it precedes a consonant, as in 'eels' iːlz. We can therefore predict which realisation of l (clear or dark) will occur in a particular context: clear l will never occur before consonants or before a pause, but only before vowels; dark l never occurs before vowels. We can say, using terminology introduced in Chapter 5, that clear l and dark l are allophones of the phoneme l in complementary distribution. Most English speakers do not consciously know about the difference between clear and dark l, yet they are quick to detect the difference when they hear English speakers with different accents, or when they hear foreign learners who have not learned the correct pronunciation. You might be able to observe that most American and lowland Scottish speakers use a "dark l" in all positions, and don't have a "clear l" in their pronunciation, while most Welsh and Irish speakers have "clear l" in all positions.

Another allophone of l is found when it follows p, k at the beginning of a stressed syllable. The l is then devoiced (i.e. produced without the voicing found in most realisations of this phoneme) and pronounced as a fricative. The situation is (as explained in Chapter 4) similar to the aspiration found when a vowel follows p, t, k in a stressed syllable: the first part of the vowel is devoiced.

## 7.3 The consonant r

AU7 (CD 1), Ex 4

This consonant is important in that considerable differences in its articulation and its distribution are found in different accents of English. As far as the articulation of the sound is concerned, there is really only one pronunciation that can be recommended to the foreign learner, and that is what is called a post-alveolar approximant. An **approximant**, as a type of consonant, is rather difficult to describe; informally, we can say that it is an articulation in which the articulators approach each other but do not get sufficiently close to each other to produce a "complete" consonant such as a plosive, nasal or fricative. The difficulty with this explanation is that articulators are always in *some* positional relationship with each other, and any vowel articulation could also be classed as an approximant – but the term "approximant" is usually used only for consonants.

The important thing about the articulation of r is that the tip of the tongue approaches the alveolar area in approximately the way it would for a t or d, but never actually makes contact with any part of the roof of the mouth. You should be able to make a long r sound and feel that no part of the tongue is in contact with the roof of the mouth at any time. This is, of course, very different from the "r-sounds" of many other languages where some kind of tongue–palate contact is made. The tongue is in fact usually slightly curled backwards with the tip raised; consonants with this tongue shape are usually called **retroflex**. If you pronounce an alternating sequence of d and r (drdrdrdrdr) while looking in a mirror you should be able to see more of the underside of the tongue in the r than in the d, where the tongue tip is not raised and the tongue is not curled back. The "curling-back" process usually carries the tip of the tongue to a position slightly further back in the mouth than that for alveolar consonants such as t, d, which is why this approximant is called "post-alveolar". A rather different r sound is found at the beginning of a syllable if it is preceded by p, t, k; it is then voiceless and fricative. This pronunciation is found in words such as 'press', 'tress', 'cress'.

One final characteristic of the articulation of r is that it is usual for the lips to be slightly rounded; learners should do this but should be careful not to exaggerate it. If the lip-rounding is too strong the consonant will sound too much like w, which is the sound that most English children produce until they have learned to pronounce r in the adult way.

The distributional peculiarity of r in the BBC accent is very easy to state: this phoneme only occurs before vowels. No one has any difficulty in remembering this rule, but foreign learners (most of whom, quite reasonably, expect that if there is a letter 'r' in the spelling then r should be pronounced) find it difficult to apply the rule to their own pronunciation. There is no problem with words like the following:

i) 'red' red 'arrive' əraɪv 'hearing' hɪərɪŋ

In these words r is followed by a vowel. But in the following words there is no r in the pronunciation:

ii) 'car' kɑː 'ever' evə 'here' hɪə
iii) 'hard' hɑːd 'verse' vɜːs 'cares' keəz

Many accents of English do pronounce r in words like those of (ii) and (iii) (e.g. most American, Scots and West of England accents). Those accents which have r in final position (before a pause) and before a consonant are called **rhotic** accents, while accents in which r only occurs before vowels (such as BBC) are called **non-rhotic**.

## 7.4 The consonants j and w

AU7 (CD 1), Ex 5

These are the consonants found at the beginning of words such as 'yet' and 'wet'. They are known as approximants (introduced in Section 7.3 above). The most important thing to remember about these phonemes is that they are phonetically like vowels but phonologically like consonants (in earlier works on phonology they were known as "semivowels"). From the phonetic point of view the articulation of j is practically the same as that of a front close vowel such as [i], but is very short. In the same way w is closely similar to [u]. If you make the initial sound of 'yet' or 'wet' very long, you will be able to hear this. But despite this vowel-like character, we use them like consonants. For example, they only occur before vowel phonemes; this is a typically consonantal distribution. We can show that a word beginning with w or j is treated as beginning with a consonant in the following way: the indefinite article is 'a' before a consonant (as in 'a cat', 'a dog'), and 'an' before a vowel (as in 'an apple', 'an orange'). If a word beginning with w or j is preceded by the indefinite article, it is the 'a' form that is found (as in 'a way', 'a year'). Another example is that of the definite article. Here the rule is that 'the' is pronounced as ðə before consonants (as in 'the dog' ðə dɒg, 'the cat' ðə kæt) and as ði before vowels (as in 'the apple' ði æpl, 'the orange' ði ɒrɪndʒ). This evidence illustrates why it is said that j, w are phonologically consonants. However, it is important to remember that to pronounce them as fricatives (as many foreign learners do), or as affricates, is a mispronunciation. Only in special contexts do we hear friction noise in j or w; this is when they are preceded by p, t, k at the beginning of a syllable, as in these words:

| | |
|---|---|
| 'pure' pjʊə | (no English words begin with pw) |
| 'tune' tjuːn | 'twin' twɪn |
| 'queue' kjuː | 'quit' kwɪt |

When p, t, k come at the beginning of a syllable and are followed by a vowel, they are aspirated, as was explained in Chapter 4. This means that the beginning of a vowel is voiceless in this context. However, when p, t, k are followed not by a vowel but by one of l, r, j, w, these voiced continuant consonants undergo a similar process, as has been mentioned earlier in this chapter: they lose their voicing and become fricative. So words like 'play' pleɪ, 'tray' treɪ, 'quick' kwɪk, 'cue' kjuː contain devoiced and fricative l, r, w, j whereas 'lay', 'ray', 'wick', 'you' contain voiced l, r, w, j. Consequently, if for example 'tray' were to be pronounced without devoicing of the r (i.e. with fully voiced r) English speakers would be likely to hear the word 'dray'.

This completes our examination of the consonant phonemes of English. It is useful to place them on a consonant chart, and this is done in Table l. On this chart, the different places of articulation are arranged from left to right and the manners of articulation are arranged from top to bottom. When there is a pair of phonemes with the same place and manner of articulation but differing in whether they are fortis or lenis (voiceless or voiced), the symbol for the fortis consonant is placed to the left of the symbol for the lenis consonant.

## Notes on problems and further reading

The notes for this chapter are devoted to giving further detail on a particularly difficult theoretical problem. The argument that ŋ is an allophone of n, not a phoneme in its own right, is so widely accepted by contemporary phonological theorists that few seem to feel it worthwhile to explain it fully. Since the velar nasal is introduced in this chapter, I have chosen to attempt this here. However, it is a rather complex theoretical matter, and you may prefer to leave consideration of it until after the discussion of problems of phonemic analysis in Chapter 13.

There are brief discussions of the phonemic status of ŋ in Chomsky and Halle (1968: 85) and Ladefoged (2006); for a fuller treatment, see Wells (1982: 60–4) and Giegerich (1992: 297–301). Everyone agrees that English has at least two contrasting nasal phonemes, m and n. However, there is disagreement about whether there is a third nasal phoneme ŋ. In favour of accepting ŋ as a phoneme is the fact that traditional phoneme theory more or less demands its acceptance despite the usual preference for making phoneme inventories as small as possible. Consider **minimal pairs** (pairs of words in which a difference in

*Table 1 Chart of English consonant phonemes*

| | | PLACE OF ARTICULATION | | | | | | | |
|---|---|---|---|---|---|---|---|---|---|
| | | Bilabial | Labiodental | Dental | Alveolar | Post-alveolar | Palatal | Velar | Glottal |
| MANNER OF ARTICULATION | Plosive | p b | | | t d | | | k g | |
| | Fricative | | f v | θ ð | s z | ʃ ʒ | | | h |
| | Affricate | | | | | tʃ dʒ | | | |
| | Nasal | m | | | n | | | ŋ | |
| | Lateral approximant | | | | l | | | | |
| | Approximant | w | | | | r | j | | |

meaning depends on the difference of just one phoneme) like these: 'sin' sɪn – 'sing' sɪŋ; 'sinner' sɪnə – 'singer' sɪŋə.

There are three main arguments against accepting ŋ as a phoneme:

i) In some English accents it can easily be shown that ŋ is an allophone of n, which suggests that something similar might be true of BBC pronunciation too.
ii) If ŋ is a phoneme, its distribution is very different from that of m and n, being restricted to syllable-final position (phonologically), and to morpheme-final position (morphologically) unless it is followed by k or g.
iii) English speakers with no phonetic training are said to feel that ŋ is not a 'single sound' like m, n. Sapir (1925) said that "no native speaker of English could be made to feel in his bones" that ŋ formed part of a series with m, n. This is, of course, very hard to establish, although that does not mean that Sapir was wrong.

We need to look at point (i) in more detail and go on to see how this leads to the argument against having ŋ as a phoneme. Please note that I am not trying to argue that this proposal must be correct; my aim is just to explain the argument. The whole question may seem of little or no practical consequence, but we ought to be interested in any phonological problem if it appears that conventional phoneme theory is not able to deal satisfactorily with it.

In some English accents, particularly those of the Midlands, ŋ is only found with k or g following. For example:

| | |
|---|---|
| 'sink' sɪŋk | 'singer' sɪŋgə |
| 'sing' sɪŋg | 'singing' sɪŋgɪŋg |

This was my own pronunciation as a boy, living in the West Midlands, but I now usually have the BBC pronunciation sɪŋk, sɪŋ, sɪŋə, sɪŋɪŋ. In the case of an accent like this, it can be shown that within the morpheme the only nasal that occurs before k, g is ŋ. Neither m nor n can occur in this environment. Thus within the morpheme ŋ is in complementary distribution with m, n. Since m, n are already established as distinct English phonemes in other contexts (mæp, næp, etc.), it is clear that for such non-BBC accents ŋ must be an allophone of one of the other nasal consonant phonemes. We choose n because when a morpheme-final n is followed by a morpheme-initial k, g it is usual for that n to change to ŋ; however, a morpheme-final m followed by a morpheme-initial k, g usually doesn't change to ŋ. Thus:

'raincoat' reɪŋkəʊt *but* 'tramcar' træmkɑː

So in an analysis which contains no ŋ phoneme, we would transcribe 'raincoat' phonemically as reɪnkəʊt and 'sing', 'singer', 'singing' as sɪng, sɪngə, sɪngɪng. The phonetic realisation of the n phoneme as a velar nasal will be accounted for by a general rule that we will call Rule 1:

*Rule 1*: n is realised as ŋ when it occurs in an environment in which it precedes either k or g.

Let us now look at BBC pronunciation. As explained in Section 7.1 above, the crucial difference between 'singer' sɪŋə and 'finger' fɪŋgə is that 'finger' is a single, indivisible morpheme whereas 'singer' is composed of two morphemes 'sing' and '-er'. When ŋ occurs without a following k or g it is always immediately before a morpheme boundary. Consequently, the sound ŋ and the sequence ŋg are in complementary distribution. But within the morpheme there is no contrast between the sequence ŋg and the sequence ng, which makes it possible to say that ŋ is also in complementary distribution with the sequence ng.

After establishing these "background facts", we can go on to state the argument as follows:

i) English has only m, n as nasal phonemes.
ii) The sound ŋ is an allophone of the phoneme n.
iii) The words 'finger', 'sing', 'singer', 'singing' should be represented phonemically as fɪngə, sɪng, sɪngə, sɪngɪng.
iv) Rule 1 (above) applies to all these phonemic representations to give these phonetic forms: fɪŋgə, sɪŋg, sɪŋgə, sɪŋgɪŋg
v) A further rule (Rule 2) must now be introduced:

*Rule 2*: g is deleted when it occurs after ŋ and before a morpheme boundary.

It should be clear that Rule 2 will not apply to 'finger' because the ŋ is not immediately followed by a morpheme boundary. However, the rule does apply to all the others, hence the final phonetic forms: fɪŋgə, sɪŋ, sɪŋə, sɪŋɪŋ.

vi) Finally, it is necessary to remember the exception we have seen in the case of comparatives and superlatives.

The argument against treating ŋ as a phoneme may not appeal to you very much. The important point, however, is that if one is prepared to use the kind of complexity and abstractness illustrated above, one can produce quite far-reaching changes in the phonemic analysis of a language.

The other consonants – l, r, w, j – do not, I think, need further explanation, except to mention that the question of whether j, w are consonants or vowels is examined on distributional grounds in O'Connor and Trim (1953).

## Written exercises

1 List all the consonant phonemes of the BBC accent, grouped according to manner of articulation.
2 Transcribe the following words phonemically:
a) sofa c) steering
b) verse d) breadcrumb

e) square g) bought
f) anger h) nineteen

3 When the vocal tract is in its resting position for normal breathing, the soft palate is usually lowered. Describe what movements are carried out by the soft palate in the pronunciation of the following words:
a) banner b) mid c) angle

# 8 The syllable

The syllable is a very important unit. Most people seem to believe that, even if they cannot define what a syllable is, they can count how many syllables there are in a given word or sentence. If they are asked to do this they often tap their finger as they count, which illustrates the syllable's importance in the rhythm of speech. As a matter of fact, if one tries the experiment of asking English speakers to count the syllables in, say, a recorded sentence, there is often a considerable amount of disagreement.

## 8.1 The nature of the syllable

When we looked at the nature of vowels and consonants in Chapter 1 it was shown that one could decide whether a particular sound was a vowel or a consonant on phonetic grounds (in relation to how much they obstructed the airflow) or on phonological grounds (vowels and consonants having different distributions). We find a similar situation with the syllable, in that it may be defined both phonetically and phonologically. Phonetically (i.e. in relation to the way we produce them and the way they sound), syllables are usually described as consisting of a centre which has little or no obstruction to airflow and which sounds comparatively loud; before and after this centre (i.e. at the beginning and end of the syllable), there will be greater obstruction to airflow and/or less loud sound. We will now look at some examples:

i) What we will call a **minimum syllable** is a single vowel in isolation (e.g. the words 'are' ɑː, 'or' ɔː, 'err' ɜː). These are preceded and followed by silence. Isolated sounds such as m, which we sometimes produce to indicate agreement, or ʃ, to ask for silence, must also be regarded as syllables.

ii) Some syllables have an **onset** – that is, instead of silence, they have one or more consonants preceding the centre of the syllable:

'bar' bɑː 'key' kiː 'more' mɔː

iii) Syllables may have no onset but have a **coda** – that is, they end with one or more consonants:

'am' æm 'ought' ɔːt 'ease' iːz

iv) Some syllables have both onset and coda:

'ran' ræn 'sat' sæt 'fill' fɪl

This is one way of looking at syllables. Looking at them from the phonological point of view is quite different. What this involves is looking at the possible combinations of English phonemes; the study of the possible phoneme combinations of a language is called **phonotactics**. It is simplest to start by looking at what can occur in initial position – in other words, what can occur at the beginning of the first word when we begin to speak after a pause. We find that the word can begin with a vowel, or with one, two or three consonants. No word begins with more than three consonants. In the same way, we can look at how a word ends when it is the last word spoken before a pause; it can end with a vowel, or with one, two, three or (in a small number of cases) four consonants. No current word ends with more than four consonants.

## 8.2 The structure of the English syllable

Let us now look in more detail at syllable onsets. If the first syllable of the word in question begins with a vowel (any vowel may occur, though ʊ is rare) we say that this initial syllable has a **zero onset**. If the syllable begins with one consonant, that initial consonant may be any consonant phoneme except ŋ; ʒ is rare.

We now look at syllables beginning with two consonants. When we have two or more consonants together we call them a **consonant cluster**. Initial two-consonant clusters are of two sorts in English. One sort is composed of s followed by one of a small set of consonants; examples of such clusters are found in words such as 'sting' stɪŋ, 'sway' sweɪ, 'smoke' sməʊk. The s in these clusters is called the **pre-initial** consonant and the other consonant (t, w, m in the above examples) the **initial** consonant. These clusters are shown in Table 2.

The other sort begins with one of a set of about fifteen consonants, followed by one of the set l, r, w, j as in, for example, 'play' pleɪ, 'try' traɪ, 'quick' kwɪk, 'few' fjuː. We call the first consonant of these clusters the **initial consonant** and the second the **post-initial**. There are some restrictions on which consonants can occur together. This can best be shown in table form, as in Table 3. When we look at three-consonant clusters we can recognise a clear relationship between them and the two sorts of two-consonant cluster described above; examples of three-consonant initial clusters are: 'split' splɪt, 'stream' striːm, 'square' skweə. The s is the pre-initial consonant, the p, t, k that follow s in the three example words are the initial consonant and the l, r, w are post-initial. In fact, the number of possible initial three-consonant clusters is quite small and they can be set out in full (words given in spelling form):

AU8 (CD 1), Ex 2

| | | POST-INITIAL | | | |
|---|---|---|---|---|---|
| | | l | r | w | j |
| | p | 'splay' | 'spray' | – | 'spew' |
| s plus initial | t | – | 'string' | – | 'stew' |
| | k | 'sclerosis' | 'screen' | 'squeak' | 'skewer' |

Table 2 *Two-consonant clusters with pre-initial* s

**Pre-initial s followed by:**

| INITIAL | | | | | | | | | | | | | | | | | |
|---|---|---|---|---|---|---|---|---|---|---|---|---|---|---|---|---|---|
| p | t | k | b | d | g | f | θ | s | ʃ | h | v | ð | z | ʒ | m | n | ŋ |
| spɪn | stɪk | skɪn | – | – | – | sfɪə | – | – | – | – | – | – | – | – | smel | snəʊ | – |

*Note:* Two-consonant clusters of s plus l, w, j are also possible (e.g. slɪp, swɪŋ, sjuː), and even perhaps sr in 'syringe' srɪndʒ for many speakers. These clusters can be analysed *either* as pre-initial s plus initial l, w, j, r *or* initial s plus post-initial l, w, j, r. There is no clear answer to the question of which analysis is better; here they are treated in the latter way, and appear in Table 3.

Table 3 *Two-consonant clusters with post-initial* l, r, w, j

| POST-INITIAL | p | t | k | b | d | g | f | θ | s | ʃ | h | v | ð | z | ʒ | m | n | ŋ | l | r | w | j |
|---|---|---|---|---|---|---|---|---|---|---|---|---|---|---|---|---|---|---|---|---|---|---|
| l | pleɪ | – | kleɪ | blæk | – | gluː | flaɪ | – | slɪp | – | – | – | – | – | – | – | – | – | – | – | – | – |
| r | preɪ | treɪ | kraɪ | brɪŋ | drɪp | grɪn | fraɪ | θrəʊ | ?[1] | ʃruː | – | – | – | – | – | – | – | – | – | – | – | – |
| w | – | twɪn | kwɪk | – | dwel | ?[2] | – | θwɔːt | swɪm | ?[3] | – | – | – | – | – | – | – | – | – | – | – | – |
| j | pjɔː | tjuːn | kjuː | bjuːti | djuː | ?[4] | fjuː | ?[5] | sjuː | – | hjuːdʒ | vjuː | – | – | – | mjuːz | njuːz | – | ljuːd | – | – | – |

*Notes in doubtful cases:*

1 Some people pronounce the word 'syringe' as srɪndʒ; there are no other cases of sr unless one counts foreign names (e.g. Sri Lanka).

2 Many Welsh names (including some well known outside Wales) – such as girls' names like Gwen and place names like the county of Gwent – have initial gw and English speakers seem to find them perfectly easy to pronounce.

3 Two cases make ʃw seem familiar: the vowel name 'schwa', and the name of the soft drinks brand Schweppes. This is, however, a very infrequent cluster for English.

4 The only possible occurrence of gj would be in the archaic (heraldic) word 'gules', which is in very few people's vocabulary.

5 θj occurs in the archaic word 'thew' only.

AU8 (CD 1), Exs 3 & 4

We now have a similar task to do in studying final consonant clusters. Here we find the possibility of up to four consonants at the end of a word. If there is no final consonant we say that there is a **zero coda**. When there is one consonant only, this is called the **final** consonant. Any consonant may be a final consonant except h, w, j. The consonant r is a special case: it doesn't occur as a final consonant in BBC pronunciation, but there are many rhotic accents of English (see Section 7.3) in which syllables may end with this consonant. There are two sorts of two-consonant final cluster, one being a final consonant preceded by a **pre-final** consonant and the other a final consonant followed by a **post-final** consonant. The pre-final consonants form a small set: m, n, ŋ, l, s. We can see these in 'bump' bʌmp, 'bent' bent, 'bank' bæŋk, 'belt' belt, 'ask' ɑːsk. The post-final consonants also form a small set: s, z, t, d, θ; example words are: 'bets' bets, 'beds' bedz, 'backed' bækt, 'bagged' bægd, 'eighth' eɪtθ. These post-final consonants can often be identified as separate morphemes (although not always – 'axe' æks, for example, is a single morpheme and its final s has no separate meaning). A point of pronunciation can be pointed out here: the release of the first plosive of a plosive-plus-plosive cluster such as the g (of gd) in bægd or the k (of kt) in bækt is usually without plosion and is therefore practically inaudible.

AU8 (CD 1), Ex 5

There are two types of final three-consonant cluster; the first is pre-final plus final plus post-final, as set out in the following table:

| | | Pre-final | Final | Post-final |
|---|---|---|---|---|
| 'helped' | he | l | p | t |
| 'banks' | bæ | ŋ | k | s |
| 'bonds' | bɒ | n | d | z |
| 'twelfth' | twe | l | f | θ |

The second type shows how more than one post-final consonant can occur in a final cluster: final plus post-final 1 plus post-final 2. Post-final 2 is again one of s, z, t, d, θ.

| | | Pre-final | Final | Post-final 1 | Post-final 2 |
|---|---|---|---|---|---|
| 'fifths' | fɪ | – | f | θ | s |
| 'next' | ne | – | k | s | t |
| 'lapsed' | læ | – | p | s | t |

Most four-consonant clusters can be analysed as consisting of a final consonant preceded by a pre-final and followed by post-final 1 and post-final 2, as shown below:

| | | Pre-final | Final | Post-final 1 | Post-final 2 |
|---|---|---|---|---|---|
| 'twelfths' | twe | l | f | θ | s |
| 'prompts' | prɒ | m | p | t | s |

A small number of cases seem to require a different analysis, as consisting of a final consonant with no pre-final but three post-final consonants:

| | | Pre-final | Final | Post-final 1 | Post-final 2 | Post-final 3 |
|---|---|---|---|---|---|---|
| 'sixths' | sɪ | – | k | s | θ | s |
| 'texts' | te | – | k | s | t | s |

To sum up, we may describe the English syllable as having the following maximum phonological structure:

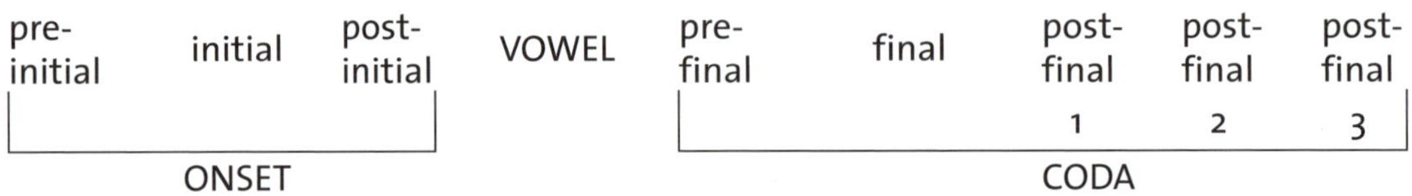


In the above structure there must be a vowel in the centre of the syllable. There is, however, a special case, that of **syllabic consonants** (which are introduced in Chapter 9); we do not, for example, analyse the word 'students' stjuːdnts as consisting of one syllable with the three-consonant cluster stj for its onset and a four-consonant final cluster dnts. To fit in with what English speakers feel, we say that the word contains two syllables, with the second syllable ending with the cluster nts; in other words, we treat the word as though there was a vowel between d and n, although a vowel only occurs here in very slow, careful pronunciation. This phonological problem will be discussed in Chapter 13.

Much present-day work in phonology makes use of a rather more refined analysis of the syllable in which the vowel and the coda (if there is one) are known as the **rhyme**; if you think of rhyming English verse you will see that the rhyming works by matching just that part of the last syllable of a line. The rhyme is divided into the **peak** (normally the vowel) and the **coda** (but note that this is optional: the rhyme may have no coda, as in a word like 'me'). As we have seen, the syllable may also have an onset, but this is not obligatory. The structure is thus the following

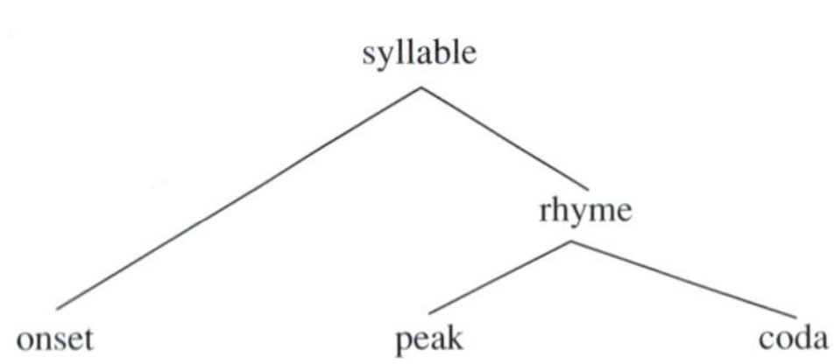


## 8.3 **Syllable division**

There are still problems with the description of the syllable: an unanswered question is how we decide on the division between syllables when we find a connected sequence of them as we usually do in normal speech. It often happens that one or more consonants from the end of one word combine with one or more at the beginning of the following word, resulting in a consonant sequence that could not occur in a single syllable. For example, 'walked through' wɔːkt θruː gives us the consonant sequence ktθr.

We will begin by looking at two words that are simple examples of the problem of dividing adjoining syllables. Most English speakers feel that the word 'morning' mɔːnɪŋ consists of two syllables, but we need a way of deciding whether the division into syllables should be mɔː and nɪŋ, or mɔːn and ɪŋ. A more difficult case is the word 'extra' ekstrə. One problem is that by some definitions the s in the middle, between k and t, could be counted as a syllable, which most English speakers would reject. They feel that the word has two syllables. However, the more controversial issue relates to where the two syllables are to be divided; the possibilities are (using the symbol . to signify a syllable boundary):

i) e.kstrə
ii) ek.strə
iii) eks.trə
iv) ekst.rə
v) ekstr.ə

How can we decide on the division? No single rule will tell us what to do without bringing up problems.

One of the most widely accepted guidelines is what is known as the **maximal onsets principle**. This principle states that where two syllables are to be divided, any consonants between them should be attached to the right-hand syllable, not the left, as far as possible. In our first example above, 'morning' would thus be divided as mɔː.nɪŋ. If we just followed this rule, we would have to divide 'extra' as (i) e.kstrə, but we know that an English syllable cannot begin with kstr. Our rule must therefore state that consonants are assigned to the right-hand syllable as far as possible *within the restrictions governing syllable onsets and codas*. This means that we must reject (i) e.kstrə because of its impossible onset, and (v) ekstr.ə because of its impossible coda. We then have to choose between (ii), (iii) and (iv). The maximal onsets rule makes us choose (ii). There are, though, many problems still remaining. How should we divide words like 'better' betə? The maximal onsets principle tells us to put the t on the right-hand syllable, giving be.tə, but that means that the first syllable is analysed as be. However, we never find isolated syllables ending with one of the vowels ɪ, e, æ, ʌ, ɒ, ʊ, so this division is not possible. The maximal onsets principle must therefore also be modified to allow a consonant to be assigned to the left syllable if that prevents one of the vowels ɪ, e, æ, ʌ, ɒ, ʊ from occurring at the end of a syllable. We can then analyse the word as bet.ə, which seems more satisfactory. There are words like 'carry' kæri which still give us problems: if we divide the word as kæ.ri, we get a syllable-final æ, but if we divide it as kær.i we have a syllable-final r, and both of these are non-occurring in BBC pronunciation. We have to decide on the lesser of two evils here, and the preferable solution is to divide the word as kær.i on the grounds that in the many rhotic accents of English (see Section 7.3) this division would be the natural one to make.

One further possible solution should be mentioned: when one consonant stands between vowels and it is difficult to assign the consonant to one syllable or the other – as in 'better' and 'carry' – we could say that the consonant belongs to *both* syllables. The term used by phonologists for a consonant in this situation is **ambisyllabic**.

## Notes on problems and further reading

The study of syllable structure is a subject of considerable interest to phonologists. If you want to read further in this area, I would recommend Giegerich (1992: Chapter 6), Katamba (1989: Chapter 9), Hogg and McCully (1987: Chapter 2) and Goldsmith (1990: Chapter 3). In the discussion of the word 'extra' ekstrə it was mentioned that the s in the middle might be classed as a syllable. This could happen if one followed the **sonority** theory of syllables: sonority corresponds to loudness, and some sounds have greater sonority than others. Vowels have the greatest sonority, and these are usually the centre of a syllable. Consonants have a lower level of sonority, and usually form the beginnings and ends of syllables. But s has greater sonority than k or t, and this could lead to the conclusion that s is the centre of a syllable in the middle of the word 'extra', which goes against English speakers' feelings. There is a thorough discussion, and a possible solution, in Giegerich (1992: Sections 6.2–6.4). Some writers believe that it is possible to describe the combinations of phonemes with little reference to the syllable as an independent unit in theoretical phonology; see, for example, Harris (1994: Section 2.3). Cruttenden (2008: Section 10.10) and Kreidler (2004: Chapters 5 and 6) describe the phonotactics of English in more detail.

A paper that had a lot of influence on more recent work is Fudge (1969). This paper brought up two ideas first discussed by earlier writers: the first is that sp, st, sk could be treated as individual phonemes, removing the pre-initial position from the syllable onset altogether and removing s from the pre-final set of consonants; the second is that since post-initial j only occurs before ʊ, uː, ʊə (which in his analysis all begin with the same vowel), one could postulate a diphthong ju and remove j from post-initial position. These are interesting proposals, but there is not enough space here to examine the arguments in full.

There are many different ways of deciding how to divide syllables. To see two different approaches, see the Introductions to the *Longman Pronunciation Dictionary* (Wells, 2008) and the *Cambridge English Pronouncing Dictionary* (Jones, eds. Roach *et al.*, 2006).

## Notes for teachers

Analysing syllable structure, as we have been doing in this chapter, can be very useful to foreign learners of English, since English has a more complex syllable structure than most languages. There are many more limitations on possible combinations of vowels and consonants than we have covered here, but an understanding of the basic structures described will help learners to become aware of the types of consonant cluster that present them with pronunciation problems. In the same way, teachers can use this knowledge to construct suitable exercises. Most learners find *some* English clusters difficult, but few find *all* of them difficult. For reading in this area, see Celce-Murcia *et al.* (1996: 80–9); Dalton and Seidlhofer (1994: 34–8); Hewings (2004: 1.4, 2.10–2.12).

## Written exercise

Using the analysis of the word 'cramped' given below as a model, analyse the structure of the following one-syllable English words:

| | Initial | Post-initial | | Pre-final | Final | Post-final |
|---|---|---|---|---|---|---|
| 'cramped' | k | r | æ | m | p | t |
| | Onset | | Peak | Coda | | |

a) squealed
b) eighths
c) splash
d) texts

# 9 Strong and weak syllables

## 9.1 Strong and weak

One of the most noticeable features of English pronunciation is that some of its syllables are **strong** while many others are **weak**; this is also true of many other languages, but it is necessary to study how these weak syllables are pronounced and where they occur in English. The distribution of strong and weak syllables is a subject that will be met in several later chapters. For example, we will look later at **stress**, which is very important in deciding whether a syllable is strong or weak. **Elision** is a closely related subject, and in considering **intonation** the difference between strong and weak syllables is also important. Finally, words with "strong forms" and "weak forms" are clearly a related matter. In this chapter we look at the general nature of weak syllables.

What do we mean by "strong" and "weak"? To begin with, we can look at how we use these terms to refer to phonetic characteristics of syllables. When we compare weak syllables with strong syllables, we find the vowel in a weak syllable tends to be shorter, of lower intensity (loudness) and different in quality. For example, in the word 'data' deɪtə the second syllable, which is weak, is shorter than the first, is less loud and has a vowel that cannot occur in strong syllables. In a word like 'bottle' bɒtl̩ the weak second syllable contains no vowel at all, but consists entirely of the consonant l̩. We call this a **syllabic consonant**.

There are other ways of characterising strong and weak syllables. We could describe them partly in terms of stress (by saying, for example, that strong syllables are stressed and weak syllables unstressed) but, until we describe what "stress" *means*, such a description would not be very useful. The most important thing to note at present is that any strong syllable will have as its peak one of the vowel phonemes (or possibly a triphthong) listed in Chapters 2 and 3, but not ə, i, u (the last two are explained in Section 9.3 below). If the vowel is one of ɪ, e, æ, ʌ, ɒ, ʊ, then the strong syllable will always have a coda as well. Weak syllables, on the other hand, as they are defined here, can only have one of a very small number of possible peaks. At the end of a word, we may have a weak syllable ending with a vowel (i.e. with no coda):

i) the vowel ə ("schwa");
ii) a close front unrounded vowel in the general area of iː, ɪ, symbolised i;
iii) a close back rounded vowel in the general area of uː, ʊ, symbolised u.

Examples would be:

i) ‘better’ betə
ii) ‘happy’ hæpi
iii) ‘thank you’ θæŋk ju

We also find weak syllables in word-final position with a coda if the vowel is ə. For example:

i) ‘open’ əʊpən
ii) ‘sharpen’ ʃɑːpən

Inside a word, we can find the above vowels acting as peaks without codas in weak syllables; for example, look at the second syllable in each of these words:

i) ‘photograph’ fəʊtəgrɑːf
ii) ‘radio’ reɪdiəʊ
iii) ‘influence’ ɪnfluəns

In addition, the vowel ɪ can act as a peak without a coda if the following syllable begins with a consonant:

iv) ‘architect’ ɑːkɪtekt

In the rest of this chapter we will look at the different types of weak syllable in more detail.

## 9.2 The ə vowel (“schwa”)

AU9 (CD 1), Ex 1

The most frequently occurring vowel in English is ə, which is always associated with weak syllables. In quality it is mid (i.e. halfway between close and open) and central (i.e. halfway between front and back). It is generally described as lax – that is, not articulated with much energy. Of course, the quality of this vowel is not always the same, but the variation is not important.

Not all weak syllables contain ə, though many do. Learners of English need to learn where ə is appropriate and where it is not. To do this we often have to use information that traditional phonemic theory would not accept as relevant – we must consider spelling. The question to ask is: if the speaker were to pronounce a particular weak syllable as if it were strong instead, which vowel would it be most likely to have, according to the usual rules of English spelling? Knowing this will not tell us which syllables in a word or utterance should be weak – that is something we look at in later chapters – but it will give us a rough guide to the correct pronunciation of weak syllables. Let us look at some examples:

i) Spelt with ‘a’; strong pronunciation would have æ
‘*a*ttend’ ətend   ‘char*a*cter’ kærəktə
‘barr*a*cks’ bærəks

ii) Spelt with 'ar'; strong pronunciation would have ɑː
'p*ar*ticular' pətɪkjələ 'mol*ar*' məʊlə
'mon*ar*chy' mɒnəki

iii) Adjectival endings spelt 'ate'; strong pronunciation would have eɪ
'intim*ate*' ɪntɪmət 'accur*ate*' ækjərət
'desol*ate*' desələt (although there are exceptions to this: 'private' is usually praɪvɪt)

iv) Spelt with 'o'; strong pronunciation would have ɒ or əʊ
't*o*morrow' təmɒrəʊ 'p*o*tato' pəteɪtəʊ
'carr*o*t' kærət

v) Spelt with 'or'; strong pronunciation would have ɔː
'f*or*get' fəget 'ambassad*or*' æmbæsədə
'opp*or*tunity' ɒpətʃuːnəti

vi) Spelt with 'e'; strong pronunciation would have e
'settlem*e*nt' setl̩mənt 'viol*e*t' vaɪələt
'postm*e*n' pəʊstmən

vii) Spelt with 'er'; strong pronunciation would have ɜː
'p*er*haps' pəhæps 'strong*er*' strɒŋgə
'sup*er*man' suːpəmæn

viii) Spelt with 'u'; strong pronunciation would have ʌ
'aut*u*mn' ɔːtəm 's*u*pport' səpɔːt
'halib*u*t' hælɪbət

ix) Spelt with 'ough' (there are many pronunciations for the letter-sequence 'ough')
'thor*ough*' θʌrə 'bor*ough*' bʌrə

x) Spelt with 'ou'; strong pronunciation might have aʊ
'graci*ou*s' greɪʃəs 'call*ou*s' kæləs

## 9.3 Close front and close back vowels

Two other vowels are commonly found in weak syllables, one close front (in the general region of iː, ɪ) and the other close back rounded (in the general region of uː, ʊ). In strong syllables it is comparatively easy to distinguish iː from ɪ or uː from ʊ, but in weak syllables the difference is not so clear. For example, although it is easy enough to decide which vowel one hears in 'beat' or 'bit', it is much less easy to decide which vowel one hears in the second syllable of words such as 'easy' or 'busy'. There are accents of English (e.g. Welsh accents) in which the second syllable sounds most like the iː in the first syllable of 'easy', and others (e.g. Yorkshire accents) in which it sounds more like the ɪ in the first syllable of 'busy'. In present-day BBC pronunciation, however, the matter is not so clear. There is uncertainty, too, about the corresponding close back rounded vowels. If we look at the words 'good to eat' and 'food to eat', we must ask if the word 'to' is pronounced with the ʊ vowel phoneme of 'good' or the uː phoneme of 'food'. Again, which vowel comes in 'to' in 'I want to'?

One common feature is that the vowels in question are more like iː or uː when they precede another vowel, less so when they precede a consonant or pause. You should notice one further thing: with the exception of one or two very artificial examples, there is really no possibility in these contexts of a phonemic contrast between iː and ɪ, or between uː and ʊ. Effectively, then, the two distinctions, which undoubtedly exist within strong syllables, are **neutralised** in weak syllables of BBC pronunciation. How should we transcribe the words 'easy' and 'busy'? We will use the close front unrounded case as an example, since it is more straightforward. The possibilities, using our phoneme symbols, are the following:

| | 'easy' | 'busy' |
|---|---|---|
| i) | iːziː | bɪziː |
| ii) | iːzɪ | bɪzɪ |

Few speakers with a BBC accent seem to feel satisfied with any of these transcriptions. There is a possible solution to this problem, but it goes against standard phoneme theory. We can symbolise this weak vowel as i – that is, using the symbol for the vowel in 'beat' but without the length mark. Thus:

iːzi bɪzi

The i vowel is neither the iː of 'beat' nor the ɪ of 'bit', and is not in contrast with them. We can set up a corresponding vowel u that is neither the uː of 'shoe' nor the ʊ of 'book' but a weak vowel that shares the characteristics of both. If we use i, u in our transcription as well as iː, ɪ, uː, ʊ, it is no longer a true phonemic transcription in the traditional sense. However, this need not be too serious an objection, and the fact that native speakers seem to think that this transcription fits better with their feelings about the language is a good argument in its favour.

🎧 AU9 (CD 1), Ex 2

Let us now look at where these vowels are found, beginning with close front unrounded ones. We find i occurring:

i) In word-final position in words spelt with final 'y' or 'ey' after one or more consonant letters (e.g. 'happy' hæpi, 'valley' væli) and in morpheme-final position when such words have suffixes beginning with vowels (e.g. 'happier' hæpiə, 'easiest' iːziəst, 'hurrying' hʌriɪŋ).
ii) In a prefix such as those spelt 're', 'pre', 'de' if it precedes a vowel and is unstressed (e.g. in 'react' riækt, 'create' krieɪt, 'deodorant' diəʊdərənt).
iii) In the suffixes spelt 'iate', 'ious' when they have two syllables (e.g. in 'appreciate' əpriːʃieɪt, 'hilarious' hɪleəriəs).
iv) In the following words when unstressed: 'he', 'she', 'we', me', 'be' and the word 'the' when it precedes a vowel.

In most other cases of syllables containing a short close front unrounded vowel we can assign the vowel to the ɪ phoneme, as in the first syllable of 'resist' rɪzɪst, 'inane' ɪneɪn, 'enough' ɪnʌf, the middle syllable of 'incident' ɪnsɪdənt, 'orchestra' ɔːkɪstrə, 'artichoke' ɑːtɪtʃəʊk, and the final syllable of 'swimming' swɪmɪŋ, 'liquid' lɪkwɪd, 'optic' ɒptɪk. It can be seen that this vowel is most often represented in spelling by the letters 'i' and 'e'.

Weak syllables with close back rounded vowels are not so commonly found. We find u most frequently in the words 'you', 'to', 'into', 'do', when they are unstressed and are not immediately preceding a consonant, and 'through', 'who' in all positions when they are unstressed. This vowel is also found before another vowel within a word, as in 'evacuation' ɪvækjueɪʃn̩, 'influenza' ɪnfluenzə.

## 9.4 Syllabic consonants

In the above sections we have looked at vowels in weak syllables. We must also consider syllables in which no vowel is found. In this case, a consonant, either l, r or a nasal, stands as the peak of the syllable instead of the vowel, and we count these as weak syllables like the vowel examples given earlier in this chapter. It is usual to indicate that a consonant is syllabic by means of a small vertical mark ( ̩ ) beneath the symbol, for example 'cattle' kætl̩.

### Syllabic l

AU9 (CD 1), Ex 3

Syllabic l is perhaps the most noticeable example of the English syllabic consonants, although it would be wrong to expect to find it in all accents. It occurs after another consonant, and the way it is produced depends to some extent on the nature of that consonant. If the preceding consonant is alveolar, as in 'bottle' bɒtl̩, 'muddle' mʌdl̩, 'tunnel' tʌnl̩, the articulatory movement from the preceding consonant to the syllabic l is quite simple. The sides of the tongue, which are raised for the preceding consonant, are lowered to allow air to escape over them (this is called **lateral release**). The tip and blade of the tongue do not move until the articulatory contact for the l is released. The l is a "dark l" (as explained in Chapter 7). In some accents – particularly London ones, and "Estuary English" – we often find a close back rounded vowel instead (e.g. 'bottle' bɒtu). Where do we find syllabic l in the BBC accent? It is useful to look at the spelling as a guide. The most obvious case is where we have a word ending with one or more consonant letters followed by 'le' (or, in the case of noun plurals or third person singular verb forms, 'les'). Examples are:

i) with alveolar consonant preceding
   'cattle' kætl̩ 'bottle' bɒtl̩
   'wrestle' resl̩ 'muddle' mʌdl̩
ii) with non-alveolar consonant preceding
   'couple' kʌpl̩ 'trouble' trʌbl̩
   'struggle' strʌgl̩ 'knuckle' nʌkl̩

Such words usually lose their final letter 'e' when a suffix beginning with a vowel is attached, but the l usually remains syllabic. Thus:

| | |
|---|---|
| 'bottle' – 'bottling' | bɒtl̩ – bɒtl̩ɪŋ |
| 'muddle' – 'muddling' | mʌdl̩ – mʌdl̩ɪŋ |
| 'struggle' – 'struggling' | strʌgl̩ – strʌgl̩ɪŋ |

Similar words not derived in this way do not have the syllabic l – it has been pointed out that the two words 'coddling' (derived from the verb 'coddle') and 'codling' (meaning "small cod", derived by adding the diminutive suffix '-ling' to 'cod') show a contrast between syllabic and non-syllabic l: 'coddling' kɒdl̩ɪŋ and 'codling' kɒdlɪŋ. In the case of words such as 'bottle', 'muddle', 'struggle', which are quite common, it would be a mispronunciation to insert a vowel between the l and the preceding consonant in the accent described here. There are many accents of English which may do this, so that, for example, 'cattle' is pronounced kætəl, but this is rarely the case in BBC pronunciation.

We also find syllabic l in words spelt, at the end, with one or more consonant letters followed by 'al' or 'el', for example:

| | |
|---|---|
| 'panel' pænl̩ | 'petal' petl̩ |
| 'kernel' kɜːnl̩ | 'pedal' pedl̩ |
| 'parcel' pɑːsl̩ | 'papal' peɪpl̩ |
| 'Babel' beɪbl̩ | 'ducal' djuːkl̩ |

In some less common or more technical words, it is not obligatory to pronounce syllabic l and the sequence əl may be used instead, although it is less likely: 'missal' mɪsl̩ or mɪsəl, 'acquittal' əkwɪtl̩ or əkwɪtəl.

### Syllabic n

🎧 AU9 (CD 1), Ex 4

Of the syllabic nasals, the most frequently found and the most important is n̩. When should it be pronounced? A general rule could be made that weak syllables which are phonologically composed of a plosive or fricative consonant plus ən are uncommon except in initial position in the words. So we can find words like 'tonight' tənaɪt, 'canary' kəneəri, 'fanatic' fənætɪk, 'sonata' sənɑːtə with ə before n, but medially and finally – as in words like 'threaten', 'threatening' – we find much more commonly a syllabic n̩: θretn̩, θretn̩ɪŋ. To pronounce a vowel before the nasal consonant would sound strange (or at best over-careful) in the BBC accent.

Syllabic n is most common after alveolar plosives and fricatives; in the case of t, d, s, z followed by n the plosive is nasally released by lowering the soft palate, so that in the word 'eaten' iːtn̩, for example, the tongue does not move in the tn̩ sequence but the soft palate is lowered at the end of t so that compressed air escapes through the nose. We do not usually find n̩ after l, tʃ, dʒ, so that for example 'sullen' must be pronounced sʌlən, 'Christian' as krɪstʃən (though this word may be pronounced with t followed by i or j) and 'pigeon' as pɪdʒən.

Syllabic n after non-alveolar consonants is not so widespread. In words where the syllable following a velar consonant is spelt 'an' or 'on' (e.g. 'toboggan', 'wagon') it is rarely heard, the more usual pronunciation being təbɒgən, wægən. After bilabial consonants, in words like 'happen', 'happening', 'ribbon' we can consider it equally acceptable to pronounce them with syllabic n (hæpn̩, hæpn̩ɪŋ, rɪbn̩) or with ən (hæpən, hæpənɪŋ, rɪbən). In a similar way, after velar consonants in words like 'thicken', 'waken', syllabic n is possible but ən is also acceptable.

After f, v, syllabic n is more common than ən (except, as with the other cases described, in word-initial syllables). Thus 'seven', 'heaven', 'often' are more usually sevn̩, hevn̩, ɒfn̩ than sevən, hevən, ɒfən.

In all the examples given so far the syllabic n has been following another consonant; sometimes it is possible for another consonant to precede that consonant, but in this case a syllabic consonant is less likely to occur. If n is preceded by l and a plosive, as in 'Wilton', the pronunciation wɪltn̩ is possible, but wɪltən is also found regularly. If s precedes, as in 'Boston', a final syllabic nasal is less frequent, while clusters formed by nasal + plosive + syllabic nasal are very unusual: thus 'Minton', 'lantern', 'London', 'abandon' will normally have ə in the last syllable and be pronounced mɪntən, læntən, lʌndən, əbændən. Other nasals also discourage a following plosive plus syllabic nasal, so that for example 'Camden' is normally pronounced kæmdən.

### Syllabic m, ŋ

We will not spend much time on the syllabic pronunciation of these consonants. Both can occur as syllabic, but only as a result of processes such as assimilation and elision that are introduced later. We find them sometimes in words like 'happen', which can be pronounced hæpm̩, though hæpn̩ and hæpən are equally acceptable, and 'uppermost', which could be pronounced as ʌpm̩əʊst, though ʌpəməʊst would be more usual. Examples of possible syllabic velar nasals would be 'thicken' θɪkŋ̍ (where θɪkən and θɪkn̩ are also possible), and 'broken key' brəʊkŋ̍ kiː, where the nasal consonant occurs between velar consonants (n or ən could be substituted for ŋ̍).

### Syllabic r

In many accents of the type called "rhotic" (introduced in Chapter 7), such as most American accents, syllabic r is very common. The word 'particular', for example, would probably be pronounced pr̩tɪkjəlr̩ in careful speech by most Americans, while BBC speakers would pronounce this word pətɪkjələ. Syllabic r is less common in BBC pronunciation: it is found in weak syllables such as the second syllable of 'preference' prefr̩əns. In most cases where it occurs there are acceptable alternative pronunciations without the syllabic consonant.

There are a few pairs of words (minimal pairs) in which a difference in meaning appears to depend on whether a particular r is syllabic or not, for example:

'hungry' hʌŋgri 'Hungary' hʌŋgr̩i

But we find no case of syllabic r where it would not be possible to substitute either non-syllabic r or ər; in the example above, 'Hungary' could equally well be pronounced hʌŋgəri.

### Combinations of syllabic consonants

It is not unusual to find two syllabic consonants together. Examples are: 'national' næʃn̩l̩, 'literal' lɪtr̩l̩, 'visionary' vɪʒn̩r̩i, 'veteran' vetr̩n̩. It is important to remember that it is often not possible to say with certainty whether a speaker has pronounced a syllabic consonant, a non-syllabic consonant or a non-syllabic consonant plus ə. For example, the word 'veteran' given above could be pronounced in other ways than vetr̩n̩. A BBC speaker might instead say vetrən, vetərn̩ or vetərən. The transcription makes it look as if the difference between these words is clear; it is not. In examining colloquial English it is often more or less a matter of arbitrary choice how one transcribes such a word. Transcription has the unfortunate tendency to make things seem simpler and more clear-cut than they really are.

## Notes on problems and further reading

**9.1** I have at this point tried to bring in some preliminary notions of stress and prominence without giving a full explanation. By this stage in the course it is important to be getting familiar with the difference between stressed and unstressed syllables, and the nature of the "schwa" vowel. However, the subject of stress is such a large one that I have felt it best to leave its main treatment until later. On the subject of schwa, see Ashby (2005: p. 29); Cruttenden (2008: Section 8.9.12).

**9.2** The introduction of i and u is a relatively recent idea, but it is now widely accepted as a convention in influential dictionaries such as the *Longman Pronunciation Dictionary* (Wells, 2008), the *Cambridge English Pronouncing Dictionary* (Jones, eds. Roach *et al.*, 2006) and the *Oxford Dictionary of Pronunciation* (Upton *et al.*, 2001). Since I mention native speakers' feelings in this connection, and since I am elsewhere rather sceptical about appeals to native speakers' feelings, I had better explain that in this case my evidence comes from the native speakers of English I have taught in practical classes on transcription over many years. A substantial number of these students have either been speakers with BBC pronunciation or had accents only slightly different from it, and their usual reaction to being told to use ɪ for the vowel at the end of 'easy', 'busy' has been one of puzzlement and frustration; like them, I cannot equate this vowel with the vowel of 'bit'. I am, however, reluctant to use iː, which suggests a stronger vowel than should be pronounced (like the final vowel in 'evacuee', 'Tennessee'). I must emphasise that the vowels i, u are not to be included in the set of English phonemes but are simply additional symbols to make the writing and reading of transcription easier. The Introduction to the *Cambridge English Pronouncing Dictionary* (Jones, eds. Roach *et al.*, 2006) discusses some of the issues involved in syllabic consonants and weak syllables: see section 2.10 and p. 492.

## Notes for teachers

Introduction of the "schwa" vowel has been deliberately delayed until this chapter, since I wanted it to be presented in the context of weak syllables in general. Since students should by now be comparatively well informed about basic segmental phonetics, it is very important that their production and recognition of this vowel should be good before moving on to the following chapters.

This chapter is in a sense a crucial point in the course. Although the segmental material of the preceding chapters is important as a foundation, the strong/weak syllable distinction and the overall prosodic characteristics of words and sentences are essential to intelligibility. Most of the remaining chapters of the course are concerned with such matters.

## Written exercise

The following sentences have been partially transcribed, but the vowels have been left blank. Fill in the vowels, taking care to identify which vowels are weak; put no vowel at all if you think a syllabic consonant is appropriate, but put a syllabic mark beneath the syllabic consonant

1 A particular problem of the boat was a leak
  p t kj l pr bl m v ð b t w z l k
2 Opening the bottle presented no difficulty
  p n ŋ ð b t l pr z nt d n d f k lt
3 There is no alternative to the government's proposal
  ð r z n lt n t v t ð g v nm nt spr p zl
4 We ought to make a collection to cover the expenses
  w t t m k k l kʃ n t k v ð ksp ns z
5 Finally they arrived at a harbour at the edge of the mountains
  f n l ð r v d t h b r t ð dʒ v ð m nt nz

# 10 Stress in simple words

## 10.1 The nature of stress

AU10 (CD 2), Ex 1

Stress has been mentioned several times already in this course without an explanation of what the word means. The nature of stress is simple enough: practically everyone would agree that the first syllable of words like 'father', 'open', 'camera' is stressed, that the middle syllable is stressed in 'potato', 'apartment', 'relation', and that the final syllable is stressed in 'about', 'receive', 'perhaps'. Also, most people feel they have some sort of idea of what the difference is between stressed and unstressed syllables, although they might explain it in different ways.

We will mark a stressed syllable in transcription by placing a small vertical line (ˈ) high up, just before the syllable it relates to; the words quoted above will thus be transcribed as follows:

| | | |
|---|---|---|
| ˈfɑːðə | pəˈteɪtəʊ | əˈbaʊt |
| ˈəʊpən | əˈpɑːtmənt | rɪˈsiːv |
| ˈkæmr̩ə | rɪˈleɪʃn̩ | pəˈhæps |

What are the characteristics of stressed syllables that enable us to identify them? It is important to understand that there are two different ways of approaching this question. One is to consider what the speaker does in producing stressed syllables and the other is to consider what characteristics of sound make a syllable seem to a listener to be stressed. In other words, we can study stress from the points of view of **production** and of **perception**; the two are obviously closely related, but are not identical. The production of stress is generally believed to depend on the speaker using more muscular energy than is used for unstressed syllables. Measuring muscular effort is difficult, but it seems possible, according to experimental studies, that when we produce stressed syllables, the muscles that we use to expel air from the lungs are often more active, producing higher subglottal pressure. It seems probable that similar things happen with muscles in other parts of our vocal apparatus.

Many experiments have been carried out on the perception of stress, and it is clear that many different sound characteristics are important in making a syllable recognisably stressed. From the perceptual point of view, all stressed syllables have one characteristic in common, and that is **prominence.** Stressed syllables are recognised as stressed because they are more prominent than unstressed syllables. What makes a syllable prominent? At least four different factors are important:

i) Most people seem to feel that stressed syllables are **louder** than unstressed syllables; in other words, loudness is a component of prominence. In a sequence of identical syllables (e.g. bɑːbɑːbɑːbɑː), if one syllable is made louder than the others, it will be heard as stressed. However, it is important to realise that it is very difficult for a speaker to make a syllable louder without changing other characteristics of the syllable such as those explained below (ii–iv); if one literally changes *only* the loudness, the perceptual effect is not very strong.
ii) The **length** of syllables has an important part to play in prominence. If one of the syllables in our "nonsense word" bɑːbɑːbɑːbɑː is made longer than the others, there is quite a strong tendency for that syllable to be heard as stressed.
iii) Every voiced syllable is said on some **pitch**; pitch in speech is closely related to the frequency of vibration of the vocal folds and to the musical notion of low- and high-pitched notes. It is essentially a *perceptual* characteristic of speech. If one syllable of our "nonsense word" is said with a pitch that is noticeably different from that of the others, this will have a strong tendency to produce the effect of prominence. For example, if all syllables are said with low pitch except for one said with high pitch, then the high-pitched syllable will be heard as stressed and the others as unstressed. To place some **movement** of pitch (e.g. rising or falling) on a syllable is even more effective in making it sound prominent.
iv) A syllable will tend to be prominent if it contains a vowel that is different in **quality** from neighbouring vowels. If we change one of the vowels in our "nonsense word" (e.g. bɑːbiːbɑːbɑː) the "odd" syllable biː will tend to be heard as stressed. This effect is not very powerful, but there is one particular way in which it is relevant in English: the previous chapter explained how the most frequently encountered vowels in weak syllables are ə, ɪ, i, u (syllabic consonants are also common). We can look on stressed syllables as occurring against a "background" of these weak syllables, so that their prominence is increased by contrast with these background qualities.

Prominence, then, is produced by four main factors: (i) loudness, (ii) length, (iii) pitch and (iv) quality. Generally these four factors work together in combination, although syllables may sometimes be made prominent by means of only one or two of them. Experimental work has shown that these factors are not equally important; the strongest effect is produced by pitch, and length is also a powerful factor. Loudness and quality have much less effect.

## 10.2 **Levels of stress**

Up to this point we have talked about stress as though there were a simple distinction between "stressed" and "unstressed" syllables with no intermediate levels; such a treatment would be a **two-level** analysis of stress. Usually, however, we have to recognise one or more intermediate levels. It should be remembered that in this chapter we are dealing only with stress *within the word*. This means that we are looking at words as they are said in isolation, which is a rather artificial situation: we do not often say words in isolation, except for a few such as 'yes', 'no', 'possibly', 'please' and interrogative words such as 'what', 'who', etc. However, looking at words in isolation does help us to see stress placement and stress levels more clearly than studying them in the context of continuous speech.

Let us begin by looking at the word 'around' ə'raʊnd, where the stress always falls clearly on the last syllable and the first syllable is weak. From the point of view of stress, the most important fact about the way we pronounce this word is that on the second syllable the pitch of the voice does not remain level, but usually falls from a higher to a lower pitch. We can diagram the pitch movement as shown below, where the two parallel lines represent the speaker's highest and lowest pitch level. The prominence that results from this pitch movement, or **tone**, gives the strongest type of stress; this is called **primary stress**.

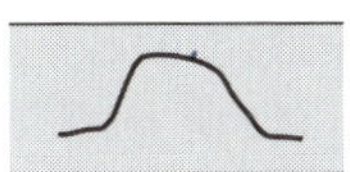

speaker's highest pitch level

speaker's lowest pitch level

In some words, we can observe a type of stress that is weaker than primary stress but stronger than that of the first syllable of 'around'; for example, consider the first syllables of the words 'photographic' fəʊtəgræfɪk, 'anthropology' ænθrəpɒlədʒi. The stress in these words is called **secondary stress**. It is usually represented in transcription with a low mark ( ˌ ) so that the examples could be transcribed as ˌfəʊtə'græfɪk, ˌænθrə'pɒlədʒi.

We have now identified two levels of stress: primary and secondary; this also implies a third level which can be called **unstressed** and is regarded as being the absence of any recognisable amount of prominence. These are the three levels that we will use in describing English stress. However, it is worth noting that unstressed syllables containing ə, ɪ, i, u, or a syllabic consonant, will sound less prominent than an unstressed syllable containing some other vowel. For example, the first syllable of 'poetic' pəʊ'etɪk is more prominent than the first syllable of 'pathetic' pə'θetɪk. This *could* be used as a basis for a further division of stress levels, giving us a third ("tertiary") level. It is also possible to suggest a tertiary level of stress in some polysyllabic words. To take an example, it has been suggested that the word 'indivisibility' shows four different levels: the syllable bɪl is the strongest (carrying primary stress), the initial syllable ɪn has secondary stress, while the third syllable vɪz has a level of stress which is weaker than those two but stronger than the second, fourth, sixth and seventh syllable (which are all unstressed). Using the symbol $_{\circ}$ to mark this tertiary stress, the word could be represented like this: ˌɪndɪ$_{\circ}$vɪzə'bɪləti. While this may be a phonetically correct account of some pronunciations, the introduction of tertiary stress seems to introduce an unnecessary degree of complexity. We will transcribe the word as ˌɪndɪˌvɪzə'bɪləti.

## 10.3 Placement of stress within the word

We now come to a question that causes a great deal of difficulty, particularly to foreign learners (who cannot simply dismiss it as an academic question): how can one select the correct syllable or syllables to stress in an English word? As is well known, English is not one of those languages where word stress can be decided simply in relation to the syllables of the word, as can be done in French (where the last syllable is usually stressed), Polish (where the syllable before the last – the penultimate syllable – is usually stressed) or Czech (where the first syllable is usually stressed). Many writers have said that English word stress is so difficult to predict that it is best to treat stress placement as a property of the individual word, to be learned when the word itself is learned. Certainly anyone who tries to analyse English stress placement has to recognise that it is a highly complex matter. However, it must also be recognised that in most cases (though certainly not all), when English speakers come across an unfamiliar word, they can pronounce it with the correct stress; in principle, it should be possible to discover what it is that the English speaker knows and to write it in the form of rules. The following summary of ideas on stress placement in nouns, verbs and adjectives is an attempt to present a few rules in the simplest possible form. Nevertheless, practically all the rules have exceptions and readers may feel that the rules are so complex that it would be easier to go back to the idea of learning the stress for each word individually.

In order to decide on stress placement, it is necessary to make use of some or all of the following information:

i) Whether the word is morphologically **simple,** or whether it is **complex** as a result either of containing one or more affixes (i.e. prefixes or suffixes) or of being a compound word.
ii) What the grammatical category of the word is (noun, verb, adjective, etc.).
iii) How many syllables the word has.
iv) What the phonological structure of those syllables is.

It is sometimes difficult to make the decision referred to in (i). The rules for complex words are different from those for simple words and these will be dealt with in Chapter 11. Single-syllable words present no problems: if they are pronounced in isolation they are said with primary stress.

Point (iv) above is something that should be dealt with right away, since it affects many of the other rules that we will look at later. We saw in Chapter 9 that it is possible to divide syllables into two basic categories: **strong** and **weak**. One component of a syllable is the **rhyme**, which contains the syllable peak and the coda. A strong syllable has a rhyme with

*either* (i) a syllable peak which is a long vowel or diphthong, with or without a following consonant (coda). Examples:

‘die’ daɪ ‘heart’ hɑːt ‘see’ siː

*or* (ii) a syllable peak which is a short vowel, one of ɪ, e, æ, ʌ, ɒ, ʊ, followed by at least one consonant. Examples:

‘bat’ bæt ‘much’ mʌtʃ ‘pull’ pʊl

A weak syllable has a syllable peak which consists of one of the vowels ə, i, u and no coda except when the vowel is ə. Syllabic consonants are also weak. Examples:

‘fa’ in ‘sofa’ ˈsəʊfə ‘zy’ in ‘lazy’ ˈleɪzi
‘flu’ in ‘influence’ ˈɪnfluəns ‘en’ in ‘sudden’ ˈsʌdn̩

The vowel ɪ may also be the peak of a weak syllable if it occurs before a consonant that is initial in the syllable that follows it. Examples:

‘bi’ in ‘herbicide’ ˈhɜːbɪsaɪd ‘e’ in ‘event’ ɪˈvent

(However, this vowel is also found frequently as the peak of stressed syllables, as in ‘thinker’ ˈθɪŋkə, ‘input’ ˈɪnpʊt.)

The important point to remember is that, although we do find unstressed strong syllables (as in the last syllable of ‘dialect’ ˈdaɪəlekt), *only* strong syllables can be stressed. Weak syllables are always unstressed. This piece of knowledge does not by any means solve all the problems of how to place English stress, but it does help in some cases.

## Two-syllable words

AU10 (CD 2), Ex 3

In the case of simple two-syllable words, either the first or the second syllable will be stressed – not both. There is a general tendency for verbs to be stressed nearer the end of a word and for nouns to be stressed nearer the beginning. We will look first at verbs. If the final syllable is weak, then the first syllable is stressed. Thus:

‘enter’ ˈentə ‘open’ ˈəʊpən
‘envy’ ˈenvi ‘equal’ ˈiːkwəl

A final syllable is also unstressed if it contains əʊ (e.g. ‘follow’ ˈfɒləʊ, ‘borrow’ ˈbɒrəʊ).

If the final syllable is strong, then that syllable is stressed even if the first syllable is also strong. Thus:

‘apply’ əˈplaɪ ‘attract’ əˈtrækt ‘rotate’ rəʊˈteɪt
‘arrive’ əˈraɪv ‘assist’ əˈsɪst ‘maintain’ meɪnˈteɪn

Two-syllable simple adjectives are stressed according to the same rule, giving:

‘lovely’ ˈlʌvli ‘divine’ dɪˈvaɪn
‘even’ ˈiːvən ‘correct’ kəˈrekt
‘hollow’ ˈhɒləʊ ‘alive’ əˈlaɪv

As with most stress rules, there are exceptions; for example: ‘honest’ ˈɒnɪst, ‘perfect’ ˈpɜːfɪkt, both of which end with strong syllables but are stressed on the first syllable.

Nouns require a different rule: stress will fall on the first syllable unless the first syllable is weak and the second syllable is strong. Thus:

| | |
|---|---|
| 'money' ˈmʌni | 'divan' dɪˈvæn |
| 'product' ˈprɒdʌkt | 'balloon' bəˈluːn |
| 'larynx' ˈlærɪŋks | 'design' dɪˈzaɪn |

Other two-syllable words such as adverbs seem to behave like verbs and adjectives.

### Three-syllable words

Here we find a more complicated picture. One problem is the difficulty of identifying three-syllable words which are indisputably simple. In simple verbs, if the final syllable is strong, then it will receive primary stress. Thus:

| | |
|---|---|
| 'entertain' ˌentəˈteɪn | 'resurrect' ˌrezəˈrekt |

If the last syllable is weak, then it will be unstressed, and stress will be placed on the preceding (penultimate) syllable if that syllable is strong. Thus:

| | |
|---|---|
| 'encounter' ɪŋˈkaʊntə | 'determine' dɪˈtɜːmɪn |

If both the second and third syllables are weak, then the stress falls on the initial syllable:

| | |
|---|---|
| 'parody' ˈpærədi | 'monitor' ˈmɒnɪtə |

Nouns require a slightly different rule. The general tendency is for stress to fall on the first syllable unless it is weak. Thus:

| | |
|---|---|
| 'quantity' ˈkwɒntəti | 'emperor' ˈempərə |
| 'custody' ˈkʌstədi | 'enmity' ˈenməti |

However, in words with a weak first syllable the stress comes on the next syllable:

| | |
|---|---|
| 'mimosa' mɪˈməʊzə | 'disaster' dɪˈzɑːstə |
| 'potato' pəˈteɪtəʊ | 'synopsis' sɪˈnɒpsɪs |

When a three-syllable noun has a strong final syllable, that syllable will not usually receive the main stress:

| | |
|---|---|
| 'intellect' ˈɪntəlekt | 'marigold' ˈmærɪgəʊld |
| 'alkali' ˈælkəlaɪ | 'stalactite' ˈstæləktaɪt |

Adjectives seem to need the same rule, to produce stress patterns such as:

| | |
|---|---|
| 'opportune' ˈɒpətjuːn | 'insolent' ˈɪnsələnt |
| 'derelict' ˈderəlɪkt | 'anthropoid' ˈænθrəpɔɪd |

The above rules certainly do not cover all English words. They apply only to major categories of lexical words (nouns, verbs and adjectives in this chapter), not to function words such as articles and prepositions. There is not enough space in this course to deal with simple words of more than three syllables, nor with special cases of loan words (words brought into the language from other languages comparatively recently). Complex and compound words are dealt with in Chapter 11. One problem that we must also leave until Chapter 11 is the fact that there are many cases of English words with alternative possible stress patterns (e.g. 'controversy' as either ˈkɒntrəvɜːsi or kənˈtrɒvəsi). Other words – which we will look at in studying connected speech – change their stress pattern according to the context they occur in. Above all, there is not space to discuss the many exceptions to the above rules. Despite the exceptions, it seems better to attempt to produce *some* stress rules (even if they are rather crude and inaccurate) than to claim that there is no rule or regularity in English word stress.

## Notes on problems and further reading

The subject of English stress has received a large amount of attention, and the references given here are only a small selection from an enormous number. As I suggested in the notes on the previous chapter, incorrect stress placement is a major cause of intelligibility problems for foreign learners, and is therefore a subject that needs to be treated very seriously.

**10.1** I have deliberately avoided using the term *accent*, which is found widely in the literature on stress – see, for example, Cruttenden (2008), p. 23. This is for three main reasons:

i) It increases the complexity of the description without, in my view, contributing much to its value.
ii) Different writers do not agree with each other about the way the term should be used.
iii) The word *accent* is used elsewhere to refer to different varieties of pronunciation (e.g. "a foreign *accent*"); it is confusing to use it for a quite different purpose. To a lesser extent we also have this problem with the word *stress*, which can be used to refer to psychological tension.

**10.2** On the question of the number of levels of stress, in addition to Laver (1994: 516), see also Wells (2008).

**10.3** It is said in this chapter that one may take one of two positions. One is that stress is not predictable by rule and must be learned word by word (see, for example, Jones 1975: Sections 920–1). The second (which I prefer) is to say that, difficult though the task is, one must try to find a way of writing rules that express what native speakers naturally tend to do in placing stress, while acknowledging that there will always be a substantial residue of cases which appear to follow no regular rules. A very thorough treatment is given by Fudge (1984). More recently, Giegerich (1992) has presented a clear analysis of English word stress (including a useful explanation of *strong*, *weak*, *heavy* and *light* syllables); see p. 146

and Chapter 7. I have not adopted the practice of labelling syllables *heavy* and *light* to denote characteristics of phonological structure (e.g. types of peak and coda), though this could have been done to avoid confusion with the more phonetically-based terms *strong* and *weak* introduced in Chapter 9. For our purposes, the difference is not important enough to need additional terminology.

There is another approach to English stress rules which is radically different. This is based on **generative phonology**, an analysis which was first presented in Chomsky and Halle (1968) and has been followed by a large number of works exploring the same field. To anyone not familiar with this type of treatment, the presentation will seem difficult or even unintelligible; within the generative approach, many different theories, all with different names, tend to come and go with changes in fashion. The following paragraph is an attempt to summarise the main characteristics of basic generative phonology, and recommends some further reading for those interested in learning about it in detail.

The level of phonology is very abstract in this theory. An old-fashioned view of speech communication would be that what the speaker intends to say is coded – or *represented* – as a string of phonemes just like a phonemic transcription, and what a hearer hears is also converted by the brain from sound waves into a similar string of phonemes. A generative phonologist, however, would say that this phonemic representation is not accurate; the representation in the brain of the speaker or hearer is much more abstract and is often quite different from the 'real' sounds recognisable in the sound wave. You may hear the word 'football' pronounced as fʊpbɔːl, but your brain recognises the word as made up of 'foot' and 'ball' and interprets it phonologically as fʊtbɔːl. You may hear ə in the first syllable of 'photography', in the second syllable of 'photograph' and in the third syllable of 'photographer', but these ə vowels are only the *surface* realizations of *underlying* vowel phonemes. An abstract phonemic representation of 'photograph' (including the relevant part of 'photography', 'photographic' and 'photographer') would be something like foːtograf; each of the three underlying vowels (for which I am using symbols different from those used in the rest of this book) would be realised differently according to the stress they received and their position in the word: the oː in the first syllable would be realized as əʊ if stressed ('photograph' ˈfəʊtəgrɑːf, 'photographic' ˌfəʊtəˈgræfɪk) and as ə if unstressed ('photography' fəˈtɒgrəfi); the o in the second syllable would be realised as ɒ if stressed ('photography' fəˈtɒgrəfi) and as ə if unstressed ('photograph' ˈfəʊtəgrɑːf), while the a in the third syllable would be realised as æ if stressed ('photographic' fəʊtəˈgræfɪk), as either ɑː or æ if in a word-final syllable ('photograph' ˈfəʊtəgrɑːf or ˈfəʊtəgræf) and as ə if unstressed in a syllable that is not word-final ('photography' fəˈtɒgrəfi). These vowel changes are brought about by *rules* – not the sort of rules that one might teach to language learners, but more like the instructions that one might build into a machine or write into a computer program. According to Chomsky and Halle, at the abstract phonological level words do not possess stress; stress (of many different levels) is the result of the application of phonological rules, which are simple enough in theory but highly complex in practice. The principles of these rules are explained first on pp. 15–43 of Chomsky and Halle (1968), and in greater detail on pp. 69–162.

There is a clear and thorough introductory account of generative phonology in Clark *et al.* (2007: Chapter 5), and they present a brief account of the generative treatment of stress in section 9.7. A briefer review is given in Katamba (1989: Chapter 11, Section 1).

## Notes for teachers

It should be clear from what is said above that from the purely practical classroom point of view, explaining English word stress in terms of generative phonology could well create confusion for learners. Finding practice and testing material for word stress is very simple, however: any modern English dictionary shows word stress patterns as part of word entries, and lists of these can be made either with stress marks for students to read from (as in Exercise 2 of Audio Unit 10), or without stress marks for students to put their own marks on (as in Exercise 1 of the same Audio Unit).

## Written exercises

Mark the stress on the following words:

1 Verbs

| | |
|---|---|
| a) protect | e) bellow |
| b) clamber | f) menace |
| c) festoon | g) disconnect |
| d) detest | h) enter |

2 Nouns

| | |
|---|---|
| a) language | e) event |
| b) captain | f) jonquil |
| c) career | g) injury |
| d) paper | h) connection |

(Native speakers of English should transcribe the words phonemically as well as marking stress.)

# 11 Complex word stress

## 11.1 Complex words

In Chapter 10 the nature of stress was explained and some broad general rules were given for deciding which syllable in a word should receive primary stress. The words that were described were called "simple" words; "simple" in this context means "not composed of more than one grammatical unit", so that, for example, the word 'care' is simple while 'careful' and 'careless' (being composed of two grammatical units each) are complex; 'carefully' and 'carelessness' are also complex, and are composed of three grammatical units each. Unfortunately, as was suggested in Chapter 10, it is often difficult to decide whether a word should be treated as complex or simple. The majority of English words of more than one syllable (**polysyllabic** words) have come from other languages whose way of constructing words is easily recognisable; for example, we can see how combining 'mit' with the prefixes 'per-', 'sub-', 'com-' produced 'permit', 'submit', 'commit' – words which have come into English from Latin. Similarly, Greek has given us 'catalogue', 'analogue', 'dialogue', 'monologue', in which the prefixes 'cata-', 'ana-', 'dia-', 'mono-' are recognisable. But we cannot automatically treat the separate grammatical units of other languages as if they were separate grammatical units of English. If we did, we would not be able to study English morphology without first studying the morphology of five or six other languages, and we would be forced into ridiculous analyses such as that the English word 'parallelepiped' is composed of four or five grammatical units (which is the case in Ancient Greek). We must accept, then, that the distinction between "simple" and "complex" words is difficult to draw.

Complex words are of two major types:

i) words made from a basic word form (which we will call the **stem**), with the addition of an **affix**; and
ii) **compound** words, which are made of two (or occasionally more) independent English words (e.g. 'ice cream', 'armchair').

We will look first at the words made with affixes. Affixes are of two sorts in English: **prefixes**, which come before the stem (e.g. prefix 'un-' + stem 'pleasant' → 'unpleasant') and **suffixes**, which come after the stem (e.g. stem 'good' + suffix '-ness' → 'goodness').

Affixes have one of three possible effects on word stress:

i) The affix itself receives the primary stress (e.g. 'semi-' + 'circle' sɜːkl̩ → 'semicircle' ˈsemɪsɜːkl̩; '-ality' + 'person' ˈpɜːsn̩ → 'personality' pɜːsn̩ˈæləti).
ii) The word is stressed as if the affix were not there (e.g. 'pleasant' ˈpleznt̩, 'unpleasant' ʌnˈpleznt̩; 'market' ˈmɑːkɪt, 'marketing' ˈmɑːkɪtɪŋ).
iii) The stress remains on the stem, not the affix, but is shifted to a different syllable (e.g. 'magnet' ˈmæɡnət, 'magnetic' mæɡˈnetɪk).

## 11.2 **Suffixes**

There are so many suffixes that it will only be possible here to examine a small proportion of them: we will concentrate on those which are common and **productive** – that is, are applied to a considerable number of stems and could be applied to more to make new English words. In the case of the others, foreign learners would probably be better advised to learn the 'stem + affix' combination as an individual item.

One of the problems that we encounter is that we find words which are obviously complex but which, when we try to divide them into stem + affix, turn out to have a stem that is difficult to imagine as an English word. For example, the word 'audacity' seems to be a complex word – but what is its stem? Another problem is that it is difficult in some cases to know whether a word has one, or more than one, suffix: for example, should we analyse 'personality' from the point of view of stress assignment, as pɜːsn̩ + æləti or as pɜːsn̩ + æl + əti? In the study of English word formation at a deeper level than we can go into here, it is necessary for such reasons to distinguish between a stem (which is what remains when affixes are removed), and a **root**, which is the smallest piece of lexical material that a stem can be reduced to. So, in 'personality', we could say that the *suffix* '-ity' is attached to the *stem* 'personal' which contains the *root* 'person' and the suffix 'al'. We will not spend more time here on looking at these problems, but go on to look at some generalisations about suffixes and stress, using only the term 'stem' for the sake of simplicity. The suffixes are referred to in their spelling form.

### Suffixes carrying primary stress themselves

AU11 (CD 2), Ex 1

In the examples given, which seem to be the most common, the primary stress is on the first syllable of the suffix. If the stem consists of more than one syllable there will be a secondary stress on one of the syllables of the stem. This cannot fall on the last syllable of the stem and is, if necessary, moved to an earlier syllable. For example, in 'Japan' dʒəˈpæn the primary stress is on the last syllable, but when we add the stress-carrying suffix '-ese' the primary stress is on the suffix and the secondary stress is placed not on the second syllable but on the first: 'Japanese' ˌdʒæpəˈniːz.

- '-ee': 'refugee' ˌrefjʊˈdʒiː; 'evacuee' ɪˌvækjuˈiː
- '-eer': 'mountaineer' ˌmaʊntɪˈnɪə; 'volunteer' ˌvɒlənˈtɪə
- '-ese': 'Portuguese' ˌpɔːtʃəˈɡiːz; 'journalese' ˌdʒɜːnl̩ˈiːz

- '-ette': 'cigarette' ˌsɪgr̩ˈet; 'launderette' ˌlɔːndr̩ˈet
- 'esque': 'picturesque' ˌpɪktʃr̩ˈesk

**Suffixes that do not affect stress placement** AU11 (CD 2), Ex 2

- '-able': 'comfort' ˈkʌmfət; 'comfortable' ˈkʌmfətəbl̩
- '-age': 'anchor' ˈæŋkə; 'anchorage' ˈæŋkr̩ɪdʒ
- '-al': 'refuse' (verb) rɪˈfjuːz; 'refusal' rɪˈfjuːzl̩
- '-en': 'wide' ˈwaɪd; 'widen' ˈwaɪdn̩
- '-ful': 'wonder' ˈwʌndə; 'wonderful' ˈwʌndəfl̩
- '-ing': 'amaze' əˈmeɪz; 'amazing' əˈmeɪzɪŋ
- '-like': 'bird' ˈbɜːd; 'birdlike' ˈbɜːdlaɪk
- '-less': 'power' ˈpaʊə; 'powerless' ˈpaʊələs
- '-ly': 'hurried' ˈhʌrɪd; 'hurriedly' ˈhʌrɪdli
- '-ment' (noun): 'punish' ˈpʌnɪʃ; 'punishment' ˈpʌnɪʃmənt
- '-ness': 'yellow' ˈjeləʊ; 'yellowness' ˈjeləʊnəs
- '-ous': 'poison' ˈpɔɪzn̩; 'poisonous' ˈpɔɪzn̩əs
- '-fy': 'glory' ˈglɔːri; 'glorify' ˈglɔːrɪfaɪ
- '-wise': 'other' ˈʌðə; 'otherwise' ˈʌðəwaɪz
- '-y' (adjective or noun): 'fun' ˈfʌn; 'funny' ˈfʌni
- ('-ish' in the case of adjectives does not affect stress placement: 'devil' ˈdevl̩; 'devilish' ˈdevl̩ɪʃ; however, verbs with stems of more than one syllable always have the stress on the syllable immediately preceding 'ish' – for example, 'replenish' rɪˈplenɪʃ, 'demolish' dɪˈmɒlɪʃ)

**Suffixes that influence stress in the stem** AU11 (CD 2), Ex 3

In these examples primary stress is on the last syllable of the stem.

- '-eous': 'advantage' ədˈvɑːntɪdʒ; 'advantageous' ˌædvənˈteɪdʒəs
- '-graphy': 'photo' ˈfəʊtəʊ; 'photography' fəˈtɒgrəfi
- '-ial': 'proverb' ˈprɒvɜːb; 'proverbial' prəˈvɜːbiəl
- '-ic': 'climate' ˈklaɪmət; 'climatic' klaɪˈmætɪk
- '-ion': 'perfect' ˈpɜːfɪkt; 'perfection' pəˈfekʃn̩
- '-ious': 'injure' ˈɪndʒə; 'injurious' ɪnˈdʒʊəriəs
- '- ty': 'tranquil' ˈtræŋkwɪl; 'tranquillity' træŋˈkwɪləti
- '-ive': 'reflex' ˈriːfleks; 'reflexive' rɪˈfleksɪv

Finally, when the suffixes '-ance', '-ant' and '-ary' are attached to single-syllable stems, the stress is almost always placed on the stem (e.g. 'guidance', 'sealant', 'dietary'). When the stem has more than one syllable, the stress is on one of the syllables in the stem. To explain this we need to use a rule based on syllable structure, as was done for simple words in the previous chapter. If the final syllable of the stem is strong, that syllable receives the stress. For example: 'importance' ɪmˈpɔːtn̩s, 'centenary' senˈtiːnr̩i.

Otherwise the syllable *before* the last one receives the stress: 'inheritance' ɪnˈherɪtəns, 'military' ˈmɪlɪtri.

## 11.3 Prefixes

We will look only briefly at prefixes. Their effect on stress does not have the comparative regularity, independence and predictability of suffixes, and there is no prefix of one or two syllables that always carries primary stress. Consequently, the best treatment seems to be to say that stress in words with prefixes is governed by the same rules as those for polysyllabic words without prefixes.

## 11.4 Compound words

AU11 (CD 2), Ex 4

The words discussed so far in this chapter have all consisted of a stem plus an affix. We now pass on to another type of word. This is called **compound,** and its main characteristic is that it can be analysed into two words, both of which can exist independently as English words. Some compounds are made of more than two words, but we will not consider these. As with many of the distinctions being made in connection with stress, there are areas of uncertainty. For example, it could be argued that 'photograph' may be divided into two independent words, 'photo' and 'graph'; yet we usually do not regard it as a compound, but as a simple word. If, however, someone drew a graph displaying numerical information about photos, this would perhaps be called a 'photo-graph' and the word would then be regarded as a compound. Compounds are written in different ways: sometimes they are written as one word (e.g. 'armchair', 'sunflower'); sometimes with the words separated by a hyphen (e.g. 'open-minded', 'cost-effective'); and sometimes with two words separated by a space (e.g. 'desk lamp', 'battery charger'). In this last case there would be no indication to the foreign learner that the pair of words was to be treated as a compound. There is no clear dividing line between two-word compounds and pairs of words that simply happen to occur together quite frequently.

As far as stress is concerned, the question is quite simple. When is primary stress placed on the first constituent word of the compound and when on the second? Both patterns are found. A few rules can be given, although these are not completely reliable. Perhaps the most familiar type of compound is the one which combines two nouns and which normally has the stress on the first element, as in:

'typewriter' ˈtaɪpraɪtə
'car ferry' ˈkɑːferi
'sunrise' ˈsʌnraɪz
'suitcase' ˈsuːtkeɪs
'teacup' ˈtiːkʌp

It is probably safest to assume that stress will normally fall in this way on other compounds; however, a number of compounds receive stress instead on the second element. The first words in such compounds often have secondary stress. For example, compounds with an adjectival first element and the *-ed* morpheme at the end have this pattern (given in spelling only):

ˌbad-ˈtempered
ˌhalf-ˈtimbered
ˌheavy-ˈhanded

Compounds in which the first element is a number in some form also tend to have final stress:

ˌthree-ˈwheeler
ˌsecond-ˈclass
ˌfive-ˈfinger

Compounds functioning as adverbs are usually final-stressed:

ˌheadˈfirst
ˌNorth-ˈEast
ˌdownˈstream

Finally, compounds which function as verbs and have an adverbial first element take final stress:

ˌdownˈgrade
ˌback-ˈpedal
ˌill-ˈtreat

## 11.5 **Variable stress**

It would be wrong to imagine that the stress pattern is always fixed and unchanging in English words. Stress position may vary for one of two reasons: either as a result of the stress on other words occurring next to the word in question, or because not all speakers agree on the placement of stress in some words. The former case is an aspect of connected speech that will be encountered again in Chapter 14: the main effect is that the stress on a final-stressed compound tends to move to a preceding syllable and change to secondary stress if the following word begins with a strongly stressed syllable. Thus (using some examples from the previous section):

| | | |
|---|---|---|
| ˌbad-ˈtempered | *but* | a ˌbad-tempered ˈteacher |
| ˌhalf-ˈtimbered | *but* | a ˌhalf-timbered ˈhouse |
| ˌheavy-ˈhanded | *but* | a ˌheavy-handed ˈsentence |

The second is not a serious problem, but is one that foreign learners should be aware of. A well-known example is 'controversy', which is pronounced by some speakers as ˈkɒntrəvɜːsi and by others as kənˈtrɒvəsi; it would be quite wrong to say that one version was correct and one incorrect. Other examples of different possibilities are 'ice cream' (either ˌaɪs kriːm or ˈaɪs kriːm), 'kilometre' (either kɪˈlɒmɪtə or ˈkɪləmiːtə) and 'formidable' (ˈfɔːmɪdəbl̩ or fɔːˈmɪdəbl̩).

## 11.6 Word-class pairs

AU11 (CD 2), Ex 5

One aspect of word stress is best treated as a separate issue. There are several dozen pairs of two-syllable words with identical spelling which differ from each other in stress placement, apparently according to word class (noun, verb or adjective). All appear to consist of prefix + stem. We shall treat them as a special type of word and give them the following rule: if a pair of prefix-plus-stem words exists, both members of which are spelt identically, one of which is a verb and the other of which is either a noun or an adjective, then the stress is placed on the second syllable of the verb but on the first syllable of the noun or adjective. Some common examples are given below (V = verb, A = adjective, N = noun):

| | | |
|---|---|---|
| abstract | ˈæbstrækt (A) | æbˈstrækt (V) |
| conduct | ˈkɒndʌkt (N) | kənˈdʌkt (V) |
| contract | ˈkɒntrækt (N) | kənˈtrækt (V) |
| contrast | ˈkɒntrɑːst (N) | kənˈtrɑːst (V) |
| desert | ˈdezət (N) | dɪˈzɜːt (V) |
| escort | ˈeskɔːt (N) | ɪˈskɔːt (V) |
| export | ˈekspɔːt (N) | ɪkˈspɔːt (V) |
| import | ˈɪmpɔːt (N) | ɪmˈpɔːt (V) |
| insult | ˈɪnsʌlt (N) | ɪnˈsʌlt (V) |
| object | ˈɒbdʒekt (N) | əbˈdʒekt (V) |
| perfect | ˈpɜːfɪkt (A) | pəˈfekt (V) |
| permit | ˈpɜːmɪt (N) | pəˈmɪt (V) |
| present | ˈpreznt̩ (N, A) | prɪˈzent (V) |
| produce | ˈprɒdjuːs (N) | prəˈdjuːs (V) |
| protest | ˈprəʊtest (N) | prəˈtest (V) |
| rebel | ˈrebl̩ (N) | rɪˈbel (V) |
| record | ˈrekɔːd (N, A) | rɪˈkɔːd (V) |
| subject | ˈsʌbdʒekt (N) | səbˈdʒekt (V) |

## Notes on problems and further reading

Most of the reading recommended in the notes for the previous chapter is relevant for this one too. Looking specifically at compounds, it is worth reading Fudge (1984: Chapter 5). See also Cruttenden (2008: 242–5). If you wish to go more deeply into compound-word stress, you should first study English word formation. Recommended reading for this is Bauer (1983). On the distinction between *stem* and *root,* see Radford *et al.* (1999: 67–8).

## Written exercises

1 Put stress marks on the following words (try to put secondary stress marks on as well).

a) shopkeeper
b) open-ended
c) Javanese
d) birthmark
e) anti-clockwise
f) confirmation
g) eight-sided
h) fruitcake
i) defective
j) roof timber

2 Write the words in phonemic transcription, including the stress marks.

# 12 Weak forms

Chapter 9 discussed the difference between strong and weak syllables in English. We have now moved on from looking at syllables to looking at words, and we will consider certain well-known English words that can be pronounced in two different ways; these are called **strong forms** and **weak forms.** As an example, the word 'that' can be pronounced ðæt (strong form) or ðət (weak form). The sentence 'I like that' is pronounced aɪ laɪk ðæt (strong form); the sentence 'I hope that she will' is pronounced aɪ həʊp ðət ʃi wɪl (weak form). There are roughly forty such words in English. It is possible to use only strong forms in speaking, and some foreigners do this. Usually they can still be understood by other speakers of English, so why is it important to learn how weak forms are used? There are two main reasons: first, most native speakers of English find an "all-strong form" pronunciation unnatural and foreign-sounding, something that most learners would wish to avoid. Second, and more importantly, speakers who are not familiar with the use of weak forms are likely to have difficulty understanding speakers who do use weak forms; since practically all native speakers of British English use them, learners of the language need to learn about these weak forms to help them to understand what they hear.

We must distinguish between weak forms and **contracted forms**. Certain English words are shortened so severely (usually to a single phoneme) and so consistently that they are represented differently in informal writing (e.g. 'it is' → 'it's'; 'we have' → 'we've'; 'do not' → 'don't'). These contracted forms are discussed in Chapter 14, and are not included here.

Almost all the words which have both a strong and weak form belong to a category that may be called **function words** – words that do not have a dictionary meaning in the way that we normally expect nouns, verbs, adjectives and adverbs to have. These function words are words such as auxiliary verbs, prepositions, conjunctions, etc., all of which are in certain circumstances pronounced in their strong forms but which are more frequently pronounced in their weak forms. It is important to remember that there are certain contexts where only the strong form is acceptable, and others where the weak form is the normal pronunciation. There are some fairly simple rules; we can say that the strong form is used in the following cases:

i) For many weak-form words, when they occur at the end of a sentence; for example, the word 'of' has the weak form əv in the following sentence:

   'I'm fond of chips' aɪm ˈfɒnd əv ˈtʃɪps

However, when it comes at the end of the sentence, as in the following example, it has the strong form ɒv:

'Chips are what I'm fond of' 'tʃɪps ə 'wɒt aɪm 'fɒnd ɒv

Many of the words given below (particularly 1–9) never occur at the end of a sentence (e.g. 'the', 'your'). Some words (particularly the pronouns numbered 10–14 below) do occur in their weak forms in final position.

ii) When a weak-form word is being contrasted with another word; for example:

'The letter's *from* him, not *to* him' ðə 'letəz 'frɒm ɪm nɒt 'tuː ɪm

A similar case is what we might call a **co-ordinated** use of prepositions:

'I travel to and from London a lot' aɪ 'trævl̩ 'tuː ən 'frɒm 'lʌndən ə 'lɒt
'A work of and about literature' ə 'wɜːk 'ɒv ən ə'baʊt 'lɪtrətʃə

iii) When a weak-form word is given stress for the purpose of emphasis; for example:

'You *must* give me more money' ju 'mʌst 'ɡɪv mi 'mɔː 'mʌni

iv) When a weak-form word is being "cited" or "quoted"; for example:

'You shouldn't put "and" at the end of a sentence'
ju 'ʃʊdn̩t pʊt 'ænd ət ði 'end əv ə 'sentəns

Another point to remember is that when weak-form words whose spelling begins with 'h' (e.g. 'her', 'have') occur at the beginning of a sentence, the pronunciation is with initial h, even though this is usually omitted in other contexts.

AU12 (CD 2), Exs 1–4

In the rest of this chapter, the most common weak-form words will be introduced.

1 'the'

Weak forms: ðə (before consonants)
'Shut the door' 'ʃʌt ðə 'dɔː
ði (before vowels)
'Wait for the end' 'weɪt fə ði 'end

2 'a', 'an'

Weak forms: ə (before consonants)
'Read a book' 'riːd ə 'bʊk
ən (before vowels)
'Eat an apple' 'iːt ən 'æpl̩

3 'and'

Weak form: ən (sometimes n̩ after t, d, s, z, ʃ)
'Come and see' 'kʌm ən 'siː
'Fish and chips' 'fɪʃ n̩ 'tʃɪps

4 'but'

Weak form: bət

'It's good but expensive' ɪts ˈgʊd bət ɪkˈspensɪv

5 'that'

This word only has a weak form when used in a relative clause; when used with a demonstrative sense it is always pronounced in its strong form.

Weak form: ðət

'The price is the thing that annoys me' ðə ˈpraɪs ɪz ðə ˈθɪŋ ðət əˈnɔɪz mi

6 'than'

Weak form: ðən

'Better than ever' ˈbetə ðən ˈevə

7 'his' (when it occurs before a noun)

Weak form: ɪz (hɪz at the beginning of a sentence)

'Take his name' ˈteɪk ɪz ˈneɪm

(Another sense of 'his', as in 'it was his', or 'his was late', always has the strong form)

8 'her'

When used with a possessive sense, preceding a noun; as an object pronoun, this can also occur at the end of a sentence.

Weak forms: ə (before consonants)

'Take her home' ˈteɪk ə ˈhəʊm

ər (before vowels)

'Take her out' ˈteɪk ər ˈaʊt

9 'your'

Weak forms: jə (before consonants)

'Take your time' ˈteɪk jə ˈtaɪm

jər (before vowels)

'On your own' ˈɒn jər ˈəʊn

10 'she', 'he', 'we', 'you'

This group of pronouns has weak forms pronounced with weaker vowels than the iː, uː of their strong forms. I use the symbols i, u (in preference to ɪ, ʊ) to represent them. There is little difference in the pronunciation in different places in the sentence, except in the case of 'he'.

Weak forms:

a) 'she' ʃi

'Why did she read it?' ˈwaɪ dɪd ʃi ˈriːd ɪt

'Who *is* she?' ˈhuː ˈɪz ʃi

b) 'he' i (the weak form is usually pronounced without h except at the beginning of a sentence)

'Which did he choose?' ˈwɪtʃ dɪd i ˈtʃuːz

'He was late, wasn't he?' hi wəz ˈleɪt ˈwɒzn̩t i

c) 'we' wi
'How can we get there?' 'haʊ kən wi 'get ðeə
'We need that, don't we?' wi 'niːd ðæt 'dəʊnt wi

d) 'you' ju
'What do you think?' 'wɒt də ju 'θɪŋk
'You like it, do you?' ju 'laɪk ɪt 'duː ju

11 'him'
Weak form: ɪm
'Leave him alone' 'liːv ɪm ə'ləʊn
'I've seen him' aɪv 'siːn ɪm

12 'her'
Weak form: ə (hə when sentence-initial)
'Ask her to come' 'ɑːsk ə tə 'kʌm
'I've met her' aɪv 'met ə

13 'them'
Weak form: ðəm
'Leave them here' 'liːv ðəm 'hɪə
'Eat them' 'iːt ðəm

14 'us'
Weak form: əs
'Write us a letter' 'raɪt əs ə 'letə
'They invited all of us' ðeɪ ɪn'vaɪtɪd 'ɔːl əv əs

The next group of words (some prepositions and other function words) occur in their strong forms when they are in final position in a sentence; examples of this are given. Number 19, 'to', is a partial exception.

15 'at'
Weak form: ət
'I'll see you at lunch' aɪl 'siː ju ət 'lʌnʃ
In final position: æt
'What's he shooting at?' 'wɒts i 'ʃuːtɪŋ æt

16 'for'
Weak form: fə (before consonants)
'Tea for two' 'tiː fə 'tuː
fər (before vowels)
'Thanks for asking' 'θæŋks fər 'ɑːskɪŋ
In final position: fɔː
'What's that for?' 'wɒts 'ðæt fɔː

17 'from'
Weak form: frəm
'I'm home from work' aɪm 'həʊm frəm 'wɜːk

In final position: frɒm
'Here's where it came from' ˈhɪəz weər ɪt ˈkeɪm frɒm

18 'of'

Weak form: əv
'Most of all' ˈməʊst əv ˈɔːl

In final position: ɒv
'Someone I've heard of' ˈsʌmwʌn aɪv ˈhɜːd ɒv

19 'to'

Weak forms: tə (before consonants)
'Try to stop' ˈtraɪ tə ˈstɒp
tu (before vowels)
'Time to eat' ˈtaɪm tu ˈiːt

In final position: tu (it is not usual to use the strong form tuː; the pre-consonantal weak form tə is never used)
'I don't want to' aɪ ˈdəʊnt ˈwɒnt tu

20 'as'

Weak form: əz
'As much as possible' əz ˈmʌtʃ əz ˈpɒsəbl̩
In final position: æz
'That's what it was sold as' ˈðæts ˈwɒt ɪt wəz ˈsəʊld æz

21 'some'

This word is used in two different ways. In one sense (typically, when it occurs before a countable noun, meaning "an unknown individual") it has the strong form:

'I think some animal broke it' aɪ ˈθɪŋk sʌm ˈænɪməl ˈbrəʊk ɪt

It is also used before uncountable nouns (meaning "an unspecified amount of") and before other nouns in the plural (meaning "an unspecified number of"); in such uses it has the weak form səm

'Have some more tea' ˈhəv səm ˈmɔː ˈtiː

In final position: sʌm
'I've got some' aɪv ˈgɒt sʌm

22 'there'

When this word has a demonstrative function, it always occurs in its strong form ðeə (ðeər before vowels); for example:

'There it is' ˈðeər ɪt ɪz
'Put it there' ˈpʊt ɪt ˈðeə

Weak forms: ðə (before consonants)
'There should be a rule' ðə ˈʃʊd bi ə ˈruːl
ðər (before vowels)
'There is' ðər ˈɪz

In final position: the pronunciation may be ðə or ðeə.
'There isn't any, is there?' ðər ˈɪzn̩t eni ɪz ðə
*or* ðər ˈɪzn̩t eni ɪz ðeə

The remaining weak-form words are all auxiliary verbs, which are always used in conjunction with (or at least implying) another ("full") verb. It is important to remember that in their negative form (i.e. combined with 'not') they never have the weak pronunciation, and some (e.g. 'don't', 'can't') have different vowels from their non-negative strong forms.

23 'can', 'could'

Weak forms: kən, kəd
'They can wait' 'ðeɪ kən 'weɪt
'He could do it' 'hiː kəd 'duː ɪt
In final position: kæn, kʊd
'I think we can' aɪ 'θɪŋk wi 'kæn
'Most of them could' 'məʊst əv ðəm 'kʊd

24 'have', 'has', 'had'

Weak forms: əv, əz, əd (with initial h in initial position)
'Which have you seen?' 'wɪtʃ əv ju 'siːn
'Which has been best?' 'wɪtʃ əz biːn 'best
'Most had gone home' 'məʊst əd gɒn 'həʊm

In final position: hæv, hæz, hæd
'Yes, we have' 'jes wi 'hæv
'I think she has' aɪ 'θɪŋk ʃi 'hæz
'I thought we had' aɪ 'θɔːt wi 'hæd

25 'shall', 'should'

Weak forms: ʃəl or ʃl̩; ʃəd
'We shall need to hurry' wi ʃl̩ 'niːd tə 'hʌri
'I should forget it' 'aɪ ʃəd fə'get ɪt

In final position: ʃæl, ʃʊd
'I think we shall' aɪ 'θɪŋk wi 'ʃæl
'So you should' 'səʊ ju 'ʃʊd

26 'must'

This word is sometimes used with the sense of forming a conclusion or deduction (e.g. 'she left at eight o'clock, so she must have arrived by now'); when 'must' is used in this way, it is less likely to occur in its weak form than when it is being used in its more familiar sense of obligation.

Weak forms: məs (before consonants)
'You must try harder' ju məs 'traɪ 'hɑːdə
məst (before vowels)
'He must eat more' hi məst 'iːt 'mɔː

In final position: mʌst
'She certainly must' ʃi 'sɜːtn̩li 'mʌst

27 'do', 'does'

Weak forms:

'do' də (before consonants)
'Why do they like it?' 'waɪ də ðeɪ 'laɪk ɪt

du (before vowels)
'Why do all the cars stop?' ˈwaɪ du ˈɔːl ðə ˈkɑːz ˈstɒp

'does' dəz
'When does it arrive?' ˈwen dəz ɪt əˈraɪv

In final position: duː, dʌz
'We don't smoke, but some people do' ˈwiː dəʊnt ˈsməʊk bət ˈsʌm piːpl̩ ˈduː
'I think John does' aɪ ˈθɪŋk ˈdʒɒn dʌz

28 'am', 'are', 'was', 'were'

Weak forms: əm
'Why am I here?' ˈwaɪ əm aɪ ˈhɪə
ə (before consonants)
'Here are the plates' ˈhɪər ə ðə ˈpleɪts
ər (before vowels)
'The coats are in there' ðə ˈkəʊts ər ɪn ˈðeə
wəz
'He was here a minute ago' hi wəz ˈhɪər ə ˈmɪnɪt əˈgəʊ
wə (before consonants)
'The papers were late' ðə ˈpeɪpəz wə ˈleɪt
wər (before vowels)
'The questions were easy' ðə ˈkwestʃənz wər ˈiːzi

In final position: æm, ɑː, wɒz, wɜː
'She's not as old as I am' ʃɪz ˈnɒt əz ˈəʊld əz ˈaɪ æm
'I know the Smiths are' aɪ ˈnəʊ ðə ˈsmɪθs ɑː
'The last record was' ðə ˈlɑːst ˈrekɔːd wɒz
'They weren't as cold as we were' ðeɪ ˈwɜːnt əz ˈkəʊld əz ˈwiː wɜː

## Notes on problems and further reading

This chapter is almost entirely practical. All books about English pronunciation devote a lot of attention to weak forms. Some of them give a great deal of importance to using these forms, but do not stress the importance of also knowing when to use the strong forms, something which I feel is very important; see Hewings (2007: 48–9). There is a very detailed study of English weak forms in Obendorfer (1998).

## Written exercise

In the following sentences, the transcription for the weak-form words is left blank. Fill in the blanks, taking care to use the appropriate form (weak or strong).

1 I want her to park that car over there.
aɪ wɒnt pɑːk kɑːr əʊvə

2 Of all the proposals, the one that you made is the silliest.
ɔːl prəpəʊzl̩z wʌn meɪd ɪz sɪliəst

3 Jane and Bill could have driven them to and from the party.
dʒeɪn bɪl drɪvn̩ pɑːti

4 To come to the point, what shall we do for the rest of the week?
kʌm pɔɪnt wɒt rest wiːk

5 Has anyone got an idea where it came from?
eniwʌn gɒt aɪdɪə weər ɪt keɪm

6 Pedestrians must always use the crossings provided.
pədestriənz ɔːlweɪz juːz krɒsɪŋz prəvaɪdɪd

7 Each one was a perfect example of the art that had been developed there.
iːtʃ wʌn pɜːfɪkt ɪgzɑːmpl̩ ɑːt biːn dɪveləpt

# 13 Problems in phonemic analysis

The concept of the phoneme was introduced in Chapter 5, and a few theoretical problems connected with phonemic analysis have been mentioned in other chapters. The general assumption (as in most phonetics books) has been that speech is composed of phonemes and that usually whenever a speech sound is produced by a speaker it is possible to identify which phoneme that sound belongs to. While this is often true, we must recognise that there are exceptions which make us consider some quite serious theoretical problems. From the comparatively simple point of view of learning pronunciation, these problems are not particularly important. However, from the point of view of learning about the phonology of English they are too important to ignore.

There are problems of different types. In some cases, we have difficulty in deciding on the overall phonemic system of the accent we are studying, while in others we are concerned about how a particular sound fits into this system. A number of such problems are discussed below.

## 13.1 Affricates

The affricates tʃ, dʒ are, phonetically, composed of a plosive followed by a fricative, as explained in Chapter 6. It is possible to treat each of the pair tʃ, dʒ as a single consonant phoneme; we will call this the **one-phoneme analysis** of tʃ, dʒ. It is also possible to say that they are composed of two phonemes each – t plus ʃ, and d plus ʒ respectively – all of which are already established as independent phonemes of English; this will be called the **two-phoneme analysis** of tʃ, dʒ. If we adopted the two-phoneme analysis, the words 'church' and 'judge' would be composed of five phonemes each, like this:

t – ʃ – ɜː – t – ʃ    d – ʒ – ʌ – d – ʒ

instead of the three phonemes that result from the one-phoneme analysis:

tʃ – ɜː – tʃ    dʒ – ʌ – dʒ

and there would be no separate tʃ, dʒ phonemes. But how can we decide which analysis is preferable? The two-phoneme analysis has one main advantage: if there are no separate tʃ, dʒ phonemes, then our total set of English consonants is smaller. Many phonologists have claimed that one should prefer the analysis which is the most "economical" in the number of phonemes it results in. The argument for this might be based on the claim that when we speak to someone we are using a code, and the most efficient codes do not employ unnecessary symbols. Further, it can be claimed that a phonological analysis is a type of scientific theory, and a scientific theory should be stated as economically as possible. However, it is the one-phoneme analysis that is generally chosen by phonologists. Why is this? There are several arguments: no single one of them is conclusive, but added together they are felt to make the one-phoneme analysis seem preferable. We will look briefly at some of these arguments.

i) One argument could be called "phonetic" or "allophonic": if it could be shown that the phonetic quality of the t and ʃ (or d and ʒ) in tʃ, dʒ is clearly different from realisations of t, ʃ, d, ʒ found elsewhere in similar contexts, this would support the analysis of tʃ, dʒ as separate phonemes. As an example, it might be claimed that ʃ in 'hutch' hʌtʃ was different (perhaps in having shorter duration) from ʃ in 'hush' hʌʃ or 'Welsh' welʃ; or it might be claimed that the place of articulation of t in 'watch apes' wɒtʃ eɪps was different from that of t in 'what shapes' wɒt ʃeɪps. This argument is a weak one: there is no clear evidence that such phonetic differences exist, and even if there were such evidence, it would be easy to produce explanations for the differences that did not depend on phonemic analyses (e.g. the position of the word boundary in 'watch apes', 'what shapes').

ii) It could be argued that the proposed phonemes tʃ, dʒ have distributions similar to other consonants, while other combinations of plosive plus fricative do not. It can easily be shown that tʃ, dʒ are found initially, medially and finally, and that no other combination (e.g. pf, dz, tθ) has such a wide distribution. However, several consonants *are* generally accepted as phonemes of the BBC accent despite *not* being free to occur in all positions (e.g. r, w, j, h, ŋ, ʒ), so this argument, although supporting the one-phoneme analysis, does not actually *prove* that tʃ, dʒ must be classed with other single-consonant phonemes.

iii) If tʃ, dʒ were able to combine quite freely with other consonants to form consonant clusters, this would support the one-phoneme analysis. In initial position, however, tʃ, dʒ never occur in clusters with other consonants. In final position in the syllable, we find that tʃ can be followed by t (e.g. 'watched' wɒtʃt) and dʒ by d (e.g. 'wedged' wedʒd). Final tʃ, dʒ can be preceded by l (e.g. 'squelch' skweltʃ, 'bulge' bʌldʒ); ʒ is never preceded by l, and ʃ is preceded by l only in a few words and names (e.g. 'Welsh' welʃ, 'Walsh' wɒlʃ). A fairly similar situation is found if we ask if n can precede tʃ, dʒ; some BBC speakers have ntʃ in 'lunch', 'French', etc., and never pronounce the sequence nʃ within a syllable, while other speakers (like me) always have nʃ in these contexts and never ntʃ. In words like 'lunge', 'flange' there seems to be no possible phonological distinction between lʌndʒ, flændʒ and lʌnʒ, flænʒ. It seems, then, that no contrast between syllable-final lʃ and ltʃ exists in the BBC accent, and the same appears to be true in relation to nʃ and ntʃ and to nʒ and ndʒ. There are no other possibilities for final-consonant clusters containing tʃ, dʒ, except that the pre-final l or n may occur in combination with post-final t, d as in 'squelched' skweltʃt, 'hinged' hɪndʒd. It could not, then, be said that tʃ, dʒ combine freely with other consonants in forming consonant clusters; this is particularly noticeable in initial position.

How would the two-phoneme analysis affect the syllable-structure framework that was introduced in Chapter 8? Initial tʃ, dʒ would have to be interpreted as initial t, d plus post-initial ʃ, ʒ, with the result that the post-initial set of consonants would have to contain l, r, w, j and also ʃ, ʒ – consonants which are rather different from the other four and which could only combine with t, d. (The only alternative would be to put t, d with s in the pre-initial category, again with very limited possibilities of combining with another consonant.)

iv) Finally, it has been suggested that if native speakers of English who have not been taught phonetics feel that tʃ, dʒ are each "one sound", we should be guided by their intuitions and prefer the one-phoneme analysis. The problem with this is that discovering what untrained (or "naïve") speakers feel about their own language is not as easy as it might sound. It would be necessary to ask questions like this: "Would you say that the word 'chip' begins with one sound – like 'tip' and 'sip' – or with two sounds – like 'trip' and 'skip'?" But the results would be distorted by the fact that two consonant letters are used in the spelling; to do the test properly one should use illiterate subjects, which raises many further problems.

This rather long discussion of the phonemic status of tʃ, dʒ shows how difficult it can be to reach a conclusion in phonemic analysis.

For the rest of this chapter a number of other phonological problems will be discussed comparatively briefly. We have already seen (in Chapter 6) problems of analysis in connection with the sounds usually transcribed hw, hj. The velar nasal ŋ, described in Chapter 7, also raises a lot of analysis problems: many writers have suggested that the correct analysis is one in which there is no ŋ phoneme, and this sound is treated as an allophone of the phoneme n that occurs when it precedes the phoneme g. It was explained in Chapter 7 that in certain contexts no g is pronounced, but it can be claimed that at an abstract level there *is* a g phoneme, although in certain contexts the g is not actually pronounced. The sound ŋ is therefore, according to this theory, an allophone of n.

## 13.2 The English vowel system

The analysis of the English vowel system presented in Chapters 2 and 3 contains a large number of phonemes, and it is not surprising that some phonologists who believe in the importance of keeping the total number of phonemes small propose different analyses which contain fewer than ten vowel phonemes and treat all long vowels and diphthongs as composed of two phonemes each. There are different ways of doing this: one way is to treat long vowels and diphthongs as composed of two vowel phonemes. Starting with a set of basic or "simple" vowel phonemes (e.g. ɪ, e, æ, ʌ, ɒ, ʊ, ə) it is possible to make up long vowels by using short vowels twice. Our usual transcription for long vowels is given in brackets:

ɪɪ (iː) ææ (ɑː) ɒɒ (ɔː) ʊʊ (uː) əə (ɜː)

This can be made to look less unusual by choosing different symbols for the basic vowels. We will use i, e, a, ʌ, ɔ, u, ə: thus iː could be transcribed as ii, ɑː as aa, ɔː as ɔɔ, uː as uu and ɜː as əə. In this approach, diphthongs would be composed of a basic vowel phoneme followed by one of i, u, ə, while triphthongs would be made from a basic vowel plus one of i, u followed by ə, and would therefore be composed of three phonemes.

Another way of doing this kind of analysis is to treat long vowels and diphthongs as composed of a vowel plus a consonant; this may seem a less obvious way of proceeding, but it was for many years the choice of most American phonologists. The idea is that long vowels and diphthongs are composed of a basic vowel phoneme followed by one of j, w, h (we should add r for rhotic accents). Thus the diphthongs would be made up like this (our usual transcription is given in brackets):

| | | |
|---|---|---|
| ej (eɪ) | əw (əʊ) | ɪh (ɪə) |
| æj (aɪ) | æw (aʊ) | eh (eə) |
| ɒj (ɔɪ) | | ʊh (ʊə) |

Long vowels:

ɪj (iː) æh (ɑː) ɒh (ɔː) əh (ɜː) ʊw (uː)

Diphthongs and long vowels are now of exactly the same phonological composition. An important point about this analysis is that j, w, h do not otherwise occur finally in the syllable. In this analysis, the inequality of distribution is corrected.

In Chapter 9 we saw how, although ɪ, iː are clearly distinct in most contexts, there are other contexts where we find a sound which cannot clearly be said to belong to one or other of these two phonemes. The suggested solution to this problem was to use the symbol i, which does not represent any single phoneme; a similar proposal was made for u. We use the term **neutralisation** for cases where contrasts between phonemes which exist in other places in the language disappear in particular contexts. There are many other ways of analysing the very complex vowel system of English, some of which are extremely ingenious. Each has its own advantages and disadvantages.

## 13.3 Syllabic consonants

A final analysis problem that we will consider is that mentioned at the end of Chapter 8: how to deal with syllabic consonants. It has to be recognised that syllabic consonants are a problem: they *are* phonologically different from their non-syllabic counterparts. How do we account for the following minimal pairs, which were given in Chapter 9?

| *Syllabic* | *Non-syllabic* |
|---|---|
| 'coddling' kɒdl̩ɪŋ | 'codling' kɒdlɪŋ |
| 'Hungary' hʌŋgr̩i | 'hungry' hʌŋgri |

One possibility is to add new consonant phonemes to our list. We could invent the phonemes l̩, r̩, n̩, etc. The distribution of these consonants would be rather limited, but the main problem would be fitting them into our pattern of syllable structure. For a word like 'button' bʌtn̩ or 'bottle' bɒtl̩, it would be necessary to add n̩, l̩ to the first post-final set; the argument would be extended to include the r̩ in 'Hungary'. But if these consonants now form part of a syllable-final consonant cluster, how do we account for the fact that English speakers hear the consonants as extra syllables? The question might be answered by saying that the new phonemes are to be classed as vowels. Another possibility is to set up a phoneme that we might name **syllabicity**, symbolised with the mark ˌ. Then the word 'codling' would consist of the following six phonemes: k – ɒ – d – l – ɪ – ŋ, while the word 'coddling' would consist of the following *seven* phonemes: k – ɒ – d – l and simultaneously ˌ – ɪ – ŋ. This is superficially an attractive theory, but the proposed phoneme is nothing like the other phonemes we have identified up to this point – putting it simply, the syllabic mark doesn't have any sound.

Some phonologists maintain that a syllabic consonant is really a case of a vowel and a consonant that have become combined. Let us suppose that the vowel is ə. We could then say that, for example, 'Hungary' is phonemically hʌŋgəri while 'hungry' is hʌŋgri; it would then be necessary to say that the ə vowel phoneme in the phonemic representation is not pronounced as a vowel, but instead causes the following consonant to become syllabic. This is an example of the abstract view of phonology where the way a word is represented phonologically may be significantly different from the actual sequence of sounds heard, so that the phonetic and the phonemic levels are quite widely separated.

## 13.4 Clusters of s with plosives

Words like 'spill', 'still', 'skill' are usually represented with the phonemes p, t, k following the s. But, as many writers have pointed out, it would be quite reasonable to transcribe them with b, d, g instead. For example, b, d, g are unaspirated while p, t, k in syllable-initial position are usually aspirated. However, in sp, st, sk we find an unaspirated plosive, and there could be an argument for transcribing them as sb, sd, sg. We do not do this, perhaps because of the spelling, but it is important to remember that the contrasts between p and b, between t and d and between k and g are neutralised in this context.

## 13.5 Schwa (ə)

It has been suggested that there is not really a contrast between ə and ʌ, since ə only occurs in weak syllables and no minimal pairs can be found to show a clear contrast between ə and ʌ in unstressed syllables (although there have been some ingenious attempts). This has resulted in a proposal that the phoneme symbol ə should be used for representing any occurrence of ə or ʌ, so that ‘cup’ (which is usually stressed) would be transcribed 'kəp and ‘upper’ (with stress on the initial syllable) as 'əpə. This new ə phoneme would thus have two allophones, one being ə and the other ʌ; the stress mark would indicate the ʌ allophone and in weak syllables with no stress it would be more likely that the ə allophone would be pronounced.

Other phonologists have suggested that ə is an allophone of several other vowels; for example, compare the middle two syllables in the words ‘economy’ ɪ'kɒnəmi and ‘economic’ ˌiːkə'nɒmɪk – it appears that when the stress moves away from the syllable containing ɒ the vowel becomes ə. Similarly, compare ‘Germanic’ dʒɜː'mænɪk with ‘German’ 'dʒɜːmən – when the stress is taken away from the syllable mæn, the vowel weakens to ə. (This view has already been referred to in the Notes for Chapter 10, Section 3.) Many similar examples could be constructed with other vowels; some possibilities may be suggested by the list of words given in Section 9.2 to show the different spellings that can be pronounced with ə. The conclusion that could be drawn from this argument is that ə is not a phoneme of English, but is an allophone of several different vowel phonemes when those phonemes occur in an unstressed syllable. The argument is in some ways quite an attractive one, but since it leads to a rather complex and abstract phonemic analysis it is not adopted for this course.

## 13.6 **Distinctive features**

Many references have been made to phonology in this course, with the purpose of making use of the concepts and analytical techniques of that subject to help explain various facts about English pronunciation as efficiently as possible. One might call this “applied phonology”; however, the phonological analysis of different languages raises a great number of difficult and interesting theoretical problems, and for a long time the study of phonology “for its own sake” has been regarded as an important area of theoretical linguistics. Within this area of what could be called “pure phonology”, problems are examined with little or no reference to their relevance to the language learner. Many different theoretical approaches have been developed, and no area of phonology has been free from critical examination. The very fundamental notion of the phoneme, for example, has been treated in many different ways. One approach that has been given a lot of importance is **distinctive feature analysis**, which is based on the principle that phonemes should be regarded not as independent and indivisible units, but instead as combinations of different features. For example, if we consider the English d phoneme, it is easy to show that it differs from the plosives b, g in its place of articulation (alveolar), from t in being lenis, from s, z in not being fricative, from n in not being nasal, and so on. If we look at each of the consonants just mentioned and see which of the features each one has, we get a table like this, where + means that a phoneme does possess that feature and – means that it does not.

If you look carefully at this table, you will see that the combination of + and – values for each phoneme is different; if two sounds were represented by exactly the same +’s and

| | d | b | g | t | s | z | n |
|---|---|---|---|---|---|---|---|
| alveolar | + | – | – | + | + | + | + |
| bilabial | – | + | – | – | – | – | – |
| velar | – | – | + | – | – | – | – |
| lenis | + | + | + | – | – | + | (+)* |
| plosive | + | + | + | + | – | – | – |
| fricative | – | – | – | – | + | + | – |
| nasal | – | – | – | – | – | – | + |

* Since there is no fortis/lenis contrast among nasals this could be left blank.

–'s, then by definition they could not be different phonemes. In the case of the limited set of phonemes used for this example, not all the features are needed: if one wished, it would be possible to dispense with, for example, the feature *velar* and the feature *nasal*. The g phoneme would still be distinguished from b, d by being neither bilabial nor alveolar, and n would be distinct from plosives and fricatives simply by being neither plosive nor fricative. To produce a complete analysis of all the phonemes of English, other features would be needed for representing other types of consonant, and for vowels and diphthongs. In distinctive feature analysis the features themselves thus become important components of the phonology.

It has been claimed by some writers that distinctive feature analysis is relevant to the study of language learning, and that pronunciation difficulties experienced by learners are better seen as due to the need to learn a particular feature or combination of features than as the absence of particular phonemes. For example, English speakers learning French or German have to learn to produce front rounded vowels. In English it is not necessary to deal with vowels which are +front, +round, whereas this is necessary for French and German; it could be said that the major task for the English-speaking learner of French or German in this case is to learn the combination of these features, rather than to learn the individual vowels y, ø and (in French) œ*.

English, on the other hand, has to be able to distinguish dental from labiodental and alveolar places of articulation, for θ to be distinct from f, s and for ð to be distinct from v, z. This requires an additional feature that most languages do not make use of, and learning this could be seen as a specific task for the learner of English. Distinctive feature phonologists have also claimed that when children are learning their first language, they acquire features rather than individual phonemes.

## 13.7 **Conclusion**

This chapter is intended to show that there are many ways of analysing the English phonemic system, each with its own advantages and disadvantages. We need to consider

* The phonetic symbols represent the following sounds: y is a close front rounded vowel (e.g. the vowel in French *tu*, German *Bühne*); ø is a close-mid front rounded vowel (e.g. French *peu*, German *schön*); œ is an open-mid front rounded vowel (e.g. French *oeuf*).

the practical goal of teaching or learning about English pronunciation, and for this purpose a very abstract analysis would be unsuitable. This is one criterion for judging the value of an analysis; unless one believes in carrying out phonological analysis for purely aesthetic reasons, the only other important criterion is whether the analysis is likely to correspond to the representation of sounds in the human brain. Linguistic theory is preoccupied with economy, elegance and simplicity, but cognitive psychology and neuropsychology show us that the brain often uses many different pathways to the same goal.

## Notes on problems and further reading

The analysis of tʃ, dʒ is discussed in Cruttenden (2008: 181–8). The phonemic analysis of the velar nasal has already been discussed above (see Notes on problems and further reading in Chapter 7). The "double vowel" interpretation of English long vowels was put forward by MacCarthy (1952) and is used by Kreidler (2004: 45–59). The "vowel-plus-semivowel" interpretation of long vowels and diphthongs was almost universally accepted by American (and some British) writers from the 1940s to the 1960s, and still pervades contemporary American descriptions. It has the advantage of being economical on phonemes and very "neat and tidy". The analysis in this form is presented in Trager and Smith (1951). In generative phonology it is claimed that, at the abstract level, English vowels are simply tense or lax. If they are lax they are realised as short vowels, if tense as diphthongs (this category includes what I have been calling long vowels). The quality of the first element of the diphthongs/long vowels is modified by some phonological rules, while other rules supply the second element automatically. This is set out in Chomsky and Halle (1968: 178–87). There is a valuable discussion of the interpretation of the English vowel system with reference to several different accents in Giegerich (1992: Chapter 3), followed by an explanation of the distinctive feature analysis of the English vowel system (Chapter 4) and the consonant system (Chapter 5). A more wide-ranging discussion of distinctive features is given in Clark *et al.*, (2007: Chapter 10).

The idea that ə is an allophone of many English vowels is not a new one. In generative phonology, ə results from vowel reduction in vowels which have never received stress in the process of the application of stress rules. This is explained – in rather difficult terms – in Chomsky and Halle (1968: 110–26). A clearer treatment of the schwa problem is in Giegerich (1992: 68–9 and 285–7).

## Note for teachers

Since this is a theoretical chapter it is difficult to provide practical work. I do not feel that it is helpful for students to do exercises on using different ways of transcribing English phonemes – just learning one set of conventions is difficult enough. Some books on phonology give exercises on the phonemic analysis of other languages (e.g. Katamba, 1989; Roca and Johnson, 1999), but although these are useful, I do not feel that it would be appropriate in this book to divert attention from English. The exercises given below therefore concentrate on bits of phonetically transcribed English which involve problems when a phonemic representation is required.

## Written exercises

All the following exercises involve different ways of looking at the phonemic interpretation of English sounds. We use square brackets here to indicate when symbols are phonetic rather than phonemic.

1 In this exercise you must look at phonetically transcribed material from an English accent different from BBC pronunciation and decide on the best way to interpret and transcribe it phonemically.
   a) 'thing' [θɪŋg]
   b) 'think' [θɪŋk]
   c) 'thinking' [θɪŋkɪŋg]
   d) 'finger' [fɪŋgə]
   e) 'singer' [sɪŋgə]
   f) 'singing' [sɪŋgɪŋg]

2 It often happens in rapid English speech that a nasal consonant disappears when it comes between a vowel and another consonant. For example, this may happen to the n in 'front': when this happens the preceding vowel becomes nasalised – some of the air escapes through the nose. We symbolise a nasalised vowel in phonetic transcription by putting the ˜ diacritic above it; for example, the word 'front' may be pronounced [frʌ̃t]. Nasalised vowels are found in the words given in phonetic transcription below. Transcribe them phonemically.
   a) 'sound' [sãʊ̃d]
   b) 'anger' [æ̃gə]
   c) 'can't' [kɑ̃ːt]
   d) 'camper' [kæ̃pə]
   e) 'bond' [bɒ̃d]

3 When the phoneme t occurs between vowels it is sometimes pronounced as a "tap": the tongue blade strikes the alveolar ridge sharply, producing a very brief voiced plosive. The IPA phonetic symbol for this is ɾ, but many books which deal with American pronunciation prefer to use the phonetic symbol t̬; this sound is frequently pronounced in American English, and is also found in a number of accents in Britain: think of a typical American pronunciation of "getting better", which we can transcribe phonetically as [get̬ɪŋ bet̬ɚ]. Look at the transcriptions of the words given below and see if you can work out (for the accent in question) the environment in which t̬ is found.
   a) 'betting' [bet̬ɪŋ]
   b) 'bedding' [bedɪŋ]
   c) 'attend' [ətʰend]
   d) 'attitude' [æt̬ətʰuːd]

e) 'time' [tʰaɪm]
f) 'tight' [tʰaɪt]

4 Distinctive feature analysis looks at different properties of segments and classes of segments. In the following exercise you must mark the value of each feature in the table for each segment listed on the top row with either a + or –; you will probably find it useful to look at the IPA chart on p. xii.

| | p | d | s | m | z |
|---|---|---|---|---|---|
| Continuant | | | | | |
| Alveolar | | | | | |
| Voiced | | | | | |

5 In the following sets of segments (a–f), all segments in the set possess some characteristic feature which they have in common and which may distinguish them from other segments. Can you identify what this common feature might be for each set?

a) English iː, ɪ, uː, ʊ; cardinal vowels [i], [e], [u], [o]
b) t d n l s tʃ dʒ ʃ ʒ r
c) b f v k g h
d) p t k f θ s ʃ tʃ
e) uː ɔː əʊ aʊ
f) l r w j

# 14 Aspects of connected speech

Many years ago scientists tried to develop machines that produced speech from a vocabulary of pre-recorded words; the machines were designed to join these words together to form sentences. For very limited messages, such as those of a "talking clock", this technique was usable, but for other purposes the quality of the speech was so unnatural that it was practically unintelligible. In recent years, developments in computer technology have led to big improvements in this way of producing speech, but the inadequacy of the original "mechanical speech" approach has many lessons to teach us about pronunciation teaching and learning. In looking at connected speech it is useful to bear in mind the difference between the way humans speak and what would be found in "mechanical speech".

## 14.1 **Rhythm**

AU14 (CD 2), Ex 1

The notion of **rhythm** involves some noticeable event happening at regular intervals of time; one can detect the rhythm of a heartbeat, of a flashing light or of a piece of music. It has often been claimed that English speech is rhythmical, and that the rhythm is detectable in the regular occurrence of stressed syllables. Of course, it is not suggested that the timing is as regular as a clock: the regularity of occurrence is only relative. The theory that English has **stress-timed rhythm** implies that stressed syllables will tend to occur at relatively regular intervals whether they are separated by unstressed syllables or not; this would not be the case in "mechanical speech". An example is given below. In this sentence, the stressed syllables are given numbers: syllables 1 and 2 are not separated by any unstressed syllables, 2 and 3 are separated by one unstressed syllable, 3 and 4 by two, and 4 and 5 by three.

| | | | | | | | | | |
|---|---|---|---|---|---|---|---|---|---|
| 1 | 2 | | 3 | | | 4 | | | 5 |
| ˈWalk | ˈdown | the | ˈpath | to | the | ˈend | of | the | caˈnal |

The stress-timed rhythm theory states that the times from each stressed syllable to the next will tend to be the same, irrespective of the number of intervening unstressed syllables. The theory also claims that while some languages (e.g. Russian, Arabic) have stress-timed rhythm similar to that of English, others (e.g. French, Telugu, Yoruba) have a different rhythmical structure called **syllable-timed rhythm;** in these languages, all syllables, whether stressed or unstressed, tend to occur at regular time intervals and the time between stressed syllables will be shorter or longer in proportion to the number of unstressed syllables. Some writers have developed theories of English rhythm in which a unit of rhythm, the **foot**, is used (with a parallel in the metrical analysis of verse). The foot begins with a stressed syllable and includes all following unstressed syllables up to (but not including) the following stressed syllable. The example sentence given above would be divided into feet as follows:

| 1 | 2 | 3 | 4 | 5 |
|---|---|---|---|---|
| ˈWalk | ˈdown the | ˈpath to the | ˈend of the ca | ˈnal |

Some theories of rhythm go further than this, and point to the fact that some feet are stronger than others, producing strong–weak patterns in larger pieces of speech above the level of the foot. To understand how this could be done, let's start with a simple example: the word 'twenty' has one strong and one weak syllable, forming one foot. A diagram of its rhythmical structure can be made, where **s** stands for "strong" and **w** stands for "weak".

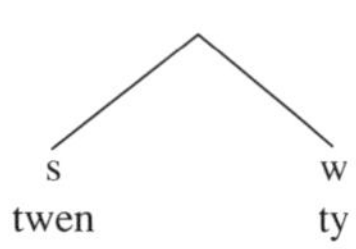


The word 'places' has the same form:

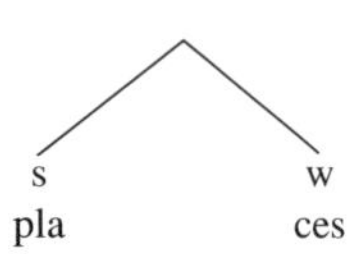


Now consider the phrase 'twenty places', where 'places' normally carries stronger stress than 'twenty' (i.e. is rhythmically stronger). We can make our "tree diagram" grow to look like this:

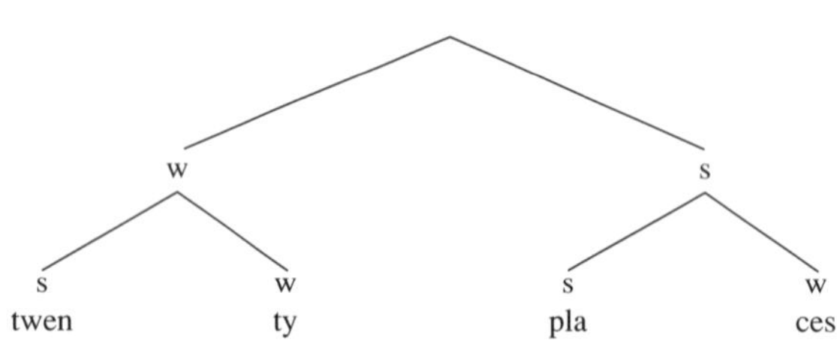


If we then look at this phrase in the context of a longer phrase 'twenty places further back', and build up the 'further back' part in a similar way, we would end up with an even more elaborate structure:

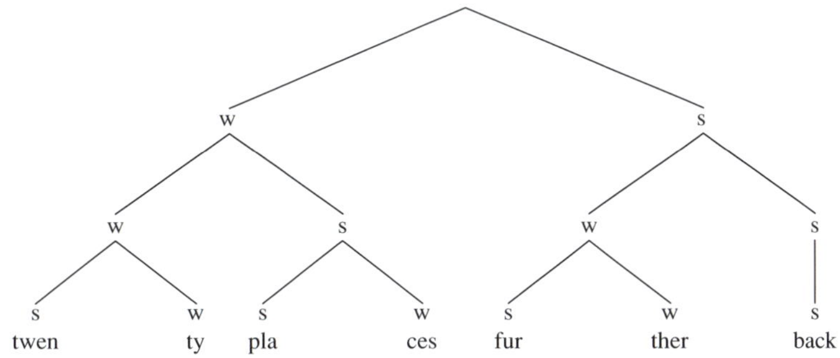


By analysing speech in this way we are able to show the relationships between strong and weak elements, and the different levels of stress that we find. The strength of any particular syllable can be measured by counting up the number of times an **s** symbol occurs above it. The levels in the sentence shown above can be diagrammed like this (leaving out syllables that have never received stress at any level):

| | | | | | | |
|---|---|---|---|---|---|---|
| | | | | | | s |
| | | s | | s | | s |
| s | | s | | s | | s |
| twen | ty | pla | ces | fur | ther | back |

The above "metrical grid" may be correct for very slow speech, but we must now look at what happens to the rhythm in normal speech: many English speakers would feel that, although in 'twenty places' the right-hand foot is the stronger, the word 'twenty' is stronger than 'places' in 'twenty places further back' when spoken in conversational style. It is widely claimed that English speech tends towards a regular alternation between stronger and weaker, and tends to adjust stress levels to bring this about. The effect is particularly noticeable in cases such as the following, which all show the effect of what is called **stress-shift**:

compact (adjective) kəm'pækt *but* compact disk 'kɒmpækt 'dɪsk
thirteen θɜː'tiːn *but* thirteenth place 'θɜːtiːnθ 'pleɪs
Westminster west'mɪnstə *but* Westminster Abbey 'westmɪnstər 'æbi

In brief, it seems that stresses are altered according to context: we need to be able to explain how and why this happens, but this is a difficult question and one for which we have only partial answers.

An additional factor is that in speaking English we vary in how rhythmically we speak: sometimes we speak very rhythmically (this is typical of some styles of public speaking) while at other times we may speak arhythmically (i.e. without rhythm) if we are hesitant or nervous. Stress-timed rhythm is thus perhaps characteristic of one style of speaking, not of English speech as a whole; one always speaks with *some* degree of rhythmicality, but the degree varies between a minimum value (arhythmical) and a maximum value (completely stress-timed rhythm).

It follows from what was stated earlier that in a stress-timed language all the feet are supposed to be of roughly the same duration. Many foreign learners of English are made to practise speaking English with a regular rhythm, often with the teacher beating time or clapping hands on the stressed syllables. It must be pointed out, however, that the evidence for the existence of truly stress-timed rhythm is not strong. There are many laboratory techniques for measuring time in speech, and measurement of the time intervals between stressed syllables in connected English speech has not shown the expected regularity; moreover, using the same measuring techniques on different languages, it has not been possible to show a clear difference between "stress-timed" and "syllable-timed" languages. Experiments have shown that we tend to hear speech as more rhythmical than it actually is, and one suspects that this is what the proponents of the stress-timed rhythm theory have been led to do in their auditory analysis of English rhythm. However, one ought to keep an open mind on the subject, remembering that the large-scale, objective study of suprasegmental aspects of real speech is difficult to carry out, and much research remains to be done.

What, then, is the practical value of the traditional "rhythm exercise" for foreign learners? The argument about rhythm should not make us forget the very important difference in English between strong and weak syllables. Some languages do not have such a noticeable difference (which may, perhaps, explain the subjective impression of "syllable-timing"), and for native speakers of such languages who are learning English it can be helpful to practise repeating strongly rhythmical utterances since this forces the speaker to concentrate on making unstressed syllables weak. Speakers of languages like Japanese, Hungarian and Spanish – which do not have weak syllables to anything like the same extent as English does – may well find such exercises of some value (as long as they are not overdone to the point where learners feel they have to speak English as though they were reciting verse).

## 14.2 **Assimilation**

The device mentioned earlier that produces "mechanical speech" would contain all the words of English, each having been recorded in isolation. A significant difference in natural connected speech is the way that sounds belonging to one word can cause changes in sounds belonging to neighbouring words. Assuming that we know how the phonemes of a particular word would be realised when the word is pronounced in isolation, in cases where we find a phoneme realised differently as a result of being near some other phoneme belonging to a neighbouring word we call this difference an instance of **assimilation**. Assimilation is something which varies in extent according to speaking rate and style: it is more likely to be found in rapid, casual speech and less likely in slow, careful speech. Sometimes the difference caused by assimilation is very noticeable, and sometimes it is very slight. Generally speaking, the cases that have most often been described are assimilations affecting consonants. As an example, consider a case where two words are combined, the first of which ends with a single final consonant (which we will call $C^f$) and the second of which starts with a single initial consonant (which we will call $C^i$); we can construct a diagram like this:

- - - - - - $C^f$ | $C^i$ - - - - - -

word boundary

If $C^f$ changes to become like $C^i$ in some way, then the assimilation is called **regressive** (the phoneme that comes first is affected by the one that comes after it); if $C^i$ changes to become like $C^f$ in some way, then the assimilation is called **progressive**. An example of the latter is what is sometimes called **coalescence**, or **coalescent assimilation**: a final t, d and an initial j following often combine to form tʃ, dʒ, so that 'not yet' is pronounced nɒtʃet and 'could you' is kʊdʒu. In what ways can a consonant change? We have seen that the main differences between consonants are of three types:

i) differences in place of articulation;
ii) differences in manner of articulation;
iii) differences in voicing.

In parallel with this, we can identify assimilation of place, of manner and of voicing in consonants. Assimilation of place is most clearly observable in some cases where a final consonant ($C^f$) with alveolar place of articulation is followed by an initial consonant ($C^i$) with a place of articulation that is *not* alveolar. For example, the final consonant in 'that' ðæt is alveolar t. In rapid, casual speech the t will become p before a bilabial consonant, as in: 'that person' ðæp pɜːsn̩; 'that man' ðæp mæn; 'meat pie' miːp paɪ. Before a dental consonant, t will change to a dental plosive, for which the phonetic symbol is t̪, as in: 'that thing' ðæt̪ θɪŋ; 'get those' get̪ ðəʊz; 'cut through' kʌt̪ θruː. Before a velar consonant, the t will become k, as in: 'that case' ðæk keɪs, 'bright colour' braɪk kʌlə, 'quite good' kwaɪk gʊd. In similar contexts d would become b, d̪ and g, respectively, and n would become m, n̪ and ŋ; examples of this would be: 'good boy' gʊb bɔɪ, 'bad thing' bæd̪ θɪŋ, 'card game' kɑːg geɪm, 'green paper' griːm peɪpə, 'fine thought' faɪn̪ θɔːt, 'ten girls' teŋ gɜːlz. However, the same is not true of the other alveolar consonants: s and z behave differently, the only noticeable change being that s becomes ʃ, and z becomes ʒ when followed by ʃ or j, as in: 'this shoe' ðɪʃ ʃuː; 'those years' ðəʊʒ jɪəz. It is important to note that the consonants that have undergone assimilation have not disappeared; in the above examples, the duration of the consonants remains more or less what one would expect for a two-consonant cluster. Assimilation of place is only noticeable in this regressive assimilation of alveolar consonants; it is not something that foreign learners need to learn to do.

Assimilation of manner is much less noticeable, and is only found in the most rapid and casual speech; generally speaking, the tendency is again for regressive assimilation and the change in manner is most likely to be towards an "easier" consonant – one which makes less obstruction to the airflow. It is thus possible to find cases where a final plosive becomes a fricative or nasal (e.g. 'that side' ðæs saɪd, 'good night' gʊn naɪt), but most unlikely that a final fricative or nasal would become a plosive. In one particular case we find progressive assimilation of manner, when a word-initial ð follows a plosive or nasal at the end of a preceding word: it is very common to find that the $C^i$ becomes identical in manner to the $C^f$ but with dental place of articulation. For example (the arrow symbol means "becomes"):

| | | | |
|---|---|---|---|
| 'in the' | ɪn ðə | → | ɪn̪n̪ə |
| 'get them' | get ðəm | → | get̪ t̪əm |
| 'read these' | riːd ðiːz | → | riːd̪ d̪iːz |

The ð phoneme frequently occurs with no discernible friction noise.

Assimilation of voice is also found, but again only in a limited way. Only regressive assimilation of voice is found across word boundaries, and then only of one type; since this matter is important for foreign learners we will look at it in some detail. If $C^f$ is a lenis (i.e. "voiced") consonant and $C^i$ is fortis ("voiceless") we often find that the lenis consonant has no voicing; for example in 'I have to' the final v becomes voiceless f because of the following voiceless t in aɪ hæf tu, and in the same way the z in 'cheese' tʃiːz becomes more like s when it occurs in 'cheesecake' tʃiːskeɪk. This is not a very noticeable case of assimilation, since, as was explained in Chapter 4, initial and final lenis consonants usually have little or no voicing anyway; these devoiced consonants do not shorten preceding vowels as true fortis consonants do. However, when $C^f$ is fortis ("voiceless") and $C^i$ lenis ("voiced"), a context in which in many languages $C^f$ would become voiced, assimilation of voice never takes place; consider the following example: 'I like that black dog' aɪ laɪk ðæt blæk dɒg. It is typical of many foreign learners of English that they allow regressive assimilation of voicing to change the final k of 'like' to g, the final t of 'that' to d and the final k of 'black' to g, giving aɪ laɪg ðæd blæg dɒg. This creates a strong impression of a foreign accent.

Up to this point we have been looking at some fairly clear cases of assimilation across word boundaries. However, similar effects are also observable across morpheme boundaries and to some extent also within the morpheme. Sometimes in the latter case it seems that the assimilation is rather different from the word-boundary examples; for example, if in a syllable-final consonant cluster a nasal consonant precedes a plosive or a fricative in the same morpheme, then the place of articulation of the nasal is always determined by the place of articulation of the other consonant; thus: 'bump' bʌmp, 'tenth' ten̪θ, 'hunt' hʌnt, 'bank' bæŋk. It could be said that this assimilation has become fixed as part of the phonological structure of English syllables, since exceptions are almost non-existent. A similar example of a type of assimilation that has become fixed is the progressive assimilation of voice with the suffixes s, z; when a verb carries a third person singular '-s' suffix, or a noun carries an '-s' plural suffix or an '-'s' possessive suffix, that suffix will be pronounced as s if the preceding consonant is fortis ("voiceless") and as z if the preceding consonant is lenis ("voiced"). Thus:

'cats' kæts 'dogs' dɒgz
'jumps' dʒʌmps 'runs' rʌnz
'Pat's' pæts 'Pam's' pæmz

Assimilation creates something of a problem for phoneme theory: when, for example, d in 'good' gʊd becomes g in the context 'good girl', giving gʊg gɜːl or b in the context 'good boy' gʊb bɔɪ, should we say that one phoneme has been substituted for another? If we do this, how do we describe the assimilation in 'good thing', where d becomes dental d̪ before the θ of 'thing', or in 'good food', where d becomes a labiodental plosive before the f in 'food'? English has no dental or labiodental plosive phonemes, so in these cases, although there is clearly assimilation, there could not be said to be a substitution of one phoneme for another. The alternative is to say that assimilation causes a phoneme to be realised by a different allophone; this would mean that, in the case of gʊg gɜːl and gʊb bɔɪ, the phoneme d of 'good' has velar and bilabial allophones. Traditionally, phonemes were supposed not to overlap in their allophones, so that the only plosives that could have allophones with bilabial place of articulation were p, b; this restriction is no longer looked on as so important. The traditional view of assimilation as a change from one phoneme to another is, therefore, naïve: modern instrumental studies in the broader field of **coarticulation** show that when assimilation happens one can often see some sort of combination of articulatory gestures. In 'good girl', for example, it is not a simple matter of the first word ending *either* in d *or* in g, but rather a matter of the extent to which alveolar and/or velar closures are achieved. There may be an alveolar closure immediately preceding and overlapping with a velar closure; there may be simultaneous alveolar and velar closure, or a velar closure followed by slight contact but not closure in the alveolar region. There are many other possibilities.

Much more could be said about assimilation but, from the point of view of learning or teaching English pronunciation, to do so would not be very useful. It is essentially a natural phenomenon that can be seen in any sort of complex physical activity, and the only important matter is to remember the restriction, specific to English, on voicing assimilation mentioned above.

## 14.3 **Elision**

AU14 (CD 2), Ex 2

The nature of **elision** may be stated quite simply: under certain circumstances sounds disappear. One might express this in more technical language by saying that in certain circumstances a phoneme may be realised as **zero**, or have **zero realisation** or be **deleted**. As with assimilation, elision is typical of rapid, casual speech. Producing elisions is something which foreign learners do not need to learn to do, but it is important for them to be aware that when native speakers of English talk to each other, quite a number of phonemes that the foreigner might expect to hear are not actually pronounced. We will look at some examples, although only a small number of the many possibilities can be given here.

i) Loss of weak vowel after p, t, k.
In words like 'potato', 'tomato', 'canary', 'perhaps', 'today', the vowel in the first syllable may disappear; the aspiration of the initial plosive takes up the whole of the middle portion of the syllable, resulting in these pronunciations (where $^{h}$ indicates aspiration in the phonetic transcription):

p$^{h}$ˈteɪtəʊ t$^{h}$ˈmɑːtəʊ k$^{h}$ˈneəri p$^{h}$ˈhæps t$^{h}$ˈdeɪ

ii) Weak vowel + n, l, r becomes syllabic consonant (see Chapter 9 for details of syllabic consonants). For example:

'tonight' tn̩aɪt 'police' pl̩iːs 'correct' kr̩ekt

iii) Avoidance of complex consonant clusters.
It has been claimed that no normal English speaker would ever pronounce all the consonants between the last two words of the following:

'George the Sixth's throne' dʒɔːdʒ ðə sɪksθs θrəʊn

Though this is not impossible to pronounce, something like sɪksθrəʊn or sɪksrəʊn is a more likely pronunciation for the last two words. In clusters of three plosives or two plosives plus a fricative, the middle plosive may disappear, so that the following pronunciations result:

'acts' æks, 'looked back' lʊk bæk, 'scripts' skrɪps

iv) Loss of final v in 'of' before consonants; for example:

'lots of them' lɒts ə ðəm, 'waste of money' weɪst ə mʌni

This last example is typical of very casual speech, and would be regarded as substandard by conservative listeners. A more common case is where the vowel of 'of' is lost, leaving either v in a voiced context (e.g. 'all of mine' ɔːl v maɪn) or f in a voiceless context (e.g. 'best of three' best f θriː).

It is difficult to know whether **contractions** of grammatical words should be regarded as examples of elision or not. The fact that they are regularly represented with special spelling forms makes them seem rather different from the above examples. The best-known cases are:

- 'had', 'would': spelt 'd, pronounced d (after vowels), əd (after consonants);
- 'is', 'has': spelt 's, pronounced s (after fortis consonants), z (after lenis consonants), except that after s, z, ʃ, ʒ, tʃ, dʒ 'is' is pronounced ɪz and 'has' is pronounced əz in contracted form;
- 'will': spelt 'll, pronounced l (after vowels), l̩ (after consonants);
- 'have': spelt 've, pronounced v (after vowels), əv (after consonants);
- 'not': spelt n't, pronounced nt (after vowels), n̩t (after consonants). There are also vowel changes associated with n't (e.g. 'can' kæn – 'can't' kɑːnt; 'do' duː – 'don't' dəʊnt; 'shall' ʃæl – 'shan't' ʃɑːnt);

- 'are': spelt 're, pronounced ə after vowels, usually with some change in the preceding vowel (e.g. 'you' juː – 'you're' jʊə or jɔː, 'we' wiː – 'we're' wɪə, 'they' ðeɪ – 'they're' ðeə); linking is used when a vowel follows, as explained in the next section. Contracted 'are' is also pronounced as ə or ər when following a consonant.

## 14.4 **Linking**

In our hypothetical "mechanical speech" all words would be separate units placed next to each other in sequence; in real connected speech, however, we link words together in a number of ways. The most familiar case is the use of **linking** r; the phoneme r does not occur in syllable-final position in the BBC accent, but when the spelling of a word suggests a final r, and a word beginning with a vowel follows, the usual pronunciation is to pronounce with r. For example:

| | | |
|---|---|---|
| 'here' hɪə | *but* | 'here are' hɪər ə |
| 'four' fɔː | *but* | 'four eggs' fɔːr egz |

BBC speakers often use r in a similar way to link words ending with a vowel, even when there is no "justification" from the spelling, as in:

'Formula A' fɔːmjələr eɪ
'Australia all out' ɒstreɪliər ɔːl aʊt
'media event' miːdiər ɪvent

This has been called **intrusive** r; some English speakers and teachers still regard this as incorrect or substandard pronunciation, but it is undoubtedly widespread.

"Linking r" and "intrusive r" are special cases of **juncture**; we need to consider the relationship between one sound and the sounds that immediately precede and follow it. If we take the two words 'my turn' maɪ tɜːn, we know that the sounds m and aɪ, t and ɜː, and ɜː and n are closely linked. The problem lies in deciding what the relationship is between aɪ and t; since we do not usually pause between words, there is no silence to indicate word division and to justify the space left in the transcription. But if English speakers hear maɪ tɜːn they can usually recognise this as 'my turn' and not 'might earn'. This is where the problem of juncture becomes apparent. What is it that makes perceptible the difference between maɪ tɜːn and maɪt ɜːn? The answer is that in one case the t is fully aspirated (initial in 'turn'), and in the other case it is not (being final in 'might'). In addition to this, the aɪ diphthong is shorter in 'might'. If a difference in meaning is caused by the difference between aspirated and unaspirated t, how can we avoid the conclusion that English has a phonemic contrast between aspirated and unaspirated t? The answer is that the position of a word boundary has some effect on the realisation of the t phoneme; this is one of the many cases in which the occurrence of different allophones can only be properly explained by making reference to units of grammar (something which was for a long time disapproved of by many phonologists).

Many ingenious minimal pairs have been invented to show the significance of juncture, a few of which are given below:

- 'might rain' maɪt reɪn (r voiced when initial in 'rain', aɪ shortened), vs.
  'my train' maɪ treɪn (r voiceless following t in 'train', aɪ longer)
- 'all that I'm after today' ɔːl ðət aɪm ɑːftə tədeɪ (t relatively unaspirated when final in 'that')
  'all the time after today' ɔːl ðə taɪm ɑːftə tədeɪ (t aspirated when initial in 'time')
- 'tray lending' treɪ lendɪŋ ("clear l" initial in 'lending')
  'trail ending' treɪl endɪŋ ("dark l" final in 'trail')
- 'keep sticking' kiːp stɪkɪŋ (t unaspirated after s)
  'keeps ticking' kiːps tɪkɪŋ (t aspirated in 'ticking')

The context in which the words occur almost always makes it clear where the boundary comes, and the juncture information is then redundant.

It should by now be clear that there is a great deal of difference between the way words are pronounced in isolation and their pronunciation in the context of connected speech.

## Notes on problems and further reading

**14.1** English rhythm is a controversial subject on which widely differing views have been expressed. On one side there have been writers such as Abercrombie (1967) and Halliday (1967) who set out an elaborate theory of the rhythmical structure of English speech (including foot theory). On the other side there are sceptics like Crystal (1969: 161–5) who reject the idea of an inherent rhythmical pattern. The distinction between physically measurable time intervals and subjective impressions of rhythmicality is discussed in Roach (1982) and Lehiste (1977). Adams (1979) presents a review and experimental study of the subject, and concludes that, despite the theoretical problems, there is practical value in teaching rhythm to learners of English. The "stress-timed / syllable-timed" dichotomy is generally agreed in modern work to be an oversimplification; a more widely accepted view is that all languages display characteristics of both types of rhythm, but each may be closer to one or the other; see Mitchell (1969) and Dauer (1983). Dauer's theory makes possible comparisons between different languages in terms of their relative positions on a scale from maximally stress-timed to maximally syllable-timed (see for example Dimitrova, 1997).

For some writers concerned with English language teaching, the notion of rhythm is a more practical matter of making a sufficiently clear difference between strong and weak syllables, rather than concentrating on a rigid timing pattern, as I suggest at the end of Section 14.1; see, for example, Taylor (1981).

The treatment of rhythmical hierarchy is based on the theory of metrical phonology. Hogg and McCully (1987) give a full explanation of this, but it is difficult material.

Goldsmith (1990: Chapter 4) and Katamba (1989: Chapter 11.1) are briefer and somewhat simpler. A paper by Fudge (1999) discusses the relationship between syllables, words and feet. James (1988) explores the relevance of metrical phonology to language learning.

**14.2** Factors such as assimilation and elision are dealt with in an interesting and original way in Shockey (2003). Assimilation is described in more conventional terms in Cruttenden (2008: 297–303). For reading on coarticulation, which studies the influences of sounds on each other in wider and more complex ways than assimilation, see Roach (2002), Ladefoged (2006: 68–71).

**14.3** An essential part of acquiring fluency in English is learning to produce connected speech without gaps between words, and this is the practical importance of linking. You can read about "linking r" and "intrusive r" in Collins and Mees (2008) and Giegerich (1992: 281–3).

An important question to be asked in relation to juncture is whether it can actually be heard. Jones (1931) implies that it can, but experimental work (e.g. O'Connor and Tooley, 1964) suggests that in many cases it is not perceptible unless a speaker is deliberately trying to avoid ambiguity. It is interesting to note that some phonologists of the 1950s and 1960s felt it necessary to invent a 'phoneme' of juncture in order to be able to transcribe minimal pairs like 'grey tape'/'great ape' unambiguously without having to refer to grammatical boundaries; see, for example, Trager and Smith (1951).

## Notes for teachers

There is a lot of disagreement about the importance of the various topics in this chapter from the language teacher's point of view. My feeling is that while the practice and study of connected speech are agreed by everyone to be very valuable, this can sometimes result in some relatively unimportant aspects of speech (e.g. assimilation, juncture) being given more emphasis than they should. It would not be practical or useful to teach all learners of English to produce assimilations; practice in making elisions is more useful, and it is clearly valuable to do exercises related to rhythm and linking. Perhaps the most important consequence of what has been described in this chapter is that learners of English must be made very clearly aware of the problems that they will meet in listening to colloquial, connected speech.

In looking at the importance of studying aspects of speech above the segmental level some writers have claimed that learners can come to identify an overall "feel" of the pronunciation of the language being learned. Differences between languages have been described in terms of their **articulatory settings** – that is, overall articulatory posture – by Honikman (1964). She describes such factors as lip mobility and tongue setting for English, French and other languages. The notion seems a useful one, although it is difficult to confirm these settings scientifically.

Audio Unit 14 is liable to come as something of a surprise to students who have not had the experience of examining colloquial English speech before. The main message to get across is that concentration on selective, analytic listening will help them to recognise what is being said, and that practice usually brings confidence.

## Written exercises

1 Divide the following sentences up into feet, using a dotted vertical line (⁞) as a boundary symbol. If a sentence starts with an unstressed syllable, leave it out of consideration – it doesn't belong in a foot.
  a) A bird in the hand is worth two in the bush.
  b) Over a quarter of a century has elapsed since his death.
  c) Computers consume a considerable amount of money and time.
  d) Most of them have arrived on the bus.
  e) Newspaper editors are invariably underworked.

2 Draw tree diagrams of the rhythmical structure of the following phrases.
  a) Christmas present
  b) Rolls-Royce
  c) pet-food dealer
  d) Rolls-Royce rally event

3 The following sentences are given in spelling and in a "slow, careful" phonemic transcription. Rewrite the phonemic transcription as a "broad phonetic" one so as to show likely assimilations, elisions and linking.

a) One cause of asthma is supposed to be allergies
wʌn kɔːz əv æsθmə ɪz səpəʊzd tə bi ælədʒiz

b) What the urban population could use is better trains
wɒt ði ɜːbən pɒpjəleɪʃn̩ kʊd juːz ɪz betə treɪnz

c) She acts particularly well in the first scene
ʃi ækts pətɪkjələli wel ɪn ðə fɜːst siːn

# 15 Intonation 1

Many of the previous chapters have been concerned with the description of phonemes, and in Section 5.2 it was pointed out that the subject of phonology includes not just this aspect (which is usually called **segmental phonology**) but also several others. In Chapters 10 and 11, for example, we studied stress. Clearly, stress has linguistic importance and is therefore an aspect of the phonology of English that must be described, but it is not usually regarded as something that is related to individual segmental phonemes; normally, stress is said to be something that is applied to (or is a property of) syllables, and is therefore part of the **suprasegmental phonology** of English. (Another name for suprasegmental phonology is **prosodic phonology** or **prosody**.) An important part of suprasegmental phonology is **intonation**, and the next five chapters are devoted to this subject.

What is intonation? No definition is completely satisfactory, but any attempt at a definition must recognise that the **pitch** of the voice plays the most important part. Only in very unusual situations do we speak with fixed, unvarying pitch, and when we speak normally the pitch of our voice is constantly changing. One of the most important tasks in analysing intonation is to listen to the speaker's pitch and recognise what it is doing; this is not an easy thing to do, and it seems to be a quite different skill from that acquired in studying segmental phonetics. We describe pitch in terms of **high** and **low**, and some people find it difficult to relate what they hear in someone's voice to a scale ranging from low to high. We should remember that "high" and "low" are arbitrary choices for end-points of the pitch scale. It would be perfectly reasonable to think of pitch as ranging instead from "light" to "heavy", for example, or from "left" to "right", and people who have difficulty in "hearing" intonation patterns are generally only having difficulty in relating what they hear (which is the same as what everyone else hears) to this "pseudo-spatial" representation.

It is very important to make the point that we are not interested in all aspects of a speaker's pitch; the only things that should interest us are those which carry some linguistic information. If a speaker tries to talk while riding fast on a horse, his or her pitch will make a lot of sudden rises and falls as a result of the irregular movement; this is something which is outside the speaker's control and therefore cannot be linguistically significant. Similarly, if we take two speakers at random we will almost certainly find that one speaker typically speaks with lower pitch than the other; the difference between the two speakers is not linguistically significant because their habitual pitch level is determined by their physical structure. But an individual speaker does have control over his or her own pitch, and may choose to speak with a higher than normal pitch; this is something which *is* potentially of linguistic significance.

A word of caution is needed in connection with the word **pitch**. Strictly speaking, this should be used to refer to an auditory sensation experienced by the hearer. The rate of vibration of the vocal folds – something which is physically measurable, and which is related to activity on the part of the speaker – is the **fundamental frequency** of voiced sounds, and should not be called "pitch". However, as long as this distinction is understood, it is generally agreed that the term "pitch" is a convenient one to use informally to refer both to the subjective sensation and to the objectively measurable fundamental frequency.

We have established that for pitch differences to be linguistically significant, it is a necessary condition that they should be under the speaker's control. There is another necessary condition and that is that a pitch difference must be **perceptible**; it is possible to detect differences in the **frequency** of the vibration of a speaker's voice by means of laboratory instruments, but these differences may not be great enough to be heard by a listener as differences in pitch. Finally, it should be remembered that in looking for linguistically significant aspects of speech we must always be looking for *contrasts*; one of the most important things about any unit of phonology or grammar is the set of items it contrasts with. We know how to establish which phonemes are in contrast with b in the context -ɪn; we can substitute other phonemes (e.g. p, s) to change the identity of the word from 'bin' to 'pin' to 'sin'. Can we establish such units and contrasts in intonation?

## 15.1 Form and function in intonation

To summarise what was said above, we want to know the answers to two questions about English speech:

i) What can we observe when we study pitch variations?
ii) What is the linguistic importance of the phenomena we observe?

These questions might be rephrased more briefly as:

i) What is the **form** of intonation?
ii) What is the **function** of intonation?

We will begin by looking at intonation in the shortest piece of speech we can find – the single syllable. At this point a new term will be introduced: we need a name for a continuous piece of speech beginning and ending with a clear pause, and we will call this an **utterance**. In this chapter, then, we are going to look at the intonation of one-syllable utterances. These are quite common, and give us a comparatively easy introduction to the subject.

Two common one-syllable utterances are 'yes' and 'no'. The first thing to notice is that we have a choice of saying these with the pitch remaining at a constant level, or with the pitch changing from one level to another. The word we use for the overall behaviour of the pitch in these examples is **tone**; a one-syllable word can be said with either a **level tone** or a **moving tone**. If you try saying 'yes' or 'no' with a level tone (rather as though you were trying to sing them on a steady note) you may find the result does not sound natural, and indeed English speakers do not use level tones on one-syllable utterances very frequently. Moving tones are more common. If English speakers want to say 'yes' or 'no' in a definite, final manner they will probably use a **falling** tone – one which descends from a higher to a lower pitch. If they want to say 'yes?' or 'no?' in a questioning manner they may say it with a **rising** tone – a movement from a lower pitch to a higher one.

Notice that already, in talking about different tones, some idea of function has been introduced; speakers are said to select from a choice of tones according to how they want the utterance to be heard, and it is implied that the listener will hear one-syllable utterances said with different tones as sounding different in some way. During the development of modern phonetics in the twentieth century it was for a long time hoped that scientific study of intonation would make it possible to state what the function of each different aspect of intonation was, and that foreign learners could then be taught rules to enable them to use intonation in the way that native speakers use it. Few people now believe this to be possible. It is certainly possible to produce a few general rules, and some will be given in this course, just as a few general rules for word stress were given in Chapters 10 and 11. However, these rules are certainly not adequate as a complete practical guide to how to use English intonation. My treatment of intonation is based on the belief that foreign learners of English at advanced levels who may use this course should be given training to make them better able to recognise and copy English intonation. The only really efficient way to learn to *use* the intonation of a language is the way a child acquires the intonation of its first language, and the training referred to above should help the adult learner of English to acquire English intonation in a similar (though much slower) way – through listening to and talking to English speakers. It is perhaps a discouraging thing to say, but learners of English who are not able to talk regularly with native speakers of English, or who are not able at least to listen regularly to colloquial English, are not likely to learn English intonation, although they may learn very good pronunciation of the segments and use stress correctly.

## 15.2. **Tone and tone languages**

🎧 AU15 (CD 2), Exs 1–4

In the preceding section we mentioned three simple possibilities for the intonation used in pronouncing the one-word utterances 'yes' and 'no'. These were: level, fall and rise. It will often be necessary to use symbols to represent tones, and for this we will use marks placed before the syllable in the following way (phonemic transcription will not be used in these examples – words are given in spelling):

Level ˍyes ˍno
Falling ╲yes ╲no
Rising ╱yes ╱no

This simple system for tone transcription could be extended, if we wished, to cover a greater number of possibilities. For example, if it were important to distinguish between a high level and low level tone for English we could do it in this way:

| | | |
|---|---|---|
| High level | ˉyes | ˉno |
| Low level | ˍyes | ˍno |

Although in English we do on occasions say ˉyes or ˉno and on other occasions ˍyes or ˍno, a speaker of English would be unlikely to say that the meaning of the words 'yes' and 'no' was different with the different tones; as will be seen below, we will not use the symbols for high and low versions of tones in the description of English intonation. But there are many languages in which the tone can determine the meaning of a word, and changing from one tone to another can completely change the meaning. For example, in Kono, a language of West Africa, we find the following (meanings given in brackets):

| | | |
|---|---|---|
| High level | ˉbɛŋ ('uncle') | ˉbuu ('horn') |
| Low level | ˍbɛŋ ('greedy') | ˍbuu ('to be cross') |

Similarly, while we can hear a difference between English ˍyes, ˏyes and ˎyes, and between ˍno, ˏno and ˎno, there is not a difference in meaning in such a clear-cut way as in Mandarin Chinese, where, for example, ˉma means 'mother', ˏma means 'hemp' and ˎma means 'scold'. Languages such as the above are called **tone languages**; although to most speakers of European languages they may seem strange and exotic, such languages are in fact spoken by a very large proportion of the world's population. In addition to the many dialects of Chinese, many other languages of South-East Asia (e.g. Thai, Vietnamese) are tone languages; so are very many African languages, particularly those of the South and West, and a considerable number of Native American languages. English, however, is not a tone language, and the function of tone is much more difficult to define than in a tone language.

## 15.3 Complex tones and pitch height

We have introduced three simple tones that can be used on one-syllable English utterances: level, fall and rise. However, other more complex tones are also used. One that is quite frequently found is the **fall–rise** tone, where the pitch descends and then rises again. Another complex tone, much less frequently used, is the **rise–fall** in which the pitch follows the opposite movement. We will not consider any more complex tones, since these are not often encountered and are of little importance.

One further complication should be mentioned here. Each speaker has his or her own normal **pitch range**: a top level which is the highest pitch normally used by the speaker, and a bottom level that the speaker's pitch normally does not go below. In ordinary speech, the intonation tends to take place within the lower part of the speaker's pitch range, but in situations where strong feelings are to be expressed it is usual to make use of extra pitch height. For example, if we represent the pitch range by drawing two parallel lines representing the highest and lowest limits of the range, then a normal unemphatic 'yes' could be diagrammed like this:

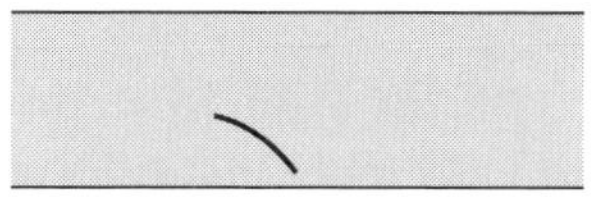

but a strong, emphatic 'yes' like this:

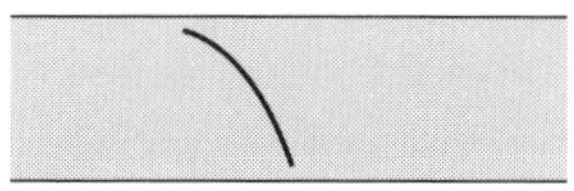

We will use a new symbol ↑(a vertical upward arrow) to indicate extra pitch height, so that we can distinguish between:

↘yes and ↑↘yes

Any of the tones presented in this chapter may be given extra pitch height, but since this course is based on normal, unemotional speech, the symbol will be used only occasionally.

## 15.4 **Some functions of English tones** 🎧 AU15 (CD 2), Ex 5

In this chapter only a very small part of English intonation has been introduced. We will now see if it is possible to state in what circumstances the different tones are used within the very limited context of the words 'yes' and 'no' said in isolation. We will look at some typical occurrences; no examples of extra pitch height will be considered here, so the examples should be thought of as being said relatively low in the speaker's pitch range.

### Fall ↘yes ↘no

This is the tone about which least needs to be said, and which is usually regarded as more or less "neutral". If someone is asked a question and replies ↘yes or ↘no it will be understood that the question is now answered and that there is nothing more to be said. The fall could be said to give an impression of "finality".

### Rise ↗yes ↗no

In a variety of ways, this tone conveys an impression that something more is to follow. A typical occurrence in a dialogue between two speakers whom we shall call A and B might be the following:

*A (wishing to attract B's attention)*: Excuse me.
*B:* ↗yes

(B's reply is, perhaps, equivalent to 'what do you want?') Another quite common occurrence would be:

*A*: Do you know John Smith?

One possible reply from B would be ↗yes, inviting A to continue with what she intends to say about John Smith after establishing that B knows him. To reply instead ↘yes would give a feeling of "finality", of "end of the conversation"; if A did have something to say about John Smith, the response with a fall would make it difficult for A to continue.

We can see similar "invitations to continue" in someone's response to a series of instructions or directions. For example:

*A*: You start off on the ring road ...
*B*: ↗yes
*A*: turn left at the first roundabout …
*B*: ↗yes
*A*: and ours is the third house on the left.

Whatever B replies to this last utterance of A, it would be most unlikely to be ↗yes again, since A has clearly finished her instructions and it would be pointless to "prompt" her to continue.

With 'no', a similar function can be seen. For example:

*A*: Have you seen Ann?

If B replies ↘no (without using high pitch at the start) he implies that he has no interest in continuing with that topic of conversation. But a reply of ↗no would be an invitation to A to explain why she is looking for Ann, or why she does not know where she is.

Similarly, someone may ask a question that implies readiness to present some new information. For example:

*A*: Do you know what the longest balloon flight was?

If B replies ↗no he is inviting A to tell him, while a response of ↘no would be more likely to mean that he does not know and is not expecting to be told. Such "do you know?" questions are, in fact, a common cause of misunderstanding in English conversation, when a question such as A's above might be a request for information or an offer to provide some.

#### Fall–rise ∨yes ∨no

The fall–rise is used a lot in English and has some rather special functions. In the present context we will only consider one fairly simple one, which could perhaps be described as "limited agreement" or "response with reservations". Examples may make this clearer:

*A*: I've heard that it's a good school.
*B*: ∨yes

B's reply would be taken to mean that he would not completely agree with what A said, and A would probably expect B to go on to explain why he was reluctant to agree. Similarly:

*A*: It's not really an expensive book, is it?
*B*: ∨no

The fall–rise in B's reply again indicates that he would not completely agree with A. Fall–rise in such contexts almost always indicates both something "given" or "conceded" and at the same time some reservation or hesitation. This use of intonation will be returned to in Chapter 19.

### Rise–fall ∧yes ∧no

This is used to convey rather strong feelings of approval, disapproval or surprise. It is not usually considered to be an important tone for foreign learners to acquire, although it is still useful practice to learn to distinguish it from other tones. Here are some examples:

*A*: You wouldn't do an awful thing like that, would you?
*B*: ∧no

*A*: Isn't the view lovely!
*B*: ∧yes

*A*: I think you said it was the best so far.
*B*: ∧yes

### Level _yes _no

This tone is certainly used in English, but in a rather restricted context: it almost always conveys (on single-syllable utterances) a feeling of saying something routine, uninteresting or boring. A teacher calling the names of students from a register will often do so using a level tone on each name, and the students are likely to respond with _yes when their name is called. Similarly, if one is being asked a series of routine questions for some purpose – such as applying for an insurance policy – one might reply to each question of a series (like 'Have you ever been in prison?', 'Do you suffer from any serious illness?', 'Is your eyesight defective?', etc.) with _no.

A few meanings have been suggested for the five tones that have been introduced, but each tone may have many more such meanings. Moreover, it would be quite wrong to conclude that in the above examples only the tones given would be appropriate; it is, in fact, almost impossible to find a context where one could not substitute a different tone. This is not the same thing as saying that any tone can be used in any context: the point is that no particular tone has a unique "privilege of occurrence" in a particular context. When we come to look at more complex intonation patterns, we will see that defining intonational "meanings" does not become any easier.

## 15.5 **Tones on other words**

We can now move on from examples of 'yes' and 'no' and see how some of these tones can be applied to other words, either single-syllable words or words of more than one syllable. In the case of polysyllabic words, it is always the most strongly stressed syllable that receives the tone; the tone mark is equivalent to a stress mark. We will underline syllables that carry a tone from this point onwards.

Examples:

**Fall** (usually suggests a "final" or "definite" feeling)

╲stop ╲eighty a╲gain

**Rise** (often suggesting a question)

╱sure ╱really to╱night

When a speaker is giving a list of items, they often use a rise on each item until the last, which has a fall, for example:

You can have it in ╱red, ╱blue, ╱green or ╲black

**Fall–rise** (often suggesting uncertainty or hesitation)

∨some ∨nearly per∨haps

Fall–rise is sometimes used instead of rise in giving lists.

**Rise–fall** (often sounds surprised or impressed)

∧oh ∧lovely i∧mmense

### Notes on problems and further reading

**15.1** The study of intonation went through many changes in the twentieth century, and different theoretical approaches emerged. In the United States the theory that evolved was based on 'pitch phonemes' (Pike, 1945; Trager and Smith, 1951): four contrastive pitch levels were established and intonation was described basically in terms of a series of movements from one of these levels to another. You can read a summary of this approach in Cruttenden (1997: 38–40). In Britain the 'tone-unit' or 'tonetic' approach was developed by (among others) O'Connor and Arnold (1973) and Halliday (1967). These two different theoretical approaches became gradually more elaborate and difficult to use. I have tried in this course to stay within the conventions of the British tradition, but to present an analysis that is simpler than most. A good introduction to the theoretical issues is Cruttenden (1997). Wells (2006) is also in the tradition of British analyses, but goes into much more detail than the present course, including a lot of recorded practice material.

**15.2** The amount of time to be spent on learning about tone languages should depend to some extent on your background. Those whose native language is a tone language should be aware of the considerable linguistic importance of tone in such languages; often it is extremely difficult for people who have spoken a tone language all their life to learn to observe their own use of tone objectively. The study of tone languages when learning English is less important for native speakers of non-tone languages, but most students seem to find it an interesting subject. A good introduction is Ladefoged (2006: 247–253). The classic work on the subject is Pike (1948) while more modern treatments are Hyman (1975: 212–29), Fromkin (1978) and Katamba (1989: Chapter 10).

Many analyses within the British approach to intonation include among tones both "high" and "low" varieties. For example, O'Connor and Arnold (1973) distinguished between "high fall" and "low fall" (the former starting from a high pitch, the latter from mid), and also between "low rise" and "high rise" (the latter rising to a higher point than the former). Some writers had high and low versions of all tones. Compared with our separate feature of *extra pitch height* (which is explained more fully in Section 18.1), this is unnecessary duplication. However, if one adds extra pitch height to a tone, one has not given all possible detail about it. If we take as an example a fall–rise without extra pitch height:

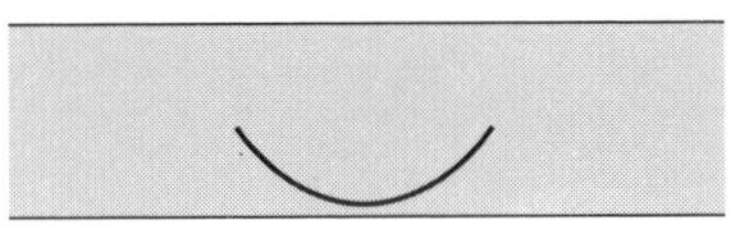

then something symbolised as ↑v could be any of the following:

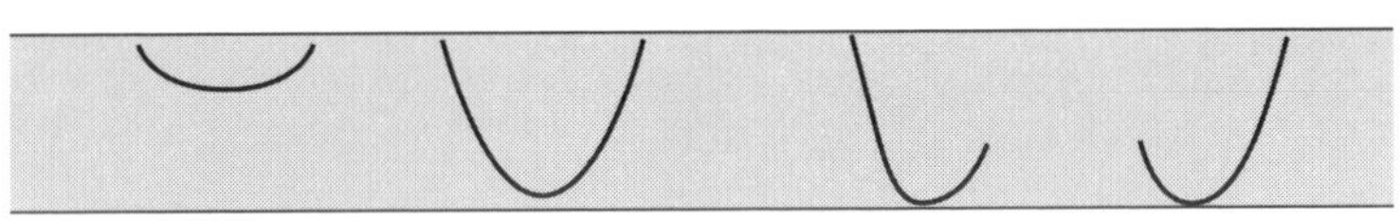

It would be possible to extend our framework to distinguish between these possibilities, but I do not believe it would be profitable to do so. Several writers have included in their set of tones **fall–rise–fall** and **rise–fall–rise**; I have seldom felt the need to recognise these as distinct from rise–fall and fall–rise respectively.

## Note for teachers

To devote five chapters to intonation may seem excessive, but I feel that this is necessary since the subject is difficult and complex, and needs to be explained at considerable length if the explanation is to be intelligible. On the positive side, working on intonation helps to improve learners' fluency and helps native speakers to understand how spoken communication works.

As explained above, some students may be perfectly well able to discriminate between tones, but have difficulty in labelling them as "fall", "rise", etc. I find that a small number of the students I teach are never able to overcome this difficulty (even though they may have perfect hearing and in some cases a high level of linguistic and musical ability). Of the remainder, a few are especially gifted and cannot understand how anyone could find the task difficult, and most others eventually learn after a few hours of practical classes. Many students find it very helpful to work with a computer showing a real-time display of their pitch movements as they speak.

## Written exercise

In the following sentences and bits of dialogue, each underlined syllable must be given an appropriate tone mark. Write a tone mark just in front of the syllable.

1 This train is for Leeds, York and Hull.
2 Can you give me a lift?
  Possibly. Where to?
3 No! Certainly not! Go away!
4 Did you know he'd been convicted of drunken driving?
  No!
5 If I give him money he goes and spends it.
  If I lend him the bike he loses it.
  He's completely unreliable.

# 16 Intonation 2

## 16.1 The tone-unit

In Chapter 15 it was explained that many of the world's languages are tone languages, in which substituting one distinctive tone for another on a particular word or morpheme can cause a change in the dictionary ("lexical") meaning of that word or morpheme, or in some aspect of its grammatical categorisation. Although tones or pitch differences are used for other purposes, English is one of the languages that do not use tone in this way. Languages such as English are sometimes called **intonation languages.** In tone languages the main suprasegmental contrastive unit is the tone, which is usually linked to the phonological unit that we call the syllable. It could be said that someone analysing the function and distribution of tones in a tone language would be mainly occupied in examining utterances syllable by syllable, looking at each syllable as an independently variable item. In Chapter 15, five tones found on English one-syllable utterances were introduced, and if English were spoken in isolated monosyllables, the job of tonal analysis would be a rather similar one to that described for tone languages. However, when we look at continuous speech in English utterances we find that these tones can only be identified on a small number of particularly prominent syllables. For the purposes of analysing intonation, a unit generally greater in size than the syllable is needed, and this unit is called the **tone-unit**; in its smallest form the tone-unit may consist of only one syllable, so it would in fact be wrong to say that it is always composed of more than one syllable. The tone-unit is difficult to define, and one or two examples may help to make it easier to understand the concept. As explained in Chapter 15, examples used to illustrate intonation transcription are usually given in spelling form, and you will notice that no punctuation is used; the reason for this is that intonation and stress are the vocal equivalents of written punctuation, so that when these are transcribed it would be unnecessary or even confusing to include punctuation as well.

AU16 (CD 2), Exs 1 & 2

Let us begin with a one-syllable utterance:

ˏyou

We underline syllables that carry a tone, as explained at the end of the previous chapter. Now consider this utterance:

is it ˏyou

The third syllable is more prominent than the other two and carries a rising tone. The other two syllables will normally be much less prominent, and be said on a level pitch. Why do we not say that each of the syllables 'is' and 'it' carries a level tone? This is a difficult question that will be examined more fully later; for the present I will answer it (rather unsatisfactorily) by saying that it is unusual for a syllable said on a level pitch to be so prominent that it would be described as carrying a level *tone*. To summarise the analysis of 'is it ⁄<u>you</u>' so far, it is an utterance of three syllables, consisting of one tone-unit; the only syllable that carries a tone is the third one. From now on, a syllable which carries a tone will be called a **tonic syllable**. It has been mentioned several times that tonic syllables have a high degree of prominence; prominence is, of course, a property of stressed syllables, and a tonic syllable not only carries a tone (which is something related to intonation) but also a type of stress that will be called **tonic stress**. (Some writers use the terms **nucleus** and **nuclear stress** for *tonic syllable* and *tonic stress*.)

The example can now be extended:

ˇ<u>John</u> is it ⁄<u>you</u>

A fall–rise tone is used quite commonly in calling someone's name. If there is a clear pause (silence) between 'ˇ<u>John</u>' and 'is it ⁄<u>you</u>', then, according to the definition of an utterance given in Chapter 15, there are two utterances; however, it is quite likely that a speaker would say 'ˇ<u>John</u> is it ⁄<u>you</u>' with no pause, so that the four syllables would make up a single utterance. In spite of the absence of any pause, the utterance would normally be regarded as divided into two tone-units: 'ˇ<u>John</u>' and 'is it ⁄<u>you</u>'. Since it is very difficult to lay down the conditions for deciding where the boundaries between tone-units exist, the discussion of this matter must wait until later.

It should be possible to see now that the tone-unit has a place in a range of phonological units that are in a hierarchical relationship: speech consists of a number of utterances (the largest units that we shall consider); each utterance consists of one or more tone-units; each tone-unit consists of one or more feet; each foot consists of one or more syllables; each syllable consists of one or more phonemes.

## 16.2 **The structure of the tone-unit**

In Chapter 8 the structure of the English syllable was examined in some detail. Like the syllable, the tone-unit has a fairly clearly defined internal structure, but the only component that has been mentioned so far is the tonic syllable. The first thing to be done is to make more precise the role of the tonic syllable in the tone-unit. Most tone-units are of a type that we call **simple**, and the sort that we call **compound** are not discussed in this chapter. Each simple tone-unit has one and only one tonic syllable; this means that the tonic syllable is an obligatory component of the tone-unit. (Compare the role of the vowel in the syllable.) We will now see what the other components may be.

### The head

Consider the following one-syllable utterance:

↘those

We can find the same tonic syllable in a long utterance (still of one tone-unit):

'give me ↘those

The rest of the tone-unit in this example is called the **head**. Notice that the first syllable has a stress mark: this is important. A head is all of that part of a tone-unit that extends from the first stressed syllable up to (but not including) the tonic syllable. It follows that if there is no stressed syllable before the tonic syllable, there cannot be a head. In the above example, the first two syllables (words) are the head of the tone-unit. In the following example, the head consists of the first five syllables:

'Bill 'called to 'give me ↘these

As was said a little earlier, if there is no stressed syllable preceding the tonic syllable, there is no head. This is the case in the following example:

in an ↘hour

Neither of the two syllables preceding the tonic syllable is stressed. The syllables 'in an' form a **pre-head**, which is the next component of the tone-unit to be introduced.

### The pre-head

The pre-head is composed of all the unstressed syllables in a tone-unit preceding the first stressed syllable. Thus pre-heads are found in two main environments:

i) when there is no head (i.e. no stressed syllable preceding the tonic syllable), as in this example:

in an ↘hour

ii) when there is a head, as in this example:

in a 'little 'less than an ↘hour

In this example, the pre-head consists of 'in a', the head consists of ''little 'less than an', and the tonic syllable is '↘hour'.

### The tail

It often happens that some syllables follow the tonic syllable. Any syllables between the tonic syllable and the end of the tone-unit are called the **tail**. In the following examples, each tone-unit consists of an initial tonic syllable and a tail:

↘look at it ↗what did you say ↘both of them were here

When it is necessary to mark stress in a tail, we will use a special symbol, a raised dot • for reasons that will be explained later. The above examples should, then, be transcribed as follows:

⟍look at it  ⟋what did you •say  ⟍both of them were •here

This completes the list of tone-unit components. If we use brackets to indicate optional components (i.e. components which may be present or may be absent), we can summarise tone-unit structure as follows:

(pre-head) (head) tonic syllable (tail)

or, more briefly, as:

(PH) (H) TS (T)

To illustrate this more fully, let us consider the following passage, which is transcribed from a recording of spontaneous speech (the speaker is describing a picture). When we analyse longer stretches of speech, it is necessary to mark the places where tone-unit boundaries occur – that is, where one tone-unit ends and another begins, or where a tone-unit ends and is followed by a pause, or where a tone-unit begins following a pause. It was mentioned above that tone-units are sometimes separated by silent pauses and sometimes not; pause-type boundaries can be marked by double vertical lines (||) and non-pause boundaries with a single vertical line (|). In practice it is not usually important to mark pauses at the beginning and end of a passage, though this is done here for completeness. The boundaries within a passage are much more important.

|| and then 'nearer to the vfront || on the ⟋left | theres a 'bit of ⟍forest | 'coming 'down to the ⟍waterside || and then a 'bit of a ⟋bay ||

We can mark their structure as follows (using dotted lines to show divisions between tone-unit components, though this is only done for this particular example):

| PH | H | TS | PH | TS | PH |
|---|---|---|---|---|---|
| and then | 'nearer to the | vfront | on the | ⟋left | theres a |

| H | TS | T | H | TS | T |
|---|---|---|---|---|---|
| 'bit of | ⟍for | est | 'coming 'down to the | ⟍wa | terside |

| PH | H | TS |
|---|---|---|
| and then a | 'bit of a | ⟋bay |

The above passage contains five tone-units. Notice that in the third tone-unit, since it is the syllable rather than the word that carries the tone, it is necessary to divide the word 'forest' into two parts, 'for-' fɒr and '-est' ɪst; in the fourth tone-unit the word 'waterside' is divided into 'wa-' wɔː (the tonic syllable) and '-terside' təsaɪd (tail). This example shows clearly how the units of phonological analysis can sometimes be seen to differ from those of grammatical analysis.

## 16.3 Pitch possibilities in the simple tone-unit

It has been said several times in this chapter that tone is carried by the tonic syllable, and it is now necessary to examine this statement more carefully. Before doing this, another general statement will be made (and will also need further explanation): intonation is carried by the tone-unit.

In a one-syllable utterance, the single syllable must have one of the five tones described in Chapter 15. In a tone-unit of more than one syllable, the tonic syllable must have one of those tones. If the tonic syllable is the final syllable, the tone will not sound much different from that of a corresponding one-syllable tone-unit. For example, the word 'here' will be said in much the same way in the following two utterances:

↗here    ˈshall we ˈsit ↗here

However, if there are other syllables following the tonic syllable (i.e. there is a tail), we find that the pitch movement of the tone is not completed on the tonic syllable. If a tail follows a tonic syllable that has a rising tone, it will almost always be found that the syllable or syllables of the tail will continue to move upwards from the pitch of the tonic syllable. For example, if the word 'what' is said on a rising tone, '↗what', it might have a pitch movement that could be diagrammed like this:

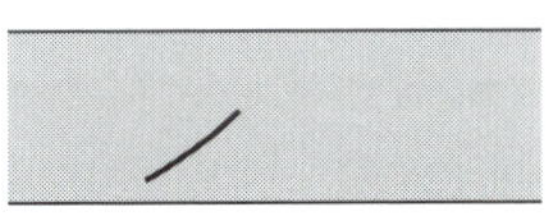

The four syllables in '↗what did you say' might be said like this:

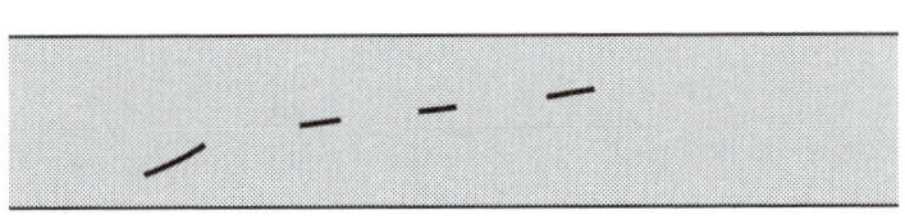

with the pitch of the syllables in the tail getting progressively higher. In such cases, the tonic syllable is the syllable on which the pitch movement of the tone begins, but that pitch movement is completed over the rest of the tone-unit (i.e. the tail). If, in rising progressively higher, the pitch reaches the highest part of the speaker's normal pitch range, subsequent syllables will continue at that top level.

We find a similar situation with the falling tone. On a single syllable '↘why', the pitch movement might be of this sort:

but if there are syllables following, the fall may not be completed on the tonic syllable:

↘why did you ·go

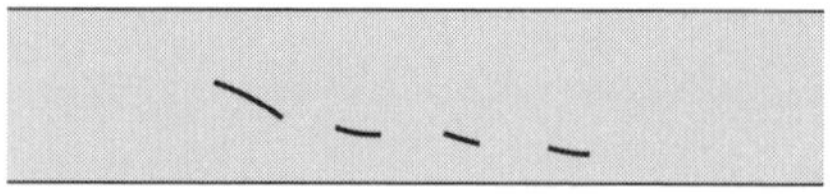

Again, if the speaker's lowest pitch is reached before the end of the tail, the pitch continues at the bottom level. In the case of a level tone, syllables following in the tail will continue at the same level; since level tone is to be treated as a rather unusual type of tone, we will not examine it in more detail at this stage. The situation is more complicated when we have a tail following a fall–rise or a rise–fall, and this is described in Chapter 17.

## Notes on problems and further reading

It would not be useful (unless you are doing research on the subject) to go into all the different ways in which English intonation has been represented, but it is worth noting that simpler approaches have been used in the past. In the earlier part of the last century, a common approach was to treat all the pitch movement in the tone-unit as a single "tune"; Tune 1 was typically descending and ending in a fall, while Tune 2 ended up rising (I was taught French intonation in this way in the 1960s). In more modern work, we can see that it is possible to represent intonation as a simple sequence of tonic and non-tonic stressed syllables, and pauses, with no higher-level organisation; an example of this is the transcription used in the Spoken English Corpus (Williams, 1996). Brown (1990, Chapter 5) uses a relatively simple analysis of intonation to present valuable examples of authentic recorded speech. Most contemporary British analyses, however, use a unit similar or identical to what I call a tone-unit divided into components such as pre-head, head, tonic syllable and tail. Different writers use different names: "tone-group", "intonation-group", "sense-group", "intonation unit" and "intonation phrase (IP)" are all more or less synonymous with "tone-unit". Good background reading on this is Cruttenden (1997: 26–55).

## Note for teachers

The move from tones to tone-units is a difficult one, and I feel it is advisable at this stage to use only slow, careful speech for exercises (Audio Units 15 and 16). More difficult exercises with more natural speech follow later (Audio Units 18 and 19).

## Written exercises

1 Here is a list of single tonic syllables. Add a number of extra syllables (as specified by the number in brackets) to make a tail. Example: go (2); Example answer: go for it

a) buy (3)
b) hear (1)
c) talk (2)

(The answers section gives some possible versions.)

2 Now expand the following tonic syllables by putting heads in front of them, containing the number of stressed syllables indicated in brackets. Example: (2) dark; Example answer: 'John was a'fraid of the dark

a) (1) step

b) (3) train

c) (2) hot

3 The following sentences are given with intonation transcribed. Draw underneath them a diagram of the pitch movements, leaving a gap between each syllable. Example:

'Would you 'like some 'more /milk

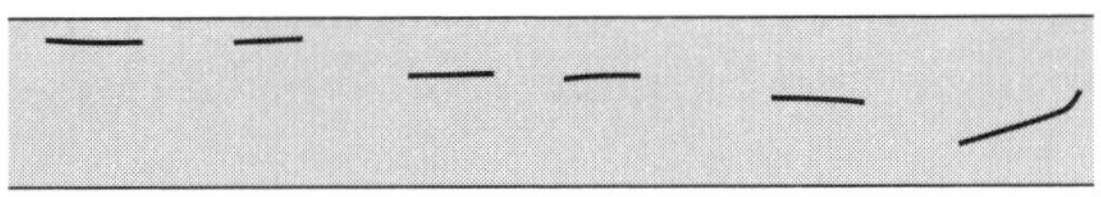

a) 'Only when the ∨wind ·blows

b) /When did you ·say

c) 'What was the \name of the ·place

# 17 Intonation 3

In Chapter 16 the structure of the tone-unit was introduced and it was explained that when a tonic syllable is followed by a tail, that tail continues and completes the tone begun on the tonic syllable. Examples were given to show how this happens in the case of rising and falling tones. We now go on to consider the rather more difficult cases of fall–rise and rise–fall tones.

## 17.1 Fall–rise and rise–fall tones followed by a tail

AU17 (CD 2), Exs 1 & 2

A rising or a falling tone is relatively easy to identify, whether it falls on a single syllable or extends over more syllables in the case of a tonic syllable followed by a tail. Fall–rise and rise–fall tones, however, can be quite difficult to recognise when they are extended over tails, since their characteristic pitch movements are often broken up or distorted by the structure of the syllables they occur on. For example, the pitch movement on 'vsome' will be something like this:

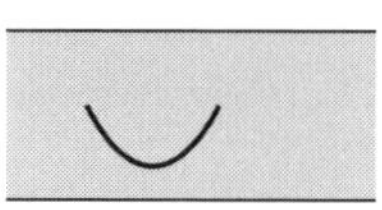

If we add a syllable, the "fall" part of the fall–rise is usually carried by the first tonic syllable and the "rise" part by the second. The result may be a continuous pitch movement very similar to the one-syllable case, if there are no voiceless medial consonants to cause a break in the voicing. This would give a pitch movement that we could draw like this:

vsome ·men

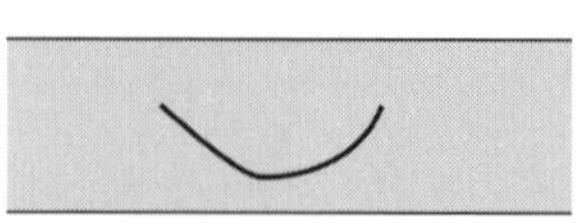

If the continuity of the voicing is broken, however, the pitch pattern might be more like this:

vsome ·chairs

In this case it would be possible to say that there is a falling tone on 'some' and a rise on 'chairs'. However, most English speakers seem to feel that the pitch movement in this case is the same as that in the previous two examples. It can be said that there is a parallel with rhyming: just as 'balloon' rhymes with 'moon', so we might say that 'vsome chairs' has what could be called a **tonal rhyme** with 'vsome'. For the rest of the chapter we will continue to break the pitch movement diagrams with gaps between syllables to make them easier to read, including cases where the voicing is continuous.

If there is a tail of two or more syllables, the normal pitch movement is for the pitch to fall on the tonic syllable and to remain low until the last stressed syllable in the tail. The pitch then rises from that point up to the end of the tone-unit. If there is no stressed syllable in the tail, the rise happens on the final syllable. Here are some examples:

i) I vmight ·buy it

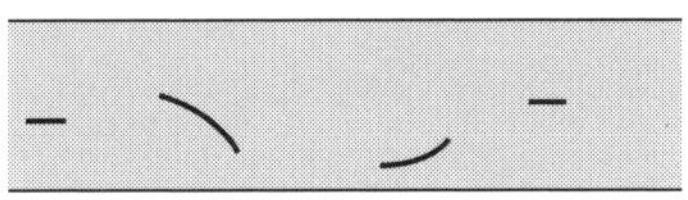

I vmight have ·thought of ·buying it

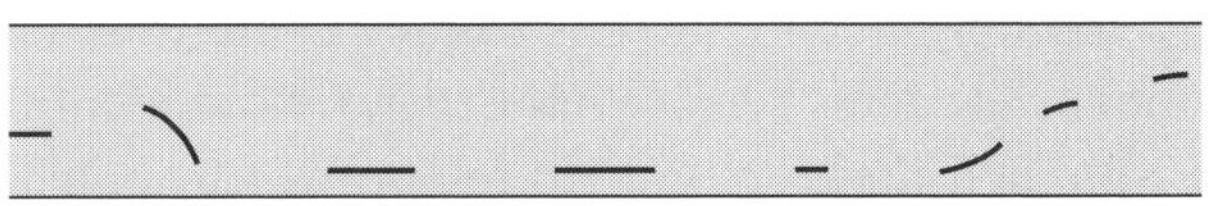

ii) vmost of them

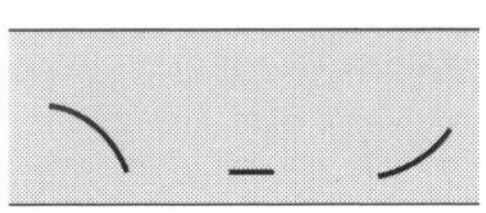

vmost of it was for them

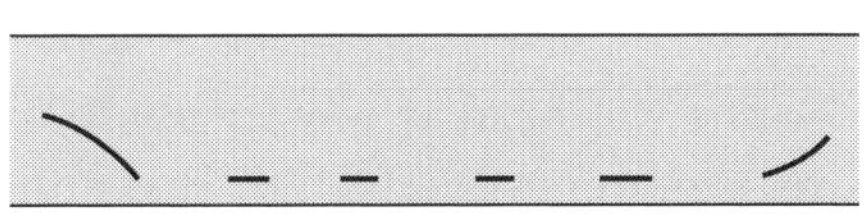

With the rise–fall tone we find a similar situation: if the tonic syllable is followed by a single syllable in the tail, the "rise" part of the tone takes place on the first (tonic) syllable and the "fall" part is on the second. Thus:

∧no ∧no one ∧no sir

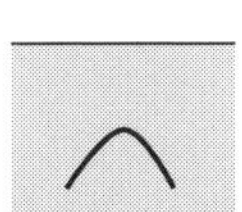

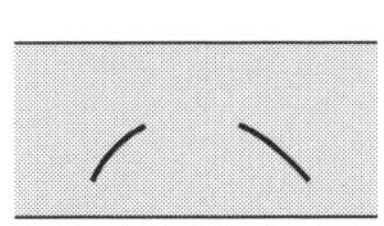

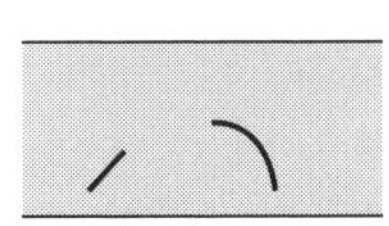

When there are two or more syllables in the tail, the syllable immediately following the tonic syllable is always higher and any following syllables are low. For example:

∧beau ti ful

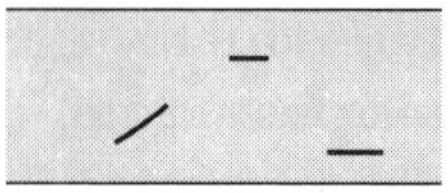

∧all of them ·went

∧thats a ·nice ·way to ·speak to your ·mother

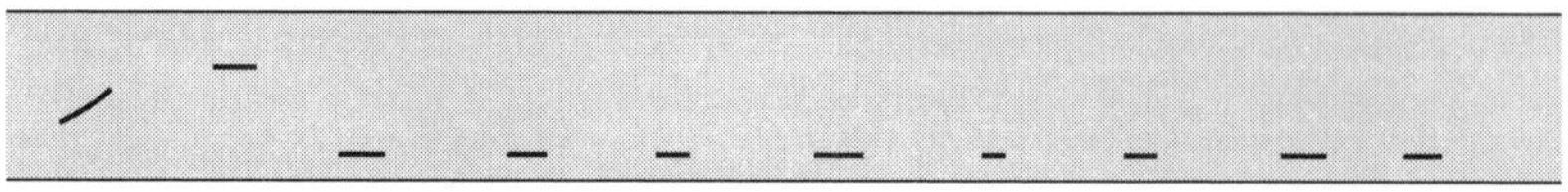

It should be clear by now that the speaker does not have a choice in the matter of the pitch of the syllables in the tail. This is completely determined by the choice of tone for the tonic syllable.

## 17.2 High and low heads

AU17 (CD 2), Ex 3

The head was defined in Chapter 16 as "all that part of a tone-unit that extends from the first stressed syllable up to, but not including, the tonic syllable". In our description of intonation up to this point, the only pitch contrasts found in the tone-unit are the different possible choices of tone for the tonic syllable. However, we can identify different pitch possibilities in the head, although these are limited to two which we will call **high head** and **low head**. In the case of the high head, the stressed syllable which begins the head is high in pitch; usually it is higher than the beginning pitch of the tone on the tonic syllable. For example:

the 'bus was ╲late

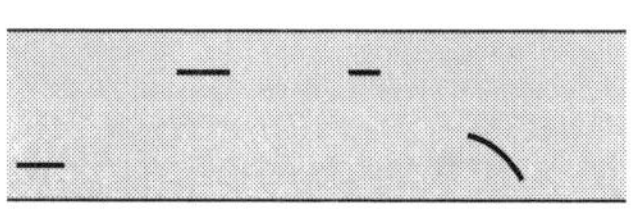

is 'that the ╱end

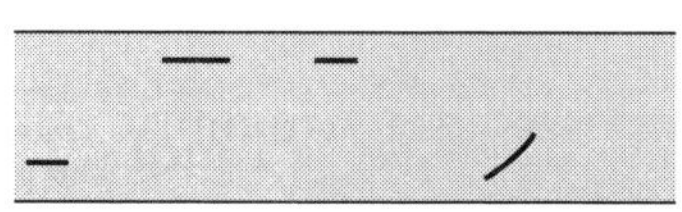

In the low head the stressed syllable which begins the head is low in pitch; usually it is lower than the beginning pitch of the tone on the tonic syllable. To mark this stressed syllable in the low head we will use a different symbol, ˌ as in 'ˌlow'. As an example, the heads of the above sentences will be changed from high to low:

the ˌbus was ╲late

is ˌthat the ╱end

The two different versions (high and low head) will usually sound slightly different to native-speaker listeners, although it is not easy to say just what the difference *is*, as will be made clear in Chapter 18.

It is usual for unstressed syllables to continue the pitch of the stressed syllable that precedes them. In the following example, the three unstressed syllables 'if it had' continue at the same pitch as the stressed syllable 'asked'.

i) with high head

we ˈasked if it had \come

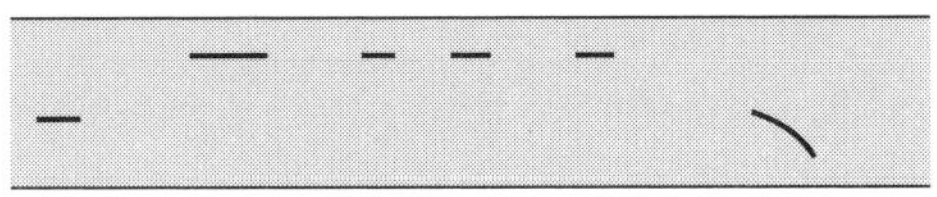

ii) with low head

we ˌasked if it had \come

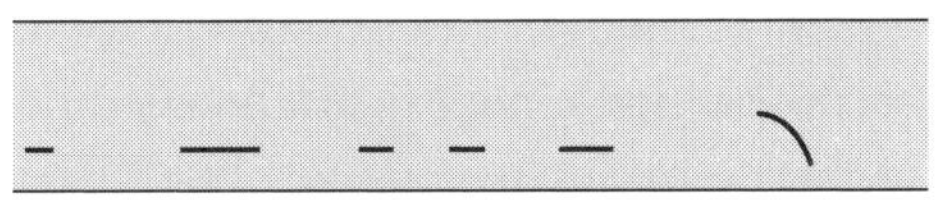

When there is more than one stressed syllable in the head there is usually a slight change in pitch from the level of one stressed syllable to that of the next, the change being in the direction of the beginning pitch of the tone on the tonic syllable. We will use some long examples to illustrate this, although heads of this length are not very frequently found in natural speech. In the first example the stressed syllables in the high head step downwards progressively to approach the beginning of the tone:

the ˈrain was ˈcoming ˈdown ˈfairly \hard

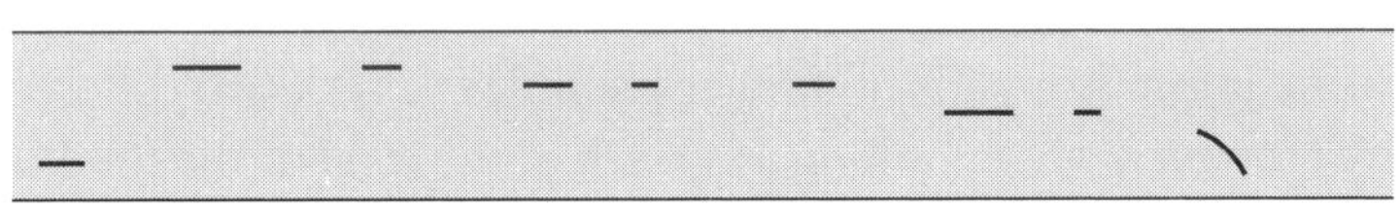

In the next example the head is low; since the tone also starts low, being a rise, there is no upward movement in the head:

ˌthats ˌnot the ˌstory you ˌtold in /court

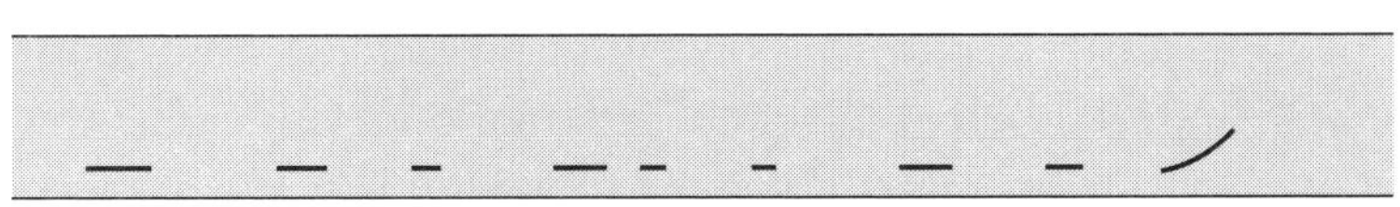

When there is a low head followed by a falling tone, successive stressed syllables in the head tend to move upwards towards the beginning pitch of the tone:

ˌI could have ˌbought it for ˌless than a \pound

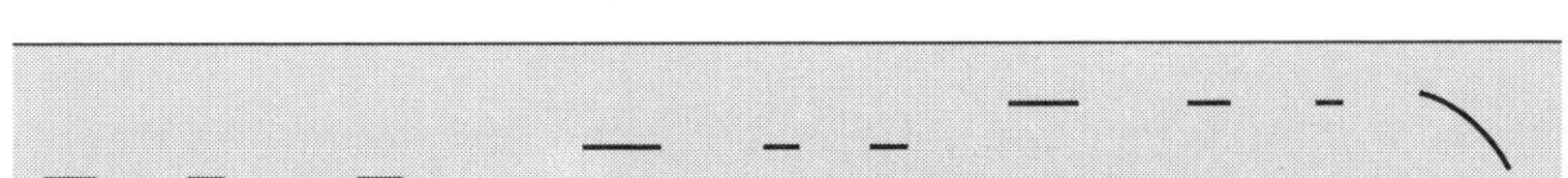

When a high head is followed by a rise the stressed syllables tend to move downwards, as one would expect, towards the beginning pitch of the tone:

'will there be a'nother 'train ⁄later

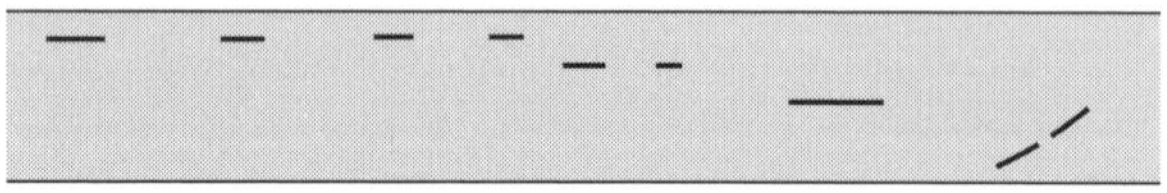

When we examine the intonation of polysyllabic heads we find much greater variety than these simple examples suggest. However, the division into high and low heads as general types is probably the most basic that can be made, and it would be pointless to set up a more elaborate system to represent differences if these differences were not recognised by most native speakers. Some writers on intonation claim that the intonation pattern starting at a fairly high pitch, with a gradual dropping down of pitch during the utterance, is the most basic, normal, "unmarked" intonation pattern; this movement is often called **declination.** The claim that declination is universally unmarked in English, or even in all languages, is a strong one. As far as English is concerned, it would be good to see more evidence from the full range of regional and national varieties in support of the claim.

It should be noted that the two marks ˈ and ˌ are being used for two different purposes in this course, as they are in many phonetics books. When stress is being discussed, the ˈ mark (blue type) indicates primary stress and ˌ indicates secondary stress. For the purposes of marking intonation, however, the mark ' (black type) indicates a stressed syllable in a high head and the mark ˌ indicates a stressed syllable in a low head. In practice this is not usually found confusing as long as one is aware of whether one is marking stress levels or intonation, and the colour difference helps to distinguish them. When the high and low marks ' and ˌ are being used to indicate intonation, it is no longer possible to mark two different levels of stress within the word. However, when looking at speech at the level of the tone-unit we are not usually interested in this; a much more important difference here is the one between tonic stress (marked by underlining the tonic syllable and placing before it one of the five tone-marks) and non-tonic stressed syllables (marked ' or ˌ in the head or · in the tail).

It needs to be emphasised that in marking intonation, only stressed syllables are marked; this implies that intonation is carried entirely by the stressed syllables of a tone-unit and that the pitch of unstressed syllables is either predictable from that of stressed syllables or is of so little importance that it is not worth marking. Remember that the additional information given in the examples above by drawing pitch levels and movements between lines is only included here to make the examples clearer and is not normally given with our system of transcription; all the important information about intonation must, therefore, be given by the marks placed in the text.

## 17.3 Problems in analysing the form of intonation

The analysis of intonational form presented in this chapter and in Chapters 15 and 16 is similar in most respects to the approaches used in many British studies of English intonation. There are certain difficulties that all of these studies have had to confront, and it is useful to give a brief summary of what the major difficulties are.

### Identifying the tonic syllable

It is often said that the tonic syllable can be identified because it is the only syllable in the tone-unit that carries a movement in pitch; this is in fact not always true. We have seen how when the tonic syllable is followed by a tail the tone is carried by the tonic plus tail together in such a way that in some cases practically no pitch movement is detectable on the tonic syllable itself. In addition, it has been claimed that one of the tones is the *level* tone, which by definition may not have any pitch movement. It is therefore necessary to say in this particular case that the tonic syllable is identified simply as the most prominent syllable.

In addition, it sometimes seems as if some tone-units (though only a small number, known as compound tone-units) contain not one but two tonic syllables, almost always with the first syllable having a fall on it and the other a rise. An example is:

Ive ↘seen ↗him

i) 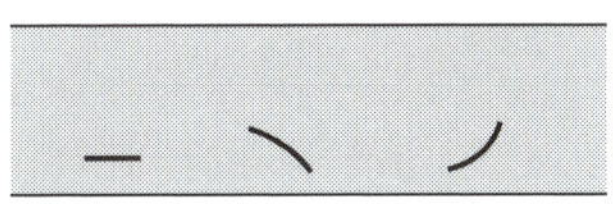

In this example there seems to be equal prominence on 'seen' and 'him'. It could be claimed that this is the same thing as:

Ive ˅seen him

ii) 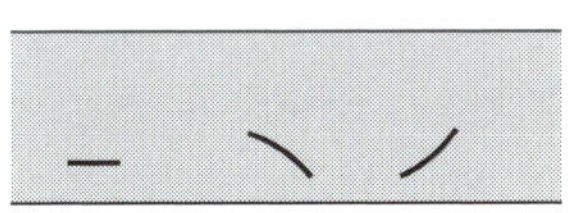

It has, however, been pointed out that the two versions are different in several ways. Since 'him' has greater prominence in (i), it cannot occur in its weak form ɪm, but must be pronounced hɪm, whereas in (ii) the pronunciation is likely to be aɪv ˅siːn ɪm. The two versions are said to convey different meanings, too. Version (i) might be said in conversation on hearing someone's name, as in this example:

*A:* ˈJohn ˈCleese is a ˈvery ˈfunny ↘actor
*B:* ˈOh ↘yes | Ive ↘seen ↗him

In version (ii), on the other hand, the word 'seen' is given the greatest prominence, and it is likely to sound as though the speaker has some reservation, or has something further to say:

*A*: ˈHave you ˈseen my ↗father ·yet
*B*: Ive ˅seen him | but I ˈhavent had ˈtime to ↘talk to him

The same is found with 'her', as in:

Ive ↘seen ↗her
aɪv ↘siːn ↗hɜː

compared with:

Ive ∨seen her
aɪv ∨siːn ə

This is a difficult problem, since it weakens the general claim made earlier that each tone-unit contains only one tonic syllable.

### Identifying tone-unit boundaries

It is a generally accepted principle in the study of grammar that utterances may contain one or more sentences, and that one can identify on grammatical grounds the places where one sentence ends and another begins. In a similar way, in suprasegmental phonology it is claimed that utterances may be divided up into tone-units, and that one can identify on phonetic or phonological grounds the places where one tone-unit ends and another tone-unit begins. However, giving rules for identifying where the boundaries are placed is not easy, except in cases where a clear pause separates tone-units. Two principles are usually mentioned: one is that it is possible in most cases to detect some sudden change from the pitch level at the end of one tone-unit to the pitch level that starts the following tone-unit, and recognition of the start of the following tone-unit is made easier by the fact that speakers tend to "return home" to a particular pitch level at the beginning of a tone-unit. The second principle used in tone-unit boundary identification is a rhythmical one: it is claimed that within the tone-unit, speech has a regular rhythm, but that rhythm is broken or interrupted at the tone-unit boundary. Both the above principles are useful guides, but one regularly finds, in analysing natural speech, cases where it remains difficult or impossible to make a clear decision; the principles may well be factually correct, but it should be emphasised that at present there is no conclusive evidence from instrumental study in the laboratory that they are.

### Anomalous tone-units

However comprehensive one's descriptive framework may be (and the one given in this course is very limited), there will inevitably be cases which do not fit within it. For example, other tones such as fall–rise–fall or rise–fall–rise are occasionally found. In the head, we sometimes find cases where the stressed syllables are not all high or all low, as in the following example:

ˌAfter ˌone of the ˈworst ˈdays of my ∨life

It can also happen that a speaker is interrupted and leaves a tone-unit incomplete – for example, lacking a tonic syllable. To return to the analogy with grammar, in natural speech one often finds sentences which are grammatically anomalous or incomplete, but this does not deter the grammarian from describing "normal" sentence structure. Similarly, although there are inevitably problems and exceptions, we continue to treat the tone-unit as something that can be described, defined and recognised.

## 17.4 Autosegmental treatment of intonation

In recent years a rather different way of analysing intonation, sometimes referred to as **autosegmental**, has become quite widely used, especially in American work. We will look briefly at this, in a simplified account that tries to introduce some basic concepts. In the autosegmental approach, all intonational phenomena can be reduced to just two basic phonological elements: H (high tone) and L (low tone). A movement of pitch from high to low (a fall) is treated as the sequence HL. Individual stressed ("accented") syllables must all be marked as H or L, or with a combination marking a pitch movement, and with an asterisk * following the syllable. In addition, H and L tones are associated with boundaries. A major tone-unit boundary (equivalent to what we have been marking with ||) is given the symbol %, but it must also be given a H or a L tone. Let us take an utterance like 'It's time to leave', which might be pronounced

its ˈtime to ╲<u>leave</u> (using our usual transcription)

The basic parts of the alternative transcription might look like this (the tone symbols may be placed above or below the line, aligned with the syllables they apply to):

```
      H*     H*L%
its time to leave
```

Instead of marking a falling tone on the word 'leave', the high-pitched part of the word is shown by the H and the low part by the L associated with the boundary %. There is another boundary (corresponding to the minor tone-unit boundary |) which is marked with –, and again this must be marked with either an H or an L. There must always be one of these boundaries marked before a % boundary. So, the following utterance would be transcribed like this in the system introduced in this book:

we ˌlooked at the ╱<u>sky</u> | and ˈsaw the ╲<u>clouds</u>

and in this way using autosegmental transcription:

```
   L*          L*H-   H*      H* L-L%
we looked at the sky and saw the clouds
```

How would this approach deal with complex tones spread over several syllables?

```
                                         H*        L-H%
v̬most of them    could be transcribed    most of them
```

(˅<u>most</u> of them — could be transcribed — H* L–H% most of them)

Although this type of analysis has some attractions, especially in the way it fits with contemporary phonological theory, it seems unlikely that it would be more useful to learners of English than the traditional analysis presented in this book.

## Notes on problems and further reading

The main concern of this chapter is to complete the description of intonational form, including analysis of perhaps the most difficult aspect: that of recognising fall–rise and rise–fall tones when they are extended over a number of syllables. This is necessary since no complete analysis of intonation can be done without having studied these "extended tones".

Cruttenden (1997: Chapters 3 and 4) gives a good introduction to the problems of analysing tones both within the traditional British framework and in autosegmental terms. On tone-unit boundaries, there is a clear explanation of the problems in Cruttenden (1997: Section 3.2), and in more detail in Crystal (1969: 204–7). A study of Scottish English by Brown *et al.* (1980) gives ample evidence that tone-units in real life are not as easy to identify as tone-units in textbooks.

Some writers follow Halliday (1967) in using the terms **tone**, **tonality** and **tonicity** (the "three Ts") to refer (respectively) to tone, to the division of speech into tone-units and to the placement of the tonic syllable; see for example Tench (1996), Wells (2006). In my experience people find it difficult to remember which is which, so I don't use these terms.

There has recently been a growth of interest in the comparative study of intonation in different languages and dialects: see Cruttenden (1997: Chapter 5); Hirst and di Cristo (1998); Ladd (1996: Chapter 4).

On declination, see Cruttenden (1997: 121–3).

For reading on autosegmental analysis (often given the name **ToBI,** which stands for **To**nes and **B**reak **I**ndices), a good introduction is Cruttenden (1997: 56–67). A fuller and more critical analysis can be read in Ladd (1996: Chapters 2 and 3); see also Roca and Johnson (1999: Chapter 14). A short account of the problems found in trying to compare this approach with the traditional British analysis is given in Roach (1994). ToBI is essentially a computer-based transcription system, and more information about it is provided on this book's website.

## Note for teachers

I would like to emphasise how valuable an exercise it is for students and teachers to attempt to analyse some recorded speech for themselves. For beginners it is best to start on slow, careful speech – such as that of newsreaders – before attempting conversational speech. One can learn more about intonation in an hour of this work than in days of reading textbooks on the subject, and one's interest in and understanding of theoretical problems becomes much more profound.

## Written exercises

1 The following sentences are given with intonation marks. Sketch the pitch within the lines below, leaving a gap between each syllable.

a) ˈWhich was the ↗cheap one did you ·say

b) I ˈonly ˈwant to ∨taste it

c) ˌShe would have ˌthought it was ∧obvious

d) There ˈwasnt ˈeven a ˈpiece of ↘bread in the ·house

e) ↘Now will you be·lieve me

2 This exercise is similar, but here you are given polysyllabic words and a tone. You must draw an appropriate pitch movement between the lines.

a) (rise) opportunity

b) (fall–rise) actually

c) (fall) confidently

d) (rise–fall) magnificent

e) (rise) relationship

f) (fall–rise) afternoon

# 18 Functions of intonation 1

The form of intonation has now been described in some detail, and we will move on to look more closely at its functions. Perhaps the best way to start is to ask ourselves what would be lost if we were to speak *without* intonation: you should try to imagine speech in which every syllable was said on the same level pitch, with no pauses and no changes in speed or loudness. This is the sort of speech that would be produced by a "mechanical speech" device (as described at the beginning of Chapter 14) that made sentences by putting together recordings of isolated words. To put it in the broadest possible terms, we can see that intonation makes it easier for a listener to understand what a speaker is trying to convey. The ways in which intonation does this are very complex, and many suggestions have been made for ways of isolating different functions. Among the most often proposed are the following:

i) Intonation enables us to express emotions and attitudes as we speak, and this adds a special kind of "meaning" to spoken language. This is often called the **attitudinal function** of intonation.
ii) Intonation helps to produce the effect of prominence on syllables that need to be perceived as stressed, and in particular the placing of tonic stress on a particular syllable marks out the word to which it belongs as the most important in the tone-unit. In this case, intonation works to **focus** attention on a particular lexical item or syllable. This has been called the **accentual function** of intonation.
iii) The listener is better able to recognise the grammar and syntactic structure of what is being said by using the information contained in the intonation; for example, such things as the placement of boundaries between phrases, clauses or sentences, the difference between questions and statements, and the use of grammatical subordination may be indicated. This has been called the **grammatical function** of intonation.
iv) Looking at the act of speaking in a broader way, we can see that intonation can signal to the listener what is to be taken as "new" information and what is already "given", can suggest when the speaker is indicating some sort of contrast or link with material in another tone-unit and, in conversation, can convey to the listener what kind of response is expected. Such functions are examples of intonation's **discourse function**.

The attitudinal function has been given so much importance in past work on intonation that it will be discussed separately in this chapter, although it should eventually become clear that it overlaps considerably with the discourse function. In the case of the other three functions, it will be argued that it is difficult to see how they could be treated as separate; for example, the placement of tonic stress is closely linked to the presentation of "new" information, while the question/statement distinction and the indication of contrast seem to be equally important in grammar and discourse. What seems to be common to accentual, grammatical and discourse functions is the indication, by means of intonation, of the relationship between some linguistic element and the context in which it occurs. The fact that they overlap with each other to a large degree is not so important if one does not insist on defining watertight boundaries between them.

The rest of this chapter is concerned with a critical examination of the attitudinal function.

## 18.1 The attitudinal function of intonation

Many writers have expressed the view that intonation is used to convey our feelings and attitudes: for example, the same sentence can be said in different ways, which might be labelled "angry", "happy", "grateful", "bored", and so on. A major factor in this is the tone used, and most books agree on some basic meanings of tones. Here are some examples (without punctuation):

1 Fall

*Finality, definiteness:* That is the end of the ╲news
Im absolutely ╲certain
Stop ╲talking

2 Rise

Most of the functions attributed to rises are nearer to grammatical than attitudinal, as in the first three examples given below; they are included here mainly to give a fuller picture of intonational function.

*General questions:* Can you ╱help me
Is it ╱over

*Listing:* ╱Red ╱brown ╱yellow or ╲blue
(a fall is usual on the last item)

*"More to follow":* I phoned them right a╱way ('and they agreed to come')
You must write it a╱gain (and this time, get it right)

*Encouraging:* It wont ╱hurt

3 Fall–rise

*Uncertainty, doubt:* You vmay be right
Its vpossible

*Requesting:* Can I vbuy it
Will you vlend it to me

4 Rise–fall

*Surprise, being impressed:* You were ʌfirst
ʌAll of them

It has also been widely observed that the form of intonation is different in different languages; for example, the intonation of languages such as Swedish, Italian or Hindi is instantly recognisable as being different from that of English. Not surprisingly, it has often been said that foreign learners of English need to learn English intonation. Some writers have gone further than this and claimed that, unless the foreign learner learns the appropriate way to use intonation in a given situation, there is a risk that he or she may unintentionally give offence; for example, the learner might use an intonation suitable for expressing boredom or discontent when what is needed is an expression of gratitude or affection. This misleading view of intonation must have caused unnecessary anxiety to many learners of the language.

Let us begin by considering how one might analyse the attitudinal function of intonation. One possibility would be for the analyst to invent a large number of sentences and to try saying them with different intonation patterns (i.e. different combinations of head and tone), noting what attitude was supposed to correspond to the intonation in each case; of course, the results are then very subjective, and based on an artificial performance that has little resemblance to conversational speech. Alternatively, the analyst could say these different sentences to a group of listeners and ask them all to write down what attitudes they thought were being expressed; however, we have a vast range of adjectives available for labelling attitudes and the members of the group would probably produce a very large number of such adjectives, leaving the analyst with the problem of deciding whether pairs such as "pompous" and "stuck-up", or "obsequious" and "sycophantic" were synonyms or represented different attitudes. To overcome this difficulty, one could ask the members of the group to choose among a small number of adjectives (or "labels") given by the analyst; the results would then inevitably be easier to quantify (i.e. the job of counting the different responses would be simpler) but the results would no longer represent the listeners' free choices of label. An alternative procedure would be to ask a lot of speakers to say a list of sentences in different ways according to labels provided by the analyst, and see what intonational features are found in common – for example, one might count how many speakers used a low head in saying something in a "hostile" way. The results of such experiments are usually very variable and difficult to interpret, not least because the range of acting talent in a randomly selected group is considerable.

A much more useful and realistic approach is to study recordings of different speakers' natural, spontaneous speech and try to make generalisations about attitudes and intonation on this basis. Many problems remain, however. In the method described previously, the analyst tries to select sentences (or passages of some other size) whose meaning is fairly "neutral" from the emotional point of view, and will tend to avoid material such as 'Why don't you leave me alone?' or 'How can I ever thank you enough?' because the lexical meaning of the words used already makes the speaker's attitude pretty clear, whereas sentences such as 'She's going to buy it tomorrow' or 'The paper has fallen under the table' are less likely to prejudice the listener. The choice of material is much less free for someone studying natural speech. Nevertheless, if we are ever to make new discoveries about intonation, it will be as a result of studying what people *really* say rather than inventing examples of what they *might* say.

The notion of "expressing an emotion or attitude" is itself a more complex one than is generally realised. First, an emotion may be expressed involuntarily or voluntarily; if I say something in a "happy" way, this may be because I *feel* happy, or because I want to convey to you the *impression* that I am happy. Second, an attitude that is expressed could be an attitude towards the listener (e.g. if I say something in a "friendly" way), towards what is being said (e.g. if I say something in a "sceptical" or "dubious" way) or towards some external event or situation (e.g. "regretful" or "disapproving").

However, one point is much more important and fundamental than all the problems discussed above. To understand this point you should imagine (or even actually perform) your pronunciation of a sentence in a number of different ways: for example, if the sentence was 'I want to buy a new car' and you were to say it in the following ways: "pleading", "angry", "sad", "happy", "proud", it is certain that at least some of your performances will be different from some others, but it is also certain that the technique for analysing and transcribing intonation introduced earlier in the course will be found inadequate to represent the different things you do. You will have used variations in loudness and speed, for example; almost certainly you will have used different voice qualities for different attitudes. You may have used your pitch range (see Section 15.3) in different ways: your pitch movements may have taken place within quite a narrow range (**narrow pitch range**) or using the full range between high and low (**wide pitch range**); if you did not use wide pitch range, you may have used different **keys: high key** (using the upper part of your pitch range), **mid key** (using the middle part of the range) or **low key** (the lower part). It is very likely that you will have used different facial expressions, and even gestures and body movements. These factors are all of great importance in conveying attitudes and emotions, yet the traditional handbooks on English pronunciation have almost completely ignored them.

If we accept the importance of these factors it becomes necessary to consider how they are related to intonation, and what intonation itself consists of. We can isolate three distinct types of suprasegmental variable: **sequential**, **prosodic** and **paralinguistic**.

### Sequential

These components of intonation are found as elements in sequences of other such elements occurring one after another (never simultaneously). These are:

i) pre-heads, heads, tonic syllables and tails (with their pitch possibilities);
ii) pauses;
iii) tone-unit boundaries.

These have all been introduced in previous chapters.

### Prosodic

These components are characteristics of speech which are constantly present and observable while speech is going on. The most important are:

i) width of pitch range;
ii) key;
iii) loudness;
iv) speed;
v) voice quality.

It is not possible to speak without one's speech having some degree or type of pitch range, loudness, speed and voice quality (with the possible exception that pitch factors are largely lost in whispered speech). Different speakers have their own typical pitch range, loudness, voice quality, etc., and contrasts among prosodic components should be seen as relative to these "background" speaker characteristics.

Each of these prosodic components needs a proper framework for categorisation, and this is an interesting area of current research. One example of the prosodic component "width of pitch range" has already been mentioned in Section 15.3, when "extra pitch height" was introduced, and the "rhythmicality" discussed in Section 14.1 could be regarded as another prosodic component. Prosodic components should be regarded as part of intonation along with sequential components.

### Paralinguistic

Mention was made above of facial expressions, gestures and body movements. People who study human behaviour often use the term **body language** for such activity. One could also mention certain vocal effects such as laughs and sobs. These paralinguistic effects are obviously relevant to the act of speaking but could not themselves properly be regarded as components of speech. Again, they need a proper descriptive and classificatory system, but this is not something that comes within the scope of this course, nor in my opinion should they be regarded as components of intonation.

## 18.2 Expressing attitudes

What advice, then, can be given to the foreign learner of English who wants to learn "correct intonation"? It is certainly true that a few generalisations can be made about the attitudinal functions of some components of intonation. We have looked at some basic examples earlier in this chapter. Generalisations such as these are, however, very broad, and foreign learners do not find it easy to learn to use intonation through studying them. Similarly, within the area of prosodic components most generalisations tend to be rather obvious: wider pitch range tends to be used in excited or enthusiastic speaking, slower speed is typical of the speech of someone who is tired or bored, and so on. Most of the generalisations one could make are probably true for a lot of other languages as well. In short, of the rules and generalisations that could be made about conveying attitudes through intonation, those which are not actually wrong are likely to be too trivial to be worth learning. I have witnessed many occasions when foreigners have unintentionally caused misunderstanding or even offence in speaking to a native English speaker, but can remember only a few occasions when this could be attributed to "using the wrong intonation"; most such cases have involved native speakers of different varieties of English, rather than learners of English. Sometimes an intonation mistake can cause a difference in apparent grammatical meaning (something that is dealt with in Chapter 19). It should not be concluded that intonation is not important for conveying attitudes. What is being claimed here is that, although it is of great importance, the complexity of the total set of sequential and prosodic components of intonation and of paralinguistic features makes it a very difficult thing to teach or learn. One might compare the difficulty with that of trying to write rules for how one might indicate to someone that one finds him or her sexually attractive; while psychologists and biologists might make detailed observations and generalisations about how human beings of a particular culture behave in such a situation, most people would rightly feel that studying these generalisations would be no substitute for practical experience, and that relying on a textbook could lead to hilarious consequences. The attitudinal use of intonation is something that is best acquired through talking with and listening to English speakers, and this course aims simply to train learners to be more aware of and sensitive to the way English speakers use intonation.

## Notes on problems and further reading

Perhaps the most controversial question concerning English intonation is what its function is; pedagogically speaking, this is a very important question, since one would not wish to devote time to teaching something without knowing what its value is likely to be. At the beginning of this chapter I list four commonly cited functions. It is possible to construct a longer list: Wells (2006) suggests six, while Lee (1958) proposed ten.

For general introductory reading on the functions of intonation, there is a good survey in Cruttenden (1997: Chapter 4). Critical views are expressed in Brazil *et al.* (1980: 98–103) and Crystal (1969: 282–308). There are many useful examples in Brazil (1994). Few people have carried out experiments on listeners' perception of attitudes through intonation, probably because it is extremely difficult to design properly controlled experiments.

Once one has recognised the importance of features other than pitch, it is necessary to devise a framework for categorising these features. There are many different views about the meaning of the term "paralinguistic". In the framework presented in Crystal and Quirk (1964), paralinguistic features of the "vocal effect" type are treated as part of intonation, and it is not made sufficiently clear how these are to be distinguished from prosodic features. Crystal (1969) defines paralinguistic features as "vocal effects which are primarily the result of physiological mechanisms other than the vocal cords, such as the direct results of the workings of the pharyngeal, oral or nasal cavities" but this does not seem to me to fit the facts. In my view, "paralinguistic" implies "outside the system of contrasts used in spoken language" – which does not, of course, necessarily mean "non-vocal". I would therefore treat prosodic variables as linguistic – and consequently part of intonation – while I would treat vocal effects like laughs or sobs as non-linguistic vocal effects to be classed with gestures and facial expressions. Brown (1990), on the other hand, uses "paralinguistic" to include what I call "prosodic", and appears to have no separate term for non-linguistic vocal effects.

The term "voice quality" needs comment, as it tends to be used with different meanings: sometimes the term is used to refer to the personal, "background" characteristics that make one person's voice recognisably different from another, mainly as a result of the complex interaction of laryngeal and supralaryngeal features (Crystal, 1969: 100–4; Laver, 1980, 1994); for some writers, however, "voice quality" is the auditory result of different types of vocal fold vibration. A better name for this is **phonation type**.

## Note for teachers

Audio Unit 18 (CD 2) consists of extracts from a recording of spontaneous dialogue. Students usually feel that listening to these unfamiliar voices chopped up into small pieces is hard work, but generally the transcription exercise is not found nearly as difficult as expected.

## Written exercise

In the following bits of conversation, you are supplied with an "opening line" and a response that you must imagine saying. You are given an indication in brackets of the feeling or attitude expressed, and you must mark on the text the intonation you think is appropriate (mark only the response). As usual in intonation work in this book, punctuation is left out, since it can cause confusion.

| | | |
|---|---|---|
| 1 | It 'looks 'nice for a ↘swim | its rather cold *(doubtful)* |
| 2 | 'Why not 'get a ↗car | because I cant afford it *(impatient)* |
| 3 | Ive ˌlost my ↘ticket | youre silly then *(stating the obvious)* |
| 4 | You 'cant 'have an 'ice ↘cream | oh please *(pleading)* |
| 5 | 'What 'times are the ↗buses | seven oclock seven thirty and eight *(listing)* |
| 6 | She got 'four ↘A ·levels | four *(impressed)* |
| 7 | 'How much ↘work have you ·got to ·do | Ive got to do the shopping *(and more things after that …)* |
| 8 | 'Will the ∨children ·go | some of them might *(uncertain)* |

# 19 Functions of intonation 2

In the previous chapter we looked at the attitudinal function of intonation. We now turn to the accentual, grammatical and discourse functions.

## 19.1 The accentual function of intonation

The term accentual is derived from "accent", a word used by some writers to refer to what in this course is called "stress". When writers say that intonation has accentual function they imply that the placement of stress is something that is determined by intonation. It is possible to argue against this view: in Chapters 10 and 11 word stress is presented as something quite independent of intonation, and subsequently (p. 140) it was said that "intonation is carried entirely by the stressed syllables of a tone-unit". This means that the presentation so far has implied that the placing of stress is independent of and prior to the choice of intonation. However, one particular aspect of stress *could* be regarded as part of intonation: this is the placement of the tonic stress within the tone-unit. It would be reasonable to suggest that while word stress is independent of intonation, the placement of tonic stress is a function (the **accentual** function) of intonation. Some older pronunciation handbooks refer to this function as "sentence stress", which is not an appropriate name: the sentence is a unit of grammar, while the location of tonic stress is a matter which concerns the tone unit, a unit of phonology.

The location of the tonic syllable is of considerable linguistic importance. The most common position for this is on the last lexical word (e.g. noun, adjective, verb, adverb as distinct from the function words introduced in Chapter 12) of the tone-unit. For contrastive purposes, however, any word may become the bearer of the tonic syllable. It is frequently said that the placement of the tonic syllable indicates the **focus** of the information. In the following pairs of examples, (i) represents normal placement and (ii) contrastive:

i) I ˌwant to ˌknow ˌwhere hes ↘<u>trav</u>elling to
(The word 'to' at the end of the sentence, being a preposition and not a lexical word, is not stressed.)

ii) (I 'dont want to 'know 'where hes 'travelling ∨<u>from</u>)
I ˌwant to ˌknow ˌwhere hes ˌtravelling ↘<u>to</u>

i) She was 'wearing a 'red ↘<u>dress</u>

ii) (She 'wasnt 'wearing a ∨<u>green</u> ·dress) | She was ˌwearing a ↘<u>red</u> ·dress

Similarly, for the purpose of emphasis we may place the tonic stress in other positions; in these examples, (i) is non-emphatic and (ii) is emphatic:

i) It was ˈvery ↘<u>bor</u>ing
ii) It was ↘<u>very</u> ·boring

i) You ˈmustnt ˈtalk so ↘<u>loud</u>ly
ii) You ↘<u>must</u>nt ·talk so ·loudly

However, it would be wrong to say that the only cases of departure from putting tonic stress on the last lexical word were cases of contrast or emphasis. There are quite a few situations where it is normal for the tonic syllable to come earlier in the tone-unit. A well-known example is the sentence 'I have plans to leave'; this is ambiguous:

i) I have ˈplans to ↘<u>leave</u>
(i.e. I am planning to leave)
ii) I have ↘<u>plans</u> to ·leave
(i.e. I have some plans/diagrams/drawings that I have to leave)

Version (ii) could not be described as contrastive or emphatic. There are many examples similar to (ii); perhaps the best rule to give is that the tonic syllable will *tend* to occur on the last lexical word in the tone-unit, but may be placed earlier in the tone-unit if there is a word there with greater importance to what is being said. This can quite often happen as a result of the last part of the tone-unit being already "given" (i.e. something which has already been mentioned or is completely predictable); for example:

i) ˈHeres that ↘<u>book</u> you ·asked me to ·bring
(The fact that you asked me to bring it is not new)
ii) Ive ˈgot to ˈtake the ↘<u>dog</u> for a ·walk
('For a walk' is by far the most probable thing to follow 'I've got to take the dog'; if the sentence ended with 'to the vet' the tonic syllable would probably be 'vet')

Placement of tonic stress is, therefore, important and is closely linked to intonation. A question that remains, however, is whether one can and should treat this matter as separate from the other functions described below.

## 19.2 The grammatical function of intonation

The word "grammatical" tends to be used in a very loose sense in this context. It is usual to illustrate the grammatical function by inventing sentences which when written are ambiguous, and whose ambiguity can only be removed by using differences of intonation. A typical example is the sentence 'Those who sold quickly made a profit'. This can be said in at least two different ways:

i) ˈThose who ˈsold ∨<u>quick</u>ly | ˌmade a ↘<u>prof</u>it
ii) ˈThose who ∨<u>sold</u> | ˌquickly ˌmade a ↘<u>prof</u>it

The difference caused by the placement of the tone-unit boundary is seen to be equivalent to giving two different paraphrases of the sentences, as in:

i) A profit was made by those who sold quickly.
ii) A profit was quickly made by those who sold.

Let us look further at the role of tone-unit boundaries, and the link between the tone-unit and units of grammar. There is a strong tendency for tone-unit boundaries to occur at boundaries between grammatical units of higher order than words; it is extremely common to find a tone-unit boundary at a sentence boundary, as in:

I 'wont have any ╱tea | I 'dont ╲like it

In sentences with a more complex structure, tone-unit boundaries are often found at phrase and clause boundaries as well, as in:

In ∨France | where ˌfarms ˌtend to be ∨smaller | the 'subsidies are 'more im╲portant

It is very unusual to find a tone-unit boundary at a place where the only grammatical boundary is a boundary between words. It would, for example, sound distinctly odd to have a tone-unit boundary between an article and a following noun, or between auxiliary and main verbs if they are adjacent (although we may, on occasions, hesitate or pause in such places within a tone-unit; it is interesting to note that some people who do a lot of arguing and debating, notably politicians and philosophers, develop the skill of pausing for breath in such intonationally unlikely places because they are less likely to be interrupted than if they pause at the end of a sentence). Tone-unit boundary placement can, then, indicate grammatical structure to the listener and we can find minimal pairs such as the following:

i) The Con'servatives who ∨like the pro·posal | are ╲pleased
ii) The Con∨servatives | who ∨like the pro·posal | are ╲pleased

The intonation makes clear the difference between (i) "restrictive" and (ii) "non-restrictive" relative clauses: (i) implies that only *some* Conservatives like the proposal, while (ii) implies that *all* the Conservatives like it.

Another component of intonation that can be said to have grammatical significance is the choice of tone on the tonic syllable. One example that is very familiar is the use of a rising tone with questions. Many languages have the possibility of changing a statement into a question simply by changing the tone from falling to rising. This is, in fact, not used very much by itself in the variety of English being described here, where questions are usually grammatically marked. The sentence 'The price is going up' can be said as a statement like this:

The ╲price is going ·up

(the tonic stress could equally well be on 'up'). It would be quite acceptable in some dialects of English (e.g. many varieties of American English) to ask a question like this:

(Why do you want to buy it now?) The ↗price is going ·up

But speakers in Britain would be more likely to ask the question like this:

(Why do you want to buy it now?) 'Is the ↗price going ·up

It is by no means true that a rising tone is always used for questions in English; it is quite usual, for example, to use a falling tone with questions beginning with one of the "wh-question-words" like 'what', 'which', 'when', etc. Here are two examples with typical intonations, where (i) does not start with a "wh-word" and has a rising tone and (ii) begins with 'where' and has a falling tone.

i) 'Did you 'park the ↗car
ii) 'Where did you 'park the ↘car

However, the fall in (ii) is certainly not obligatory, and a rise is quite often heard in such a question. A fall is also possible in (i).

The intonation of **question-tags** (e.g. 'isn't it', 'can't he', 'should she', 'won't they', etc.) is often quoted as a case of a difference in meaning being due to the difference between falling and rising tone. In the following example, the question-tag is 'aren't they'; when it has a falling tone, as in (i), the implication is said to be that the speaker is comparatively certain that the information is correct, and simply expects the listener to provide confirmation, while the rising tone in (ii) is said to indicate a lesser degree of certainty, so that the question-tag functions more like a request for information.

i) They 'are 'coming on ↘Tuesday | ↘arent they
ii) They 'are 'coming on ↘Tuesday | ↗arent they

The difference illustrated here could reasonably be said to be as much attitudinal as grammatical. Certainly there is overlap between these two functions.

## 19.3 The discourse function of intonation

If we think of linguistic analysis as usually being linked to the sentence as the maximum unit of grammar, then the study of discourse attempts to look at the larger contexts in which sentences occur. For example, consider the four sentences in the following:

*A*: Have you got any free time this morning?
*B*: I might have later on if that meeting's off.
*A*: They were talking about putting it later.
*B*: You can't be sure.

Each sentence could be studied in isolation and be analysed in terms of grammatical construction, lexical content, and so on. But it is clear that the sentences form part of some larger act of conversational interaction between two speakers; the sentences contain several references that presuppose shared knowledge (e.g. 'that meeting' implies that both speakers know which meeting is being spoken about), and in some cases the meaning of a sentence can only be correctly interpreted in the light of knowledge of what has preceded it in the conversation (e.g. 'You can't be sure').

If we consider how intonation may be studied in relation to discourse, we can identify two main areas: one of them is the use of intonation to focus the listener's attention on aspects of the message that are most important, and the other is concerned with the regulation of conversational behaviour. We will look at these in turn.

In the case of "attention focusing", the most obvious use has already been described: this is the placing of tonic stress on the appropriate syllable of one particular word in the tone-unit. In many cases it is easy to demonstrate that the tonic stress is placed on the word that is in some sense the "most important", as in:

She 'went to ↘<u>Scot</u>land

Sometimes it seems more appropriate to describe tonic stress placement in terms of "information content": the more predictable a word's occurrence is in a given context, the lower is its information content. Tonic stress will tend to be placed on words with high information content, as suggested above when the term *focus* was introduced. This is the explanation that would be used in the case of the sentences suggested in Section 19.1:

i) Ive 'got to 'take the ↘<u>dog</u> for a ·walk
ii) Ive 'got to 'take the 'dog to the ↘<u>vet</u>

The word 'vet' is less predictable (has a higher information content) than 'walk'. However, we still find many cases where it is difficult to explain tonic placement in terms of "importance" or "information". For example, in messages like:

| | |
|---|---|
| Your coat's on fire | The wing's breaking up |
| The radio's gone wrong | Your uncle's died |

probably the majority of English speakers would place the tonic stress on the subject noun, although it is difficult to see how this is more important than the last lexical word in each of the sentences. The placement of tonic stress is still to some extent an unsolved mystery; it is clear, however, that it is at least partly determined by the larger context (linguistic and non-linguistic) in which the tone-unit occurs.

We can see at least two other ways in which intonation can assist in focusing attention. The tone chosen can indicate whether the tone-unit in which it occurs is being used to present new information or to refer to information which is felt to be already possessed by speaker and hearer. For example, in the following sentence:

'Since the ∨<u>last</u> time we ·met | 'when we 'had that 'huge ∨<u>dinn</u>er |
Ive ˌbeen on a ↘<u>di</u>et

the first two tone-units present information which is relevant to what the speaker is saying, but which is not something new and unknown to the listener. The final tone-unit, however, does present new information. Writers on discourse intonation have proposed that the falling tone indicates new information while rising (including falling–rising) tones indicate "shared" or "given" information.

Another use of intonation connected with the focusing of attention is **intonational subordination**; we can signal that a particular tone-unit is of comparatively low importance and as a result give correspondingly greater importance to adjacent tone-units. For example:

i) As I exˌpect youve ↘heard | theyre ˈonly adˈmitting e↘mergency ·cases
ii) The ˈJapa∨nese | for ˌsome ˌreason or ↗other | ˈdrive on the ↘left | like ↘us

In a typical conversational pronunciation of these sentences, the first tone-unit of (i) and the second and fourth tone-units of (ii) might be treated as intonationally subordinate; the prosodic characteristics marking this are usually:

i) a drop to a lower part of the pitch range ("low key");
ii) increased speed;
iii) narrower range of pitch; and
iv) reduced loudness, relative to the non-subordinate tone-unit(s).

The use of these components has the result that the subordinate tone-units are less easy to hear. Native speakers can usually still understand what is said, if necessary by guessing at inaudible or unrecognisable words on the basis of their knowledge of what the speaker is talking about. Foreign learners of English, on the other hand, having in general less "common ground" or shared knowledge with the speaker, often find that these subordinate tone-units – with their "throwaway", parenthetic style – cause serious difficulties in understanding.

We now turn to the second main area of intonational discourse function: the regulation of conversational behaviour. We have already seen how the study of sequences of tone-units in the speech of one speaker can reveal information carried by intonation which would not have been recognised if intonation were analysed only at the level of individual tone-units. Intonation is also important in the conversational interaction of two or more speakers. Most of the research on this has been on conversational interaction of a rather restricted kind – such as between doctor and patient, teacher and student, or between the various speakers in court cases. In such material it is comparatively easy to identify what each speaker is actually doing in speaking – for example, questioning, challenging, advising, encouraging, disapproving, etc. It is likely that other forms of conversation can be analysed in the same way, although this is considerably more difficult. In a more general way, it can be seen that speakers use various prosodic components to indicate to others that they have finished speaking, that another person is expected to speak, that a particular type of response is required, and so on. A familiar example is that quoted above (p. 156), where the difference between falling and rising intonation on question-tags is supposed to indicate to the listener what sort of response is expected. It seems that key (the part of the pitch range used) is important in signalling information about conversational interaction. We can observe many examples in non-linguistic behaviour of the use of signals to regulate turn-taking: in many sports, for example, it is necessary to do this – footballers can indicate that they are looking for someone to pass the ball to, or that they are ready to receive the ball, and doubles partners in tennis can indicate to each other who is to play a shot. Intonation, in conjunction with "body language" such as eye contact, facial expression, gestures and head-turning, is used for similar purposes in speech, as well as for establishing or confirming the status of the participants in a conversation.

## 19.4 **Conclusions**

It seems clear that studying intonation in relation to discourse makes it possible to explain much more comprehensively the uses that speakers make of intonation. Practically all the separate functions traditionally attributed to intonation (attitudinal, accentual and grammatical) could be seen as different aspects of discourse function. The risk, with such a broad approach, is that one might end up making generalisations that were too broad and had little power to predict with any accuracy the intonation that a speaker would use in a particular context. It is still too early to say how useful the discourse approach will be, but even if it achieves nothing else, it can at least be claimed to have shown the inadequacy of attempting to analyse the function of intonation on the basis of isolated sentences or tone-units, removed from their linguistic and situational context.

## Notes on problems and further reading

Important work was done on the placement of tonic stress by Halliday (1967); his term for this is "tonicity", and he adopts the widely-used linguistic term "marked" for tonicity that deviates from what I have called (for the sake of simplicity) "normal". Within generative phonology there has been much debate about whether one can determine the placing of tonic ("primary") stress without referring to the non-linguistic context in which the speaker says something. This debate was very active in the 1970s, well summarised and criticised in Schmerling (1976), but see Bolinger (1972). For more recent accounts, see Couper-Kuhlen (1986: Chapters 7 and 8) and Ladd (1996: 221–35).

One of the most interesting developments of recent years has been the emergence of a theory of discourse intonation. Readers unfamiliar with the study of discourse may find some initial difficulty in understanding the principles involved; the best introduction is Brazil *et al.* (1980), while the ideas set out there are given more practical expression in Brazil (1994). I have not been able to do more than suggest the rough outline of this approach.

The treatment of intonational subordination is based not on the work of Brazil but on Crystal and Quirk (1964: 52–6) and Crystal (1969: 235–52). The basic philosophy is the same, however, in that both views illustrate the fact that there is in intonation some organisation at a level higher than the isolated tone-unit; see Fox (1973). A parallel might be drawn with the relationship between the sentence and the paragraph in writing. It seems likely that a considerable amount of valuable new research on pronunciation will grow out of the study of discourse.

### Note for teachers

Audio Unit 19 (CD 2) is short and intensive. It is meant primarily to give a reminder that English spoken at something like full conversational speed is very different from the slow, careful pronunciation of the early Audio Units.

### Written exercises

1 In the following exercise, read the "opening line" and then decide on the most suitable place for tonic stress placement (underline the syllable) in the response.

| | |
|---|---|
| a) Id 'like you to ↘help me | (right) can I do the shopping for you |
| b) I 'hear youre 'offering to 'do the ↘shopping for someone | (right) can I do the shopping for you |
| c) 'What was the 'first 'thing that ↘happened | first the professor explained her theory |
| d) 'Was the 'theory ex'plained by the ↗students | (no) first the professor explained her theory |
| e) 'Tell me 'how the ↘theory was pre·sented | first she explained her theory |
| f) I 'think it 'starts at 'ten to ↘three | (no) ten past three |
| g) I 'think it 'starts at 'quarter past ↘three | (no) ten past three |
| h) I 'think it 'starts at 'ten past ↘four | (no) ten past three |

2 The following sentences are given without punctuation. Underline the appropriate tonic syllable places and mark tone-unit boundaries where you think they are most appropriate.

a) (*he wrote the letter in a sad way*) he wrote the letter sadly
b) (*it's regrettable that he wrote the letter*) he wrote the letter sadly
c) four plus six divided by two equals five
d) four plus six divided by two equals seven
e) we broke one thing after another fell down
f) we broke one thing after another that night

# 20 Varieties of English pronunciation

In Chapter 1 there was some discussion of different types of English pronunciation and the reasons for choosing the accent that is described in this book. The present chapter returns to this topic to look in more detail at differences in pronunciation.

## 20.1 The study of variety

Differences between accents are of two main sorts: **phonetic** and **phonological**. When two accents differ from each other only phonetically, we find the same set of phonemes in both accents, but some or all of the phonemes are realised differently. There may also be differences in stress or intonation, but not such as would cause a change in meaning. As an example of phonetic differences at the segmental level, it is said that Australian English has the same set of phonemes and phonemic contrasts as BBC pronunciation, yet Australian pronunciation is so different from that accent that it is easily recognised.

Many accents of English also differ noticeably in intonation without the difference being such as would cause a difference in meaning; some Welsh accents, for example, have a tendency for unstressed syllables to be higher in pitch than stressed syllables. Such a difference is, again, a phonetic one. An example of a phonetic (non-phonological) difference in stress would be the stressing of the final syllable of verbs ending in '-ise' in some Scottish and Northern Irish accents (e.g. 'realise' rɪəˈlaɪz).

Phonological differences are of various types: again, we can divide these into segmental and suprasegmental. Within the area of segmental phonology the most obvious type of difference is where one accent has a different number of phonemes (and hence of phonemic contrasts) from another. Many speakers with northern English accents, for example, do not have a contrast between ʌ and ʊ, so that 'luck' and 'look' are pronounced identically (both as lʊk); in the case of consonants, many accents do not have the phoneme h, so that there is no difference in pronunciation between 'art' and 'heart'. The phonemic system of such accents is therefore different from that of the BBC accent. On the other hand, some accents differ from others in having *more* phonemes and phonemic contrasts. For example, many northern English accents have a long eː sound as the realisation of the phoneme symbolised eɪ in BBC pronunciation (which is a simple phonetic difference); but in some northern accents there is both an eɪ diphthong phoneme and also a contrasting long vowel phoneme that can be symbolised as eː. Words like 'eight', 'reign' are pronounced eɪt, reɪn, while 'late', 'rain' (with no 'g' in the spelling) are pronounced leːt, reːn.

A more complicated kind of difference is where, without affecting the overall set of phonemes and contrasts, a phoneme has a distribution in one accent that is different from the distribution of the same phoneme in another accent. The clearest example is r, which is restricted to occurring in pre-vocalic position in BBC pronunciation, but in many other accents is not restricted in this way. Another example is the occurrence of j between a consonant and uː, ʊ or ʊə. In BBC pronunciation we can find the following: 'pew' pjuː, 'tune' tjuːn, 'queue' kjuː. However, in most American accents and in some English accents of the south and east we find that, while 'pew' is pronounced pjuː and 'queue' as kjuː, 'tune' is pronounced tuːn; this absence of j is found after the other alveolar consonants; hence; 'due' duː, 'new' nuː. In Norwich, and other parts of East Anglia, we find many speakers who have no consonant + j clusters at the beginning of a syllable, so that 'music' is pronounced muːzɪk and 'beautiful' as buːtɪfl̩.

We also find another kind of variation: in the example just given above, the occurrence of the phonemes being discussed is determined by their phonological context; however, sometimes the determining factor is lexical rather than phonological. For example, in many accents of the Midlands and north-western England a particular set of words containing a vowel represented by 'o' in the spelling is pronounced with ʌ in BBC but with ɒ in these other accents; the list of words includes 'one', 'none', 'nothing', 'tongue', 'mongrel', 'constable', but does not include some other words of similar form such as 'some' sʌm and 'ton' tʌn. One result of this difference is that such accents have different pronunciations for the two members of pairs of words that are pronounced identically (i.e. are homophones) in BBC – for example, 'won' and 'one', 'nun' and 'none'. In my own pronunciation when I was young, I had ɒ instead of ʌ in these words, so that 'won' was pronounced wʌn and 'one' as wɒn, 'nun' as nʌn and 'none' as nɒn; this has not completely disappeared from my accent.

It would be satisfying to be able to list examples of phonological differences between accents in the area of stress and intonation but, unfortunately, straightforward examples are not available. We do not yet know enough about the phonological functions of stress and intonation, and not enough work has been done on comparing accents in terms of these factors. It will be necessary to show how one accent is able to make some difference in meaning with stress or intonation that another accent is unable to make. Since some younger speakers seem not to distinguish between the noun 'protest' and the verb 'protest', pronouncing both as ˈprəʊtest, we could say that in their speech a phonological distinction in stress has been lost, but this is a very limited example. It is probable that such differences will in the future be identified by suitable research work.

## 20.2 Geographical variation

For a long time, the study of variation in accents was part of the subject of **dialectology**, which aimed to identify all the ways in which a language differed from place to place. Dialectology in its traditional form is therefore principally interested in geographical differences; its best-known data-gathering technique was to send researchers (usually called "field workers") mainly into rural areas (where the speakers were believed to be less likely to have been influenced by other accents), to find elderly speakers (whose speech was believed to have been less influenced by other accents and to preserve older forms of the dialect) and to use lists of questions to find information about vocabulary and pronunciation, the questions being chosen to concentrate on items known to vary a lot from region to region. Surveys of this kind have provided the basis for many useful generalisations about geographical variation, but they have serious weaknesses: dialectology concentrated too much on rural varieties, tended to be interested in archaic forms of the language and took little notice of variation due to social class, education and other such factors. More recent research has tended to be carried out within the framework of **sociolinguistics**, and has tried to cover urban speech with a balanced coverage of ages and social classes.

Studies of different accents often concentrate on small communities, but for our purposes it will be more useful to look briefly at differences between some of the largest groups of speakers of English. A word of caution should be given here: it is all too easy to talk about such things as "Scottish English", "American English", and so on, and to ignore the variety that inevitably exists within any large community of speakers. Each individual's speech is different from any other's; it follows from this that no one speaker can be taken to represent a particular accent or dialect, and it also follows that the idea of a standard pronunciation is a convenient fiction, not a scientific fact.

### American

In many parts of the world, the fundamental choice for learners of English is whether to learn an American or a British pronunciation, though this is by no means true everywhere. Since we have given very little attention to American pronunciation in this course, it will be useful at this stage to look at the most important differences between American accents and the BBC accent. It is said that the majority of American speakers of English have an accent that is often referred to as **General American** (**GA**); since it is the American accent most often heard on international radio and television networks, it is also called **Network English**. Most Canadian speakers of English have a very similar accent (few British people can hear the difference between the Canadian and American accents, as is the case with the difference between Australian and New Zealand accents). Accents in America different from GA are mainly found in New England and in the "deep south" of the country, but isolated rural communities everywhere tend to preserve different accents; there is also a growing section of American society whose native language is Spanish (or who are children of Spanish speakers) and they speak English with a pronunciation influenced by Spanish.

The most important difference between GA and BBC is the distribution of the r phoneme, GA being rhotic (i.e. r occurs in all positions, including before consonants and at the end of utterances). Thus where BBC pronounces 'car' as kɑː and 'cart' as kɑːt, GA has kɑːr and kɑːrt. Long vowels and diphthongs that are written with an 'r' in the spelling are pronounced in GA as simple vowels followed by r. We can make the following comparisons:

| | BBC | GA |
|---|---|---|
| 'car' | kɑː | kɑːr |
| 'more' | mɔː | mɔːr |
| 'fear' | fɪə | fɪr |
| 'care' | keə | ker |
| 'tour' | tʊə | tʊr |

American vowels followed by r are strongly "r-coloured", to the extent that one often hears the vowel at the centre of a syllable as a long r with no preceding vowel. The GA vowel in 'fur', for example, could be transcribed as ɜːr (with a transcription that matched those for the other long vowels in the list above), but it is more often transcribed ɝ with a diacritic ˞ to indicate that the whole vowel is "r-coloured". Similarly, the short "schwa" in GA may be r-coloured and symbolised ɚ as in 'minor' maɪnɚ. It would be wrong to assume that GA has no long vowels like those of the BBC accent: in words like 'psalm', 'bra', 'Brahms', where there is no letter 'r' following the 'a' in the spelling, a long non-rhotic vowel is pronounced, whose pronunciation varies from region to region.

One vowel is noticeably different: the ɒ of 'dog', 'cot' in BBC pronunciation is not found in GA. In most words where the BBC accent has ɒ we find ɑː or ɔː, so that 'dog', which is dɒg in BBC, is dɑːg or dɔːg in American pronunciation. In this case, we have a phonological difference, since one phoneme that is present in BBC pronunciation is absent in American accents. Other segmental differences are phonetic: the l phoneme, which was introduced in Section 2 of Chapter 7, is almost always pronounced as a "dark l" in American English: the sound at the beginning of 'like' is similar to that at the end of 'mile'. The pronunciation of t is very different in American English when it occurs at the end of a stressed syllable and in front of an unstressed vowel. In a word like 'betting', which in BBC pronunciation is pronounced with a t that is plosive and slightly aspirated, American speakers usually have what is called a "flapped r" in which the tip of the tongue makes very brief contact with the alveolar ridge, a sound similar to the r sound in Spanish and many other languages. This is sometimes called "voiced t", and it is usually represented with the symbol t̬.

There are many other differences between American and English pronunciation, many of them the subject of comic debates such as "You say tomato (tə'meɪt̬əʊ) and I say tomato (tə'mɑːtəʊ)."

### Scottish

There are many accents of British English, but one that is spoken by a large number of people and is radically different from BBC English is the Scottish accent. There is much variation from one part of Scotland to another; the accent of Edinburgh is the one most usually described. Like the American accent described above, Scottish English pronunciation is essentially rhotic and an 'r' in the spelling is always pronounced; the words 'shore' and 'short' can be transcribed as ʃɔr and ʃɔrt. The Scottish r sound is usually pronounced as a "flap" or "tap" similar to the r sound in Spanish.

It is in the vowel system that we find the most important differences between BBC pronunciation and Scottish English. As with American English, long vowels and diphthongs that correspond to spellings with 'r' are composed of a vowel and the r consonant, as mentioned above. The distinction between long and short vowels does not exist, so that 'good', 'food' have the same vowel, as do 'Sam', 'psalm' and 'caught', 'cot'. The BBC diphthongs eɪ, əʊ are pronounced as pure vowels e, o, but the diphthongs eɪ, aɪ, ɔɪ exist as in the BBC accent (though with phonetic differences).

This brief account may cover the most basic differences, but it should be noted that these and other differences are so radical that people from England and from parts of lowland Scotland have serious difficulty in understanding each other. It often happens that foreigners who have learned to pronounce English as it is spoken in England find life very difficult when they go to Scotland, though in time they do manage to deal with the pronunciation differences and communicate successfully.

## 20.3 Other sources of variation

We do not have space for a detailed examination of all the different types of variation in pronunciation, but a few more are worth mentioning.

### Age

Everybody knows that younger people speak differently from older people. This seems to be true in every society, and many people believe that younger people do this specially to annoy their parents and other people of the older generation, or to make it difficult for their parents to understand what they are saying to their friends. We can look at how younger people speak and guess at how the pronunciation of the language will develop in the future, but such predictions are of limited value: elderly professors can safely try to predict how pronunciation will change over the coming decades because they are not likely to be around to find themselves proved wrong. The speech of young people tends to show more elisions than that of older people. This seems to be true in all cultures, and is usually described by older speakers as "sloppy" or "careless". A sentence like the following: 'What's the point of going to school if there's no social life?' might be pronounced in a careful way as (in phonemic transcription) wɒts ðə pɔɪnt əv gəʊɪŋ tə skuːl ɪf ðəz nəʊ səʊʃl̩ laɪf, but a young speaker talking to a friend might (in the area of England where I live) say it in a way that might be transcribed phonetically as s pɔ̃ɪʔ gæʊʔ skɔʊ f s næʊ sæʊʃ lɔɪf.

There is an aspect of intonation that has often been quoted in relation to age differences: this is the use of rising intonation in making statements, a style of speaking that is sometimes called "upspeak" or "uptalk". Here is a little invented example:

> I was in Marks and Spencer's. In the food section. They had this chocolate cake. I just had to buy some.

A typical adult pronunciation would be likely to use a sequence of falling tones, like this:

> I was in 'Marks and ↘Spencers | In the ↘food section | They had this ↘chocolate cake | I just 'had to ↘buy some

But the "upspeak" version would sound like this:

> I was in 'Marks and ↗Spencers | In the ↗food section | They had this ↗chocolate cake | I just 'had to ↘buy some

(with a falling tone only on the last tone-unit). It is widely believed that this style of intonation arose from copying young actors in Australian and American soap operas. One thing that keeps it alive in young people's speech is that older people find it so intensely irritating. It is, I believe, a passing fashion that will not last long.

### Social and class differences

We can find differences in pronunciation (as well as in other fields of linguistic analysis) resulting from various factors including (in addition to geographical origin) one's age and sex, social class, educational background, occupation and personality. In addition, various situational factors influence pronunciation, such as the social relationship between speaker and hearer, whether one is speaking publicly or privately, and the purposes for which one is using language. Some people (who usually turn out to do well in phonetic training) find that in speaking to someone with a different accent their pronunciation gets progressively more like that of the person they are speaking to, like a chameleon adapting its colour to its environment.

### Style

Many linguists have attempted to produce frameworks for the analysis of style in language. There is not space for us to consider this in detail, but we should note that, for foreign learners, a typical situation – regrettably, an almost inevitable one – is that they learn a style of pronunciation which could be described as careful and formal. Probably their teachers speak to them in this style, although what the learners are likely to encounter when they join in conversations with native speakers is a "rapid, casual" style. We all have the ability to vary our pronunciation to suit the different styles of speech that we use. Speaking to one's own children, for example, is a very different activity from that of speaking to adults that one does not know well. In broadcasting, there is a very big difference between formal news-reading style and the casual speech used in chat shows and game shows. Some politicians change their pronunciation to suit the context: it was often noticed that Tony Blair, when he was prime minister, would adopt an "Estuary English" style of pronunciation when he wanted to project an informal "man of the people" style, but a BBC accent when speaking on official state occasions. In the former style, it was not unusual to hear him say something like 'We've got a problem' with a glottal stop replacing the t in 'got': wiv gɒʔ ə prɒbləm. I can't remember any other prime minister doing this.

Rhythm forms an important part of style: careful, deliberate speech tends to go with regular rhythm and slow speed. Casual speech, as well as being less rhythmical and faster, tends to include a lot of "fillers" – such as hesitation noises (usually written 'um' or 'er') or exaggeratedly long vowels to cover a hesitation.

It should now be clear that the pronunciation described in this course is only one of a vast number of possible varieties. The choice of a slow, careful style is made for the sake of convenience and simplicity; learners of English need to be aware of the fact that this style is far from being the only one they will meet, and teachers of English to foreigners should do their best to expose their students to other varieties.

## Notes on problems and further reading

**20.1** For general reading about sociolinguistics and dialectology, see Trudgill (1999); Foulkes and Docherty (1999); Spolsky (1998).

**20.2** There are some major works on geographical variation in English pronunciation. Wells (1982) is an important source of information in this field. For a brief overview, with recorded examples, see Collins and Mees (2008: Section C). To find out more about American and Scottish pronunciation, see Cruttenden (2001: Sections 7.6.1 and 7.6.2); there is a good account of the vowel systems of American, Scottish and BBC English in Giegerich (1992: Chapter 3). In a more practical way, it can be useful to compare the accounts of American and British pronunciation in pronunciation dictionaries such as Jones (eds. Roach *et al.*, 2006) or Wells (2008); the CDs of these dictionaries allow you to listen to the British and American pronunciations of all the words in the dictionary, and to compare your own pronunciation.

**20.3** On "upspeak" or "uptalk", see Wells (2006: Section 2.9); Cruttenden (1997: 129–130). Collins and Mees (2008) reproduce a valuable extract from the work of Barbara Bradford, who has done pioneering work in this area. Shockey (2003) shows the great variation between formal and informal styles of speech.

## Note for teachers

In talking about differences in pronunciation between younger and older speakers, we should consider what I would like to call the Pronunciation Teaching Paradox: this is that the books and other teaching materials, syllabuses and examination standards are usually produced by middle-aged or old teachers, while the people who are taught are usually young. The model accent for pronunciation practice is almost always that of middle-aged English people. It would in theory be possible to teach young foreign learners of English to speak like young native speakers of English, and many students from other countries who have a period of study in a British university or language school manage to acquire something of the accent of young people in the area, but in my own experience it is likely that when they get back home they risk being given a lower mark by their (middle-aged) examiners in an oral examination than students producing a more traditional accent. I regret this, but I can't change it.

The comment about Audio Unit 18 at the end of Chapter 18 applies also to Audio Unit 20 (CD 2). At first hearing it seems very difficult, but when worked on step by step it is far from impossible. If there is time, students should now be encouraged to go back to some of the more difficult Audio Units dealing with connected speech (say from Audio Unit 12 onwards, missing out Audio Unit 15); they will probably discover a lot of things they did not notice before.

## Written exercise

Phonological differences between accents are of various types. For each of the following sets of phonetic data, based on non-BBC accents, say what you can conclude about the phonology of that accent.

| | | |
|---|---|---|
| 1 | 'sing' sɪŋ | 'finger' fɪŋgə |
| | 'sung' sʌŋ | 'running' rʌnɪn |
| | 'singing' sɪŋɪn | 'ring' rɪŋ |
| 2 | 'day' deː | 'you' juː |
| | 'buy' baɪ | 'me' miː |
| | 'go' goː | 'more' mɔː |
| | 'now' naʊ | 'fur' fɜː |
| | 'own' oːn | 'eight' eːt |
| 3 | 'mother' mʌvə | 'father' fɑːvə |
| | 'think' fɪŋk | 'breath' bref |
| | 'lip' lɪp | 'pill' pɪw |
| | 'help' ewp | 'hill' ɪw |
| 4 | 'mother' mʌðər | 'father' fɑːðər |
| | 'car' kɑːr | 'cart' kɑːrt |
| | 'area' eːriəl | 'aerial' eːriəl |
| | 'idea' aɪdɪəl | 'ideal' aɪdɪəl |
| | 'India' ɪndiəl | 'Norma' nɔːməl |
| 5 | 'cat' kat | 'plaster' plaːstər |
| | 'cart' kɑːrt | 'grass' graːs |
| | 'calm' kɑːm | 'gas' gas |

# Recorded exercises

These exercises are mainly intended for students whose native language is not English; however, those exercises which involve work with transcription (exercises 1.2, 2.2, 3.3, 3.5, 3.7, 4.5, 5.3, 5.4, 6.2, 7.6, 9.5, 10.1, 10.2, 11.5, 12.3, 13.1, 13.2, 13.3, all of Audio Unit 14 and Exercise 19.2) and those which give practice in intonation (Audio Units 15–20) will be useful to native speakers as well.

Each Audio Unit corresponds to a chapter of this book. As far as possible I have tried to relate the content of each Audio Unit to the material of the chapter; however, where the chapter is devoted to theoretical matters I have taken advantage of this to produce revision exercises going back over some of the subjects previously worked on.

In some of the exercises you are asked to put stress or intonation marks on the text. It would be sensible to do this in such a way that will make it possible for you, or someone else, to erase these marks and use the exercise again.

As with the chapters of the book, these exercises are intended to be worked through from first to last. Those at the beginning are concerned with individual vowels and consonants, and the words containing them are usually pronounced in isolation in a slow, careful style. Pronouncing isolated words in this way is a very artificial practice, but the recorded exercises are designed to lead the student towards the study of comparatively natural and fluent speech by the end of the course. In some of the later exercises you will find it necessary to stop the recording in order to allow yourself enough time to write a transcription. You will also need to stop the recording to check your answers. The answers section for the Recorded Exercises is on pages 210–18.

## Audio Unit 1 Introduction

To give you practice in using the audio exercises in this book, here are two simple exercises on English word stress.

*Exercise 1 Repetition*

Each word is shown with a diagram showing which syllables are strong (●) and which are weak (•). Listen to each word and repeat it.

| | | |
|---|---|---|
| 1 | • ● • | potato |
| 2 | ● • • | optimist |
| 3 | • ● | decide |

4 • • ● • reservation
5 ● • • quantity

*Exercise 2 Stress pattern notation*
You will hear five words. After each word, write down the stress pattern using the two symbols used above. (1–5)

Check your answers.

## Audio Unit 2 English short vowels

The exercises in this Unit practise the six short vowels introduced in Chapter 2. When pronouncing them, you should take care to give the vowels the correct length *and* the correct quality.

*Exercise 1 Repetition*
Listen and repeat:

ɪ
bit bɪt bid bɪd hymn hɪm miss mɪs
e
bet bet bed bed hen hen mess mes
æ
bat bæt bad bæd ham hæm mass mæs
ʌ
cut kʌt bud bʌd bun bʌn bus bʌs
ɒ
pot pɒt cod kɒd Tom tɒm loss lɒs
ʊ
put pʊt wood wʊd pull pʊl push pʊʃ

*Exercise 2 Identification*
Write the symbol for the vowel you hear in each word. (1–10)

Check your answers.

*Exercise 3 Production*
When you hear the number, pronounce the word (which is given in spelling and in phonetic symbols). Repeat the correct pronunciation when you hear it.
*Example:* 1 'mad'

1 mad mæd
2 mud mʌd
3 bit bɪt
4 bet bet
5 cut kʌt
6 cot kɒt

| | |
|---|---|
| 7 put pʊt | 10 man mæn |
| 8 pot pɒt | 11 fun fʌn |
| 9 men men | 12 fan fæn |

*Exercise 4 Short vowels contrasted*

Listen and repeat (words given in spelling):

| ɪ and | e | e and | æ | æ and | ʌ |
|---|---|---|---|---|---|
| bit | bet | hem | ham | lack | luck |
| tin | ten | set | sat | bad | bud |
| fill | fell | peck | pack | fan | fun |
| built | belt | send | sand | stamp | stump |
| lift | left | wreck | rack | flash | flush |

| ʌ and | ɒ | ɒ and | ʊ |
|---|---|---|---|
| dug | dog | lock | look |
| cup | cop | cod | could |
| rub | rob | pot | put |
| stuck | stock | shock | shook |
| luck | lock | crock | crook |

*Exercise 5 Repetition of sentences with short vowels*

Listen and repeat:

| | |
|---|---|
| 1 Six fat men stopped | sɪks fæt men stɒpt |
| 2 That bus is full | ðæt bʌs ɪz fʊl |
| 3 Tim hid Jan's bag | tɪm hɪd dʒænz bæg |
| 4 This dog gets cats mad | ðɪs dɒg gets kæts mæd |
| 5 Bring back ten cups | brɪŋ bæk ten kʌps |
| 6 Tom picked up twelve books | tɒm pɪkt ʌp twelv bʊks |
| 7 What bad luck | wɒt bæd lʌk |
| 8 Ken pushed Sam's truck | ken pʊʃt sæmz trʌk |

## Audio Unit 3 Long vowels, diphthongs and triphthongs

### Long vowels

*Exercise 1 Repetition*

Listen and repeat:

iː

| | | | |
|---|---|---|---|
| beat biːt | bead biːd | bean biːn | beef biːf |

ɑː

| | | | |
|---|---|---|---|
| heart hɑːt | hard hɑːd | harm hɑːm | hearth hɑːθ |

ɔː

| | | | |
|---|---|---|---|
| caught kɔːt | cord kɔːd | corn kɔːn | course kɔːs |

uː

| | | | |
|---|---|---|---|
| root ruːt | rude ruːd | room ruːm | roof ruːf |

ɜː

| | | | |
|---|---|---|---|
| hurt hɜːt | heard hɜːd | earn ɜːn | earth ɜːθ |

*Exercise 2 Production*

When you hear the number, pronounce the word. Repeat the correct pronunciation when you hear it.

| | |
|---|---|
| 1 heard hɜːd | 6 heart hɑːt |
| 2 bean biːn | 7 cord kɔːd |
| 3 root ruːt | 8 beef biːf |
| 4 hearth hɑːθ | 9 rude ruːd |
| 5 caught kɔːt | 10 earn ɜːn |

*Exercise 3 Transcription*

Write the symbol for the vowel you hear in each word. (1–10)

Check your answers.

*Exercise 4 Long–short vowel contrasts*

Listen and repeat (words in spelling):

| iː and | ɪ | ɑː and | ʌ | ɑː and | æ |
|---|---|---|---|---|---|
| feel | fill | calm | come | part | pat |
| bead | bid | cart | cut | lard | lad |
| steel | still | half | huff | calm | Cam |
| reed | rid | lark | luck | heart | hat |
| bean | bin | mast | must | harms | hams |

| ɔː and | ɒ | uː and | ʊ | ɜː and | ʌ | ɑː and | ɒ |
|---|---|---|---|---|---|---|---|
| caught | cot | pool | pull | hurt | hut | dark | dock |
| stork | stock | suit | soot | turn | ton | part | pot |
| short | shot | Luke | look | curt | cut | lark | lock |
| cord | cod | wooed | wood | girl | gull | balm | bomb |
| port | pot | fool | full | bird | bud | large | lodge |

*Exercise 5 Transcription*

Write the symbol for the vowel (long or short) you hear in each word. (1–10)

Check your answers.

## Diphthongs

*Exercise 6 Repetition*

Listen and repeat, making sure that the second part of the diphthong is weak.

| | | | |
|---|---|---|---|
| eɪ | | | |
| mate meɪt | made meɪd | main meɪn | mace meɪs |
| aɪ | | | |
| right raɪt | ride raɪd | rhyme raɪm | rice raɪs |
| ɔɪ | | | |
| quoit kɔɪt | buoyed bɔɪd | Boyne bɔɪn | Royce rɔɪs |
| əʊ | | | |
| coat kəʊt | code kəʊd | cone kəʊn | close kləʊs |
| aʊ | | | |
| gout gaʊt | loud laʊd | gown gaʊn | louse laʊs |
| ɪə | | | |
| | feared fɪəd | | fierce fɪəs |
| eə | | | |
| | cared keəd | cairn keən | scarce skeəs |
| ʊə | | | |
| | moored mʊəd | | |

*Exercise 7 Transcription*
Write the symbol for the diphthong you hear in each word. (1–12)

Check your answers.

**Tripthongs**

*Exercise 8 Repetition*
Listen and repeat:

| | | | |
|---|---|---|---|
| eɪə | layer leɪə | əʊə | lower ləʊə |
| aɪə | liar laɪə | aʊə | tower taʊə |
| ɔɪə | loyal lɔɪəl | | |

## Audio Unit 4 Plosives

*Exercise 1 Repetition of initial plosives*
INITIAL FORTIS p, t, k
Each word begins with a fortis plosive; notice that the plosive is aspirated. Listen and repeat:

| | |
|---|---|
| paw pɔː | care keə |
| tea tiː | two tuː |
| car kɑː | key kiː |
| pie paɪ | tar tɑː |
| toe təʊ | pay peɪ |

INITIAL LENIS b, d, g

Each word begins with a lenis plosive; notice that there is practically no voicing of the plosive. Listen and repeat:

| | |
|---|---|
| bee biː | gear gɪə |
| door dɔː | boy bɔɪ |
| go gəʊ | dear dɪə |
| bear beə | bough baʊ |
| do duː | day deɪ |

INITIAL sp, st, sk

The plosive must be unaspirated. Listen and repeat:

| | |
|---|---|
| spy spaɪ | score skɔː |
| store stɔː | spear spɪə |
| ski skiː | stay steɪ |
| spare speə | sky skaɪ |
| steer stɪə | spar spɑː |

### *Exercise 2 Repetition of final plosives*

In the pairs of words in this exercise one word ends with a fortis plosive and the other ends with a lenis plosive. Notice the length difference in the vowel. Listen to each pair and repeat:

FORTIS FOLLOWED BY LENIS

| | |
|---|---|
| mate made | meɪt meɪd |
| rope robe | rəʊp rəʊb |
| leak league | liːk liːg |
| cart card | kɑːt kɑːd |
| back bag | bæk bæg |

LENIS FOLLOWED BY FORTIS

| | |
|---|---|
| code coat | kəʊd kəʊt |
| bid bit | bɪd bɪt |
| lobe lope | ləʊb ləʊp |
| heard hurt | hɜːd hɜːt |
| brogue broke | brəʊg brəʊk |

### *Exercise 3 Identification of final plosives*

a) You will hear the twenty words of Exercise 2. Each will be one of a pair. You must choose whether the word is the one ending with a fortis plosive or the one ending with a lenis plosive. When you hear the word, say "fortis" if you hear the word on the left, or "lenis" if you hear the word on the right. You will then hear the correct answer and the word will be said again for you to repeat.

*Example*: 'coat'

| Fortis | Lenis | Fortis | Lenis |
|---|---|---|---|
| coat kəʊt | code kəʊd | mate meɪt | made meɪd |
| leak liːk | league liːg | coat kəʊt | code kəʊd |
| hurt hɜːt | heard hɜːd | leak liːk | league liːg |
| bit bɪt | bid bɪd | rope rəʊp | robe rəʊb |
| mate meɪt | made meɪd | hurt hɜːt | heard hɜːd |
| lope ləʊp | lobe ləʊb | broke brəʊk | brogue brəʊg |
| back bæk | bag bæg | lope ləʊp | lobe ləʊb |
| cart kɑːt | card kɑːd | bit bɪt | bid bɪd |
| broke brəʊk | brogue brəʊg | back bæk | bag bæg |
| rope rəʊp | robe rəʊb | cart kɑːt | card kɑːd |

b) Each of the words which follow ends with a plosive. Write the symbol for each plosive when you hear the word. Each will be said twice. (1–10)

Check your answers.

### *Exercise 4 Repetition of words containing plosives*

The following words contain several plosives. They are given in spelling and in transcription. Listen and repeat:

potato pəteɪtəʊ
topic tɒpɪk
petticoat petɪkəʊt
partake pɑːteɪk
cupboard kʌbəd
decapitated dɪkæpɪteɪtɪd
pocket pɒkɪt

carpeted kɑːpɪtɪd
bodyguard bɒdigɑːd
tobacco təbækəʊ
doubted daʊtɪd
decode diːkəʊd
bigoted bɪgətɪd
about əbaʊt

### *Exercise 5 Reading of words in transcription*

When you hear the number, pronounce the word given in transcription taking care to pronounce the plosives correctly and putting the strongest stress on the syllable preceded by the stress mark ˈ. You will then hear the correct pronunciation, which you should repeat.

1 dɪˈbeɪt
2 ˈkɒpɪd
3 ˈbʌtəkʌp
4 ˈkʊkuː
5 dɪˈkeɪd
6 ˈgɑːdɪd
7 ˈdedɪkeɪtɪd
8 ˈpædək
9 buːˈtiːk
10 ˈæpɪtaɪt

(You will find these words in spelling form in the answers section.)

## Audio Unit 5 Revision

### *Exercise 1 Vowels and diphthongs*

Listen and repeat:

| ɑː | and ɜː | eɪ | and e | aɪ | and ɑː |
|---|---|---|---|---|---|
| barn | burn | fade | fed | life | laugh |
| are | err | sale | sell | tight | tart |
| fast | first | laid | led | pike | park |
| cart | curt | paste | pest | hide | hard |
| lark | lurk | late | let | spike | spark |

| ɔɪ | and ɔː | əʊ | and ɔː | ɪə | and iː |
|---|---|---|---|---|---|
| toy | tore | phone | fawn | fear | fee |
| coin | corn | boat | bought | beard | bead |
| boil | ball | code | cord | mere | me |
| boy | bore | stoke | stork | steered | steed |
| foil | fall | bowl | ball | peer | pea |

| eə | and eɪ | eə | and ɪə | ʊə | and ɔː |
|---|---|---|---|---|---|
| dare | day | fare | fear | poor | paw |
| stared | stayed | pair | pier | sure | shore |
| pairs | pays | stare | steer | moor | more |
| hair | hay | air | ear | dour | door |
| mare | may | snare | sneer | tour | tore |

### *Exercise 2 Triphthongs*

Listen and repeat:

| | | |
|---|---|---|
| eɪə | player | pleɪə |
| aɪə | tyre | taɪə |
| ɔɪə | loyal | lɔɪəl |
| əʊə | mower | məʊə |
| aʊə | shower | ʃaʊə |

### *Exercise 3 Transcription of words*

You should now be able to recognise all the vowels, diphthongs and triphthongs of English, and all the plosives. In the next exercise you will hear one-syllable English words composed of these sounds. Each word will be said twice. You must transcribe these words using the phonemic symbols that you have learned in the first three chapters. When you hear the word, write it with phonemic symbols. (1–20)

Now check your answers.

### *Exercise 4 Production*

The following are all English words; they are given only in phonemic transcription. When you hear the number you should say the word. You will then hear the correct pronunciation, which you should repeat. If you want to see how these words are spelt when you have finished the exercise, you will find them in the answers section.

| | | | |
|---|---|---|---|
| 1 | kiːp | 11 | dʌk |
| 2 | bəʊt | 12 | kəʊp |
| 3 | kʌp | 13 | dɒg |
| 4 | dɜːt | 14 | kaʊəd |
| 5 | baɪk | 15 | beɪk |
| 6 | kæb | 16 | taɪd |
| 7 | geɪt | 17 | bɪəd |
| 8 | keəd | 18 | pʊt |
| 9 | taɪəd | 19 | bʌg |
| 10 | bɜːd | 20 | daʊt |

*Exercise 5 Fortis/Lenis discrimination*

When you hear the word, say "fortis" if you hear it as ending with a fortis consonant, and "lenis" if you hear it as ending with a lenis consonant. You will then hear the correct answer and the word will be said again for you to repeat.

| | Fortis | Lenis |
|---|---|---|
| 1 | right raɪt | ride raɪd |
| 2 | bat bæt | bad bæd |
| 3 | bet bet | bed bed |
| 4 | leak liːk | league liːg |
| 5 | feet fiːt | feed fiːd |
| 6 | right raɪt | ride raɪd |
| 7 | tack tæk | tag tæg |
| 8 | rope rəʊp | robe rəʊb |
| 9 | mate meɪt | made meɪd |
| 10 | beat biːt | bead biːd |

## Audio Unit 6 Fricatives and affricates

*Exercise 1 Repetition of words containing fricatives*

Listen and repeat (words given in spelling and transcription):

| | | | |
|---|---|---|---|
| f | fin fɪn | offer ɒfə | laugh lɑːf |
| v | vat væt | over əʊvə | leave liːv |
| θ | thing θɪŋ | method meθəd | breath breθ |
| ð | these ðiːz | other ʌðə | breathe briːð |
| s | sad sæd | lesser lesə | moss mɒs |
| z | zoo zuː | lazy leɪzi | lose luːz |
| ʃ | show ʃəʊ | washing wɒʃɪŋ | rush rʌʃ |

| | | |
|---|---|---|
| ʒ | measure meʒə | rouge ruːʒ |
| h hot hɒt | beehive biːhaɪv | |

*Exercise 2 Identification*

Write the symbol for the fricative you hear in each word.

a) initial position (1–5)
b) medial position (6–10)
c) final position (11–15)

Now check your answers.

*Exercise 3 Production*

When you hear the number, pronounce the word, giving particular attention to the fricatives. You will then hear the correct pronunciation, which you should repeat.

| | |
|---|---|
| 1 ðiːz these | 6 fɪfθ fifth |
| 2 feɪθ faith | 7 ʃɪvəz shivers |
| 3 heðə heather | 8 bɪheɪv behave |
| 4 siːʃɔː seashore | 9 siːʒə seizure |
| 5 feðəz feathers | 10 læʃɪz lashes |

*Exercise 4 Repetition of fricative and affricate pairs*

Listen and repeat:

a) Initial ʃ and tʃ
ʃɒp tʃɒp (shop, chop)
ʃiːt tʃiːt (sheet, cheat)
ʃuːz tʃuːz (shoes, choose)

b) Medial ʃ and tʃ
liːʃɪz liːtʃɪz (leashes, leeches)
wɒʃɪŋ wɒtʃɪŋ (washing, watching)
bæʃɪz bætʃɪz (bashes, batches)

c) Final ʃ and tʃ
mæʃ mætʃ (mash, match)
kæʃ kætʃ (cash, catch)
wɪʃ wɪtʃ (wish, witch)

d) Medial ʒ and dʒ
leʒə ledʒə (leisure, ledger)
pleʒə pledʒə (pleasure, pledger)
liːʒən liːdʒən (lesion, legion)

*Exercise 5 Discrimination between fricatives and affricates*

You will hear some of the words from Exercise 4. When you hear the word, say “A” if you hear the word on the left, or “B” if you hear the word on the right. You will then hear the correct answer and the word will be said again for you to repeat.

| A | B |
|---|---|
| ʃɒp | tʃɒp |
| kæʃ | kætʃ |
| wɒʃɪŋ | wɒtʃɪŋ |
| ʃuːz | tʃuːz |
| liːʒən | liːdʒən |
| bæʃɪz | bætʃɪz |
| ʃiːt | tʃiːt |
| leʒə | ledʒə |
| liːʃɪz | liːtʃɪz |
| wɪʃ | wɪtʃ |
| pleʒə | pledʒə |
| mæʃ | mætʃ |

*Exercise 6 Repetition of sentences containing fricatives and affricates*
Listen and repeat:

1 See the size of the fish — siː ðə saɪz əv ðə fɪʃ
2 Jeff chose four sausages — dʒef tʃəʊz fɔː sɒsɪdʒɪz
3 The view is the chief feature — ðə vjuː ɪz ðə tʃiːf fiːtʃə
4 She has five choices — ʃi hæz faɪv tʃɔɪsɪz
5 I watch the house for Suzie — aɪ wɒtʃ ðə haʊs fə suːzi
6 Save this cheese for the chef — seɪv ðɪs tʃiːz fə ðə ʃef

## Audio Unit 7 Further consonants

*Exercise 1 Repetition of words containing a velar nasal*
Listen and repeat; take care not to pronounce a plosive after the velar nasal.

| | |
|---|---|
| hæŋ | hæŋə |
| sɪŋɪŋ | rɒŋ |
| rʌŋ | bæŋɪŋ |
| θɪŋ | rɪŋ |

*Exercise 2 Velar nasal with and without* g
WORDS OF ONE MORPHEME
Listen and repeat:

| | |
|---|---|
| fɪŋgə | finger |
| æŋgə | anger |
| bæŋgə | Bangor |
| hʌŋgə | hunger |
| æŋgl̩ | angle |

WORDS OF TWO MORPHEMES
Listen and repeat:

| | |
|---|---|
| sɪŋə | singer |
| hæŋə | hanger |
| lɒŋɪŋ | longing |
| rɪŋɪŋ | ringing |
| bæŋə | banger |

***Exercise 3 "Clear" and "dark"*** l

"CLEAR l" BEFORE VOWELS
Listen and repeat:

| | |
|---|---|
| laɪ lie | ləʊ low |
| luːs loose | laʊd loud |
| liːk leak | lɔː law |

"DARK l" BEFORE PAUSE
Listen and repeat:

| | |
|---|---|
| fɪl fill | peɪl pale |
| bel bell | maɪl mile |
| niːl kneel | kɪl kill |

"DARK l" BEFORE CONSONANTS
Listen and repeat:

| | |
|---|---|
| help help | feɪld failed |
| fɪlθ filth | mɪlk milk |
| belt belt | welʃ Welsh |

***Exercise 4*** r

Listen and repeat, concentrating on not allowing the tongue to make contact with the roof of the mouth in pronouncing this consonant:

| | |
|---|---|
| eərɪŋ airing | reərə rarer |
| riːraɪt rewrite | herɪŋ herring |
| terərɪst terrorist | mɪrə mirror |
| ærəʊ arrow | rɔːrɪŋ roaring |

***Exercise 5*** j ***and*** w

Listen and repeat:

| | |
|---|---|
| juː you | weɪ way |
| jɔːn yawn | wɔː war |
| jɪə year | wɪn win |
| jʊə your | weə wear |

*Exercise 6 Dictation of words*
When you hear the word, write it down using phonemic symbols. Each word will be said three times; you should pause the CD if you need more time for writing. (1–12)

Check your answers.

*Exercise 7 Repetition of sentences with nasal consonants and* l, r, w, j
Listen and repeat:

| | | |
|---|---|---|
| 1 | One woman was the winner | wʌn wʊmən wəz ðə wɪnə |
| 2 | I'm on a really new liner | aɪm ɒn ə rɪəli njuː laɪnə |
| 3 | Will you learn rowing | wɪl ju lɜːn rəʊɪŋ |
| 4 | No way will Mary marry you | nəʊ weɪ wɪl meəri mæri juː |
| 5 | We were away a year | wi wər əweɪ ə jɪə |
| 6 | Wear the yellow woollen one | weə ðə jeləʊ wʊlən wʌn |

## Audio Unit 8 Consonant clusters

*Exercise 1 Devoicing of* l, r, w, j
When l, r, w, j follow p, t or k in syllable-initial position they are produced as voiceless, slightly fricative sounds.
Listen and repeat:

| | | |
|---|---|---|
| pleɪ play | treɪ tray | klɪə clear |
| preɪ pray | twɪn twin | kraɪ cry |
| pjuː pew | tjuːn tune | kjuː queue |

*Exercise 2 Repetition of initial clusters*
TWO CONSONANTS
Listen and repeat:

| | |
|---|---|
| spɒt spot | plaʊ plough |
| stəʊn stone | twɪst twist |
| skeɪt skate | kriːm cream |
| sfɪə sphere | pjʊə pure |
| smaɪl smile | fleɪm flame |
| snəʊ snow | ʃrɪŋk shrink |
| slæm slam | vjuː view |
| swɪtʃ switch | θwɔːt thwart |

THREE CONSONANTS
Listen and repeat:

| | | |
|---|---|---|
| spleɪ splay | streɪ stray | skruː screw |
| spreɪ spray | stjuː stew | skwɒʃ squash |
| spjuː spew | | skjuː skew |

### *Exercise 3 Final plosive-plus-plosive clusters*

a) When one plosive is followed by another at the end of a syllable, the second plosive is usually the only one that can be clearly heard. In this exercise, take care not to make an audible release of the first plosive.
Listen and repeat:

| | |
|---|---|
| pækt packed | rɪgd rigged |
| bægd bagged | dʌkt duct |
| drɒpt dropped | lept leapt |
| rɒbd robbed | græbd grabbed |

b) It is difficult to hear the difference between, for example, 'dropped back' and 'drop back', since in the normal pronunciation only the last plosive of the cluster (the b of bæk) is audibly released. The main difference is that the three-consonant cluster is longer.
Listen and repeat:

| A | B |
|---|---|
| græbd bəʊθ grabbed both | græb bəʊθ grab both |
| laɪkt ðəm liked them | laɪk ðəm like them |
| hɒpt bæk hopped back | hɒp bæk hop back |
| lʊkt fɔːwəd looked forward | lʊk fɔːwəd look forward |
| pegd daʊn pegged down | peg daʊn peg down |
| wɪpt kriːm whipped cream | wɪp kriːm whip cream |

### *Exercise 4 Recognition*

Look at the items of Exercise 3(b) above. When you hear one of them, say "A" if you hear an item from the left-hand column, or "B" if you hear one from the right-hand column. You will then hear the correct answer and the item will be said again for you to repeat. (1–6)

### *Exercise 5 Final clusters of three or four consonants*

Listen and repeat:

| | |
|---|---|
| helps helps | nekst next |
| sɪksθ sixth | reɪndʒd ranged |
| θæŋkt thanked | rɪsks risks |
| edʒd edged | riːtʃt reached |
| twelfθs twelfths | teksts texts |

### *Exercise 6 Pronouncing consonant clusters*

When you hear the number, say the word. You will then hear the correct pronunciation, which you should repeat.

| | |
|---|---|
| 1 skreɪpt | 3 kləʊðz |
| 2 grʌdʒd | 4 skrɪpts |

5 krʌnʃt
6 θrəʊnz
7 plʌndʒd
8 kwenʃ

(The spelling of these words is given in the answers section.)

*Exercise 7 Repetition of sentences with consonant clusters*

Listen and repeat:

1 Strong trucks climb steep gradients strɒŋ trʌks klaɪm stiːp greɪdiənts
2 He cycled from Sloane Square through Knightsbridge hi saɪkl̩d frəm sləʊn skweə θruː naɪtsbrɪdʒ
3 Old texts rescued from the floods were preserved əʊld teksts reskjuːd frəm ðə flʌdz wə prɪzɜːvd
4 Six extra trays of drinks were spread around sɪks ekstrə treɪz əv drɪŋks wə spred əraʊnd
5 Thick snowdrifts had grown swiftly θɪk snəʊdrɪfts əd grəʊn swɪftli
6 Spring prompts flowers to grow sprɪŋ prɒmpts flaʊəz tə grəʊ

## Audio Unit 9 Weak syllables

*Exercise 1 "Schwa"*

TWO-SYLLABLE WORDS WITH WEAK FIRST SYLLABLE AND STRESS ON THE SECOND SYLLABLE

Listen and repeat:

Weak syllable spelt 'a'

| | | |
|---|---|---|
| about ə'baʊt | ahead ə'hed | again ə'gen |

Spelt 'o'

| | | |
|---|---|---|
| obtuse əb'tjuːs | oppose ə'pəʊz | offend ə'fend |

Spelt 'u'

| | | |
|---|---|---|
| suppose sə'pəʊz | support sə'pɔːt | suggest sə'dʒest |

Spelt 'or'

| | | |
|---|---|---|
| forget fə'get | forsake fə'seɪk | forbid fə'bɪd |

Spelt 'er'

| | | |
|---|---|---|
| perhaps pə'hæps | per cent pə'sent | perceive pə'siːv |

Spelt 'ur'

| | | |
|---|---|---|
| survive sə'vaɪv | surprise sə'praɪz | survey (verb) sə'veɪ |

TWO-SYLLABLE WORDS WITH WEAK SECOND SYLLABLE AND STRESS ON THE FIRST SYLLABLE

Listen and repeat:

Weak syllable spelt 'a'

| | | |
|---|---|---|
| ballad 'bæləd | Alan 'ælən | necklace 'nekləs |

Spelt 'o'

| | | |
|---|---|---|
| melon 'melən | paddock 'pædək | purpose 'pɜːpəs |

| | | |
|---|---|---|
| Spelt 'e' | | |
| hundred ˈhʌndrəd | sullen ˈsʌlən | open ˈəʊpən |
| Spelt 'u' | | |
| circus ˈsɜːkəs | autumn ˈɔːtəm | album ˈælbəm |
| Spelt 'ar' | | |
| tankard ˈtæŋkəd | custard ˈkʌstəd | standard ˈstændəd |
| Spelt 'or' | | |
| juror ˈðʒʊərə | major ˈmeɪdʒə | manor ˈmænə |
| Spelt 'er' | | |
| longer ˈlɒŋgə | eastern ˈiːstən | mother ˈmʌðə |
| Spelt 'ure' | | |
| nature ˈneɪtʃə | posture ˈpɒstʃə | creature ˈkriːtʃə |
| Spelt 'ous' | | |
| ferrous ˈferəs | vicious ˈvɪʃəs | gracious ˈgreɪʃəs |
| Spelt 'ough' | | |
| thorough ˈθʌrə | borough ˈbʌrə | |
| Spelt 'our' | | |
| saviour ˈseɪvjə | succour ˈsʌkə | colour ˈkʌlə |

THREE-SYLLABLE WORDS WITH WEAK SECOND SYLLABLE AND STRESS ON THE FIRST SYLLABLE

Listen and repeat:

| | |
|---|---|
| Weak syllable spelt 'a' | |
| workaday ˈwɜːkədeɪ | roundabout ˈraʊndəbaʊt |
| Spelt 'o' | |
| customer ˈkʌstəmə | pantomime ˈpæntəmaɪm |
| Spelt 'u' | |
| perjury ˈpɜːdʒəri | venturer ˈventʃərə |
| Spelt 'ar' | |
| standardise ˈstændədaɪz | jeopardy ˈdʒepədi |
| Spelt 'er' | |
| wonderland ˈwʌndəlænd | yesterday ˈjestədeɪ |

***Exercise 2 Close front vowels***

WEAK INITIAL SYLLABLES

Listen and repeat:

| | |
|---|---|
| excite ɪkˈsaɪt | resume rɪˈzjuːm |
| exist ɪgˈzɪst | relate rɪˈleɪt |
| inane ɪˈneɪn | effect ɪˈfekt |
| device dɪˈvaɪs | ellipse ɪˈlɪps |

WEAK FINAL SYLLABLES

Listen and repeat:

| | |
|---|---|
| city ˈsɪti | many ˈmeni |
| funny ˈfʌni | lazy ˈleɪzi |
| easy ˈiːzi | only ˈəʊnli |
| busy ˈbɪzi | lady ˈleɪdi |

*Exercise 3 Syllabic* l

Listen and repeat:

| | | |
|---|---|---|
| bottle ˈbɒtl̩ | bottled ˈbɒtl̩d | bottling ˈbɒtl̩ɪŋ |
| muddle ˈmʌdl̩ | muddled ˈmʌdl̩d | muddling ˈmʌdl̩ɪŋ |
| tunnel ˈtʌnl̩ | tunnelled ˈtʌnl̩d | tunnelling ˈtʌnl̩ɪŋ |
| wrestle ˈresl̩ | wrestled ˈresl̩d | wrestling ˈresl̩ɪŋ |

*Exercise 4 Syllabic* n

Listen and repeat:

| | | |
|---|---|---|
| burden ˈbɜːdn̩ | burdened ˈbɜːdn̩d | burdening ˈbɜːdn̩ɪŋ |
| frighten ˈfraɪtn̩ | frightened ˈfraɪtn̩d | frightening ˈfraɪtn̩ɪŋ |
| listen ˈlɪsn̩ | listened ˈlɪsn̩d | listening ˈlɪsn̩ɪŋ |

*Exercise 5 Transcription*

Transcribe the following words when you hear them, giving particular attention to the weak syllables. Each word will be said twice. If you need more time for writing, pause the CD and restart it when you are ready for the next word. (1–10)

Now check your answers.

## Audio Unit 10 Word stress

*Exercise 1 Stress marking*

When you hear the word, repeat it, then place a stress mark (ˈ) before the stressed syllable.

| | |
|---|---|
| enəmi enemy | səbtrækt subtract |
| kəlekt collect | elɪfənt elephant |
| kæpɪtl̩ capital | əbzɜːvə observer |
| kɑːneɪʃn̩ carnation | prɒfɪt profit |
| pærədaɪs paradise | entəteɪn entertain |

Now check your marking with the correct version.

*Exercise 2 Pronouncing from transcription*

The following are British place names. When you hear the number, pronounce them with the stress as marked. You will then hear the correct pronunciation, which you should repeat.

| | |
|---|---|
| 1 'ʃrəʊzbr̩i | 6 'bɜːmɪŋəm |
| 2 pɒl'perəʊ | 7 ˌnɔː'θæmptən |
| 3 ˌæbə'diːn | 8 dʌn'diː |
| 4 ˌwʊlvə'hæmptən | 9 'kæntəbr̩i |
| 5 ˌæbə'rɪstwəθ | 10 'beɪzɪŋstəʊk |

(The spelling for these names is given in the answers section.)

### *Exercise 3 Placing stress on verbs, adjectives and nouns*

When you hear the number, pronounce the word with the appropriate stress. You will then hear the correct pronunciation, which you should repeat.

TWO-SYLLABLE WORDS

VERBS

| | |
|---|---|
| 1 dɪsiːv deceive | 6 əbdʒekt object |
| 2 ʃɑːpən sharpen | 7 kɒŋkə conquer |
| 3 kəlekt collect | 8 rɪkɔːd record |
| 4 prənaʊns pronounce | 9 pɒlɪʃ polish |
| 5 kɒpi copy | 10 dɪpend depend |

ADJECTIVES

| | |
|---|---|
| 1 iːzi easy | 6 jeləʊ yellow |
| 2 kəmpliːt complete | 7 ɜːli early |
| 3 meɪdʒə major | 8 səblaɪm sublime |
| 4 ələʊn alone | 9 hevi heavy |
| 5 bɪləʊ below | 10 əlaɪv alive |

NOUNS

| | |
|---|---|
| 1 bɪʃəp bishop | 6 ɒfɪs office |
| 2 æspekt aspect | 7 əreɪ array |
| 3 əfeə affair | 8 pətrəʊl patrol |
| 4 kɑːpɪt carpet | 9 dentɪst dentist |
| 5 dɪfiːt defeat | 10 ɔːtəm autumn |

THREE-SYLLABLE WORDS

VERBS

| | |
|---|---|
| 1 entəteɪn entertain | 6 ɪlɪsɪt elicit |
| 2 rezərekt resurrect | 7 kɒməndɪə commandeer |
| 3 əbændən abandon | 8 ɪmædʒɪn imagine |
| 4 dɪlɪvə deliver | 9 dɪtɜːmɪn determine |
| 5 ɪntərʌpt interrupt | 10 sepəreɪt separate |

ADJECTIVES

1 ɪmpɔːtn̩t important
2 ɪnɔːməs enormous
3 derəlɪkt derelict
4 desɪml̩ decimal
5 æbnɔːməl abnormal
6 ɪnsl̩ənt insolent
7 fæntæstɪk fantastic
8 negətɪv negative
9 ækjərət accurate
10 ʌnlaɪkli unlikely

NOUNS

1 fɜːnɪtʃə furniture
2 dɪzɑːstə disaster
3 dɪsaɪpl̩ disciple
4 æmbjələns ambulance
5 kwɒntəti quantity
6 kəθiːdrəl cathedral
7 hɒləkɔːst holocaust
8 trænzɪstə transistor
9 æksɪdn̩t accident
10 təmɑːtəʊ tomato

## Audio Unit 11 Complex word stress

### *Exercise 1 Stress-carrying suffixes*

a) When you hear the number, pronounce the word with stress on the suffix. You will then hear the correct pronunciation, which you should repeat.

1 -ain: entertain ˌentə'teɪn
2 -ee: refugee ˌrefjʊ'dʒiː
3 -eer: mountaineer ˌmaʊntɪ'nɪə
4 -ese: Portuguese ˌpɔːtʃə'giːz
5 -ette: cigarette ˌsɪgr̩'et
6 -esque: picturesque ˌpɪktʃr̩'esk

b) When you hear the stem word, say the word with the given suffix, putting the stress on that suffix. In these examples, a secondary stress comes on the penultimate syllable of the stem.

employ+-ee
engine+-eer (engineer)
Sudan+-ese
usher+-ette
absent+-ee
profit+-eer
Pekin+-ese
statue+-ette (statuette)

### *Exercise 2 Neutral suffixes*

When you hear the stem word, add the suffix, without changing the stress.

comfort+-able
anchor+-age
refuse+-al (refusal)
wide+-en (widen)
wonder+-ful
amaze+-ing (amazing)
devil+-ish
bird+-like
power+-less
hurried+-ly
punish+-ment
yellow+-ness
poison+-ous
glory+-fy (glorify)
other+-wise
fun+-y (funny)

### *Exercise 3 Stress-moving suffixes*

When you hear the stem word, say it with the suffix added and put the stress on the last syllable of the stem.

| | |
|---|---|
| advantage+-ous | injure+-ious (injurious) |
| photo+-graphy | tranquil+-ity (tranquillity) |
| proverb+-ial | reflex+-ive |
| climate+ -ic (climatic) | embryo+-logy |

### *Exercise 4 Compound words*

When you hear the number, say the item.

a) First element adjectival, stress on second element

| | |
|---|---|
| 1 loudspeaker | 4 second-class |
| 2 bad-tempered | 5 three-wheeler |
| 3 headquarters | |

b) First element nominal, stress on first element

| | |
|---|---|
| 1 typewriter | 4 suitcase |
| 2 car ferry | 5 teacup |
| 3 sunrise | |

c) Mixture of types (a) and (b)

| | |
|---|---|
| 1 long-suffering | 4 red-blooded |
| 2 gunman | 5 gearbox |
| 3 shoelace | 6 overweight |

### *Exercise 5 Word-class pairs*

You will hear the number of the item and its word-class. Stress the second syllable if it is a verb; stress the first syllable if it is a noun or adjective.

| | |
|---|---|
| 1 abstract (adjective) | 10 object (noun) |
| 2 conduct (verb) | 11 perfect (adjective) |
| 3 contract (noun) | 12 permit (verb) |
| 4 contrast (verb) | 13 present (adjective) |
| 5 desert (noun) | 14 produce (verb) |
| 6 escort (noun) | 15 protest (noun) |
| 7 export (verb) | 16 rebel (verb) |
| 8 import (noun) | 17 record (noun) |
| 9 insult (verb) | 18 subject (noun) |

## Audio Unit 12 Weak forms

Words occurring in their weak forms are printed in smaller type than stressed words and strong forms, for example:

ˈwe can ˈwait  ˈwiː kən ˈweɪt

*Exercise 1 Sentences for repetition*

Listen and repeat:

We can ˈwait for the ˈbus wi kən ˈweɪt fə ðə ˈbʌs
ˈHow do the ˈlights ˈwork? ˈhaʊ də ðə ˈlaɪts ˈwɜːk
There are some ˈnew ˈbooks I must ˈread ðər ə səm ˈnjuː ˈbʊks aɪ məs ˈriːd
She ˈtook her ˈaunt for a ˈdrive ʃi ˈtʊk ər ˈɑːnt fər ə ˈdraɪv
The ˈbasket was ˈfull of ˈthings to ˈeat ðə ˈbɑːskɪt wəz ˈfʊl əv ˈθɪŋz tu ˈiːt
ˈWhy should a ˈman ˈearn ˈmore than a ˈwoman? ˈwaɪ ʃəd ə ˈmæn ˈɜːn ˈmɔː ðən ə ˈwʊmən
You ˈought to ˈhave your ˈown ˈcar ju ˈɔːt tə ˈhæv jər ˈəʊn ˈkɑː
He ˈwants to ˈcome and ˈsee us at ˈhome hi ˈwɒnts tə ˈkʌm ən ˈsiː əs ət ˈhəʊm
ˈHave you ˈtaken them from ˈthat ˈbox? ˈhæv ju ˈteɪkən ðəm frəm ˈðæt ˈbɒks
It's ˈtrue that he was ˈlate, but his ˈcar could have ˈbroken ˈdown ɪts ˈtruː ðət i wəz ˈleɪt bət ɪz ˈkɑː kəd əv ˈbrəʊkən ˈdaʊn
I shall ˈtake as ˈmuch as I ˈwant aɪ ʃl̩ ˈteɪk əz ˈmʌtʃ əz aɪ ˈwɒnt
ˈWhy am I ˈtoo ˈlate to ˈsee him toˈday? ˈwaɪ əm aɪ ˈtuː ˈleɪt tə ˈsiː ɪm təˈdeɪ

*Exercise 2 Weak forms with pre-vocalic and pre-consonantal forms*

DIFFERENT VOWELS

When you hear the number, say the phrase, using the appropriate weak form:

| | | |
|---|---|---|
| the | 1 the apple ði æpl̩ | 2 the pear ðə peə |
| to | 3 to Edinburgh tu edn̩brə | 4 to Leeds tə liːdz |
| do | 5 so do I səʊ du aɪ | 6 so do they səʊ də ðeɪ |

LINKING CONSONANT

| | | |
|---|---|---|
| a/an | 7 an ear ən ɪə | 8 a foot ə fʊt |

(The other words in this section have "linking r".)

| | | |
|---|---|---|
| her | 9 her eyes hər aɪz | 10 her nose hə nəʊz |
| your | 11 your uncle jər ʌŋkl̩ | 12 your friend jə frend |
| for | 13 for Alan fər ælən | 14 for Mike fə maɪk |
| there | 15 there aren't ðər ɑːnt | 16 there couldn't ðə kʊdn̩t |
| are | 17 these are ours ðiːz ər aʊəz | 18 these are mine ðiːz ə maɪn |
| were | 19 you were out juː wər aʊt | 20 you were there juː wə ðeə |

*Exercise 3 Transcription*

(*Note:* this exercise is a long one, and it is possible to go directly to Exercise 4 if you wish.)

Write the following sentences in transcription, taking care to give the correct weak forms for the words printed in smaller type.

1 ˈLeave the ˈrest of the ˈfood for ˈlunch
2 ˈAren't there some ˈletters for her to ˈopen?
3 ˈWhere do the ˈeggs ˈcome from?
4 ˈRead his ˈbook and ˈwrite some ˈnotes
5 At ˈleast we can ˈtry and ˈhelp

Now correct your transcription, using the version in the answers section.

*Exercise 4 Pronunciation of weak forms*

This exercise uses the sentences of Exercise 3. When you hear the number, say the sentence, giving particular attention to the weak forms. (1–5)

## Audio Unit 13 Revision

*Exercise 1 Reading unfamiliar words from transcription*

The following are British place names written in transcription*. When you hear the number, say the word, making sure that the stress is correctly placed. You will then hear the correct pronunciation, which you should repeat.

1 ˈkəʊltʃɪstə
2 kɑːˈlaɪl
3 ˈherɪfəd
4 ˈskʌnθɔːp
5 gləˈmɔːgən
6 ˌhɒliˈhed
7 ˈfræmlɪŋəm
8 saʊθˈend
9 ˈtʃeltn̩əm
10 ˌɪnvəˈnes

*Exercise 2 Transcription of unfamiliar words*

The following are also place names. Each will be said twice; write what you hear in transcription, including stress marks. (1–10)

Now check your transcriptions with the correct version.

*Exercise 3 Stress placement in sentences*

Put a stress mark ˈ before each syllable you would expect to be stressed in the following sentences. For example, given the sentence 'I think I'll be late for work' you should mark the words 'think', 'late' and 'work' like this:

I ˈthink Ill be ˈlate for ˈwork

* Spelling is given in the Answers section.

1 James decided to type the letter himself
2 The plane was approaching the runway at high speed
3 Try to see the other persons point of view
4 You put your brakes on when the light turns to red
5 In a short time the house was full of children

Now correct your stress marking by looking at the versions given in the answers section.

### *Exercise 4 Pronunciation of stressed syllables*

When you hear the number, say the sentence from the list in Exercise 3, taking care to stress the correct syllables. You will then hear the correct version, which you should repeat. (1–5)

### *Exercise 5 Weak forms*

In the following sentences, those words which are not stressed must be pronounced in their weak forms. When you hear the number, say the sentence:

1 ˈHeres a ˈpresent for your ˈbrother
2 ˈThese are ˈall the ˈpictures that are ˈleft
3 There ˈcould be a ˈbit of ˈrain at the ˈend of the ˈmorning
4 A ˈfew ˈpeople ˈasked him a ˈquestion
5 Coˈllect your ˈluggage beˈfore ˈleaving the ˈtrain

## Audio Unit 14 Elisions and rhythm

### *Exercise 1 Rhythm and the foot*

Listen to the following sentences. Put a stress mark ˈ on each stressed syllable, then divide the sentences into feet by placing a dotted line ┆ at each foot boundary.
*Example:* ┆ ˈCome to the ┆ ˈparty on ┆ ˈMonday ┆ ˈevening ┆

1 Each person in the group was trained in survival
2 About three hundred soldiers were lined up
3 Buying a new computer is a major expense
4 All the people who came to the wedding were from England
5 Try to be as tactful as you can when you talk to him

### *Exercise 2 Elisions*

### *Read this before starting this exercise*

This Audio Unit gives you practice in recognising places where elision occurs in natural speech (i.e. where one or more phonemes which would be pronounced in careful speech are not pronounced). The examples are extracted from dialogues between speakers who are discussing differences between two similar pictures. Each extract is given three times. You must transcribe each item, using phonemic symbols so that the elision can be seen in the transcription. For example, if you heard ‘sixth time’ pronounced without the θ fricative at the end of the first word you would write sɪks taɪm, and the elision would be clearly indicated in this way. You can use the ʰ symbol to indicate a devoiced weak vowel, as in ‘potato’ pʰteɪtəʊ.

You will probably need to pause your CD or tape to give yourself more time to write the transcription. This is a difficult exercise, but explanatory notes are given in the answers section.

*Transcription*
ONE ELISION

1 a beautiful girl
2 we seem to have a definite one there
3 could it be a stool rather than a table
4 a fifth in
5 any peculiarities about that
6 and how many stripes on yours
7 well it appears to button up its got three
8 or the what do you call it the sill

TWO ELISIONS

9 by column into columns all right
10 diamond shaped patch
11 and I should think from experience of kitchen knives
12 what shall we do next go down

THREE ELISIONS

13 the top of the bottle is projecting outwards into the room

Now check your transcriptions.

## Audio Unit 15 Tones

### *Exercise 1 Repetition of tones*
Listen and repeat:

| | | | | |
|---|---|---|---|---|
| Fall: | ╲yes | ╲no | ╲well | ╲four |
| Rise: | ╱yes | ╱no | ╱well | ╱four |
| Fall–rise: | ∨yes | ∨no | ∨well | ∨four |
| Rise–fall: | ∧yes | ∧no | ∧well | ∧four |
| Level: | _yes | _no | _well | _four |

### *Exercise 2 Production of tones*
When you hear the number, say the syllable with the tone indicated:

1 ╱them
2 ╲why
3 ∨well

4 \John
5 /what
6 ∧no
7 \here
8 /you
9 /now
10 \end

***Exercise 3 Identification***

You will hear each syllable twice. Write an appropriate tone symbol. (1–10)

Now check your answers.

***Exercise 4 Repetition of tones on polysyllabic words***

Listen and repeat:

| | | | |
|---|---|---|---|
| Fall: | \obviously | de\lightful | maga\zine |
| Rise: | /positive | re/lated | disa/ppeared |
| Fall–rise: | ∨normally | a∨pparently | a∨round |
| Rise–fall: | ∧terrible | e∧normous | disa∧gree |

***Exercise 5 Production in context***

When you hear the sentence, say the response with the tone indicated.

| | |
|---|---|
| Hello, is that 661071? | /yes |
| Do you know any scientists? | ∨some |
| Keep away from that road! | \why |
| How many dogs have you got? | \two |
| Have you ever heard such a terrible thing? | ∧no |
| What colour is your car? | \red |
| Do you want my plate? | /please |
| Don't you like it? | ∨yes |
| You haven't seen my watch, have you? | /no |
| What was the weather like? | \wet |

## Audio Unit 16 The tone-unit

***Exercise 1 Identifying the tonic syllable***

Listen and repeat, then underline the tonic syllable.

1 We could go by bus
2 Of course its broken
3 The car was where Id left it
4 How much is the biggest one
5 I knew it would go wrong
6 It was too cold

7 Here it is
8 That was a loud noise
9 We could go from Manchester
10 Have you finished

Now check your answers.

*Exercise 2 Pronouncing the tonic syllable*
When you hear the number, say the item with the tonic syllable in the place indicated, using a falling tone:

1 Dont do that
2 Dont do that
3 Dont do that
4 Write your name
5 Write your name
6 Write your name
7 Heres my pen
8 Heres my pen
9 Heres my pen
10 Why dont you try
11 Why dont you try
12 Why dont you try
13 Why dont you try

*Exercise 3 Repetition of tone-units*
Listen and repeat, trying to copy the intonation exactly; no transcription is given.

What time will they come
A day return to London
The North Pole would be warmer
Have you decided to buy it
I recorded them on cassette

*Exercise 4 Partial analysis of tone-units*
The items of Exercise 3 will now be said again twice, and you must do the following things:

a) Identify the tonic syllable and underline it.
b) Identify the tone (in these items the only tones used are fall and rise) and place the appropriate tone mark before the tonic syllable.
c) Identify any stressed syllables preceding the tonic syllable and place a stress mark ˈ before each.

You may need to pause the CD to allow enough time to complete the analysis of each item.

1 What time will they come
2 A day return to London
3 The North Pole would be warmer
4 Have you decided to buy it
5 I recorded them on cassette

Now check your transcription.

***Exercise 5 Reading intonation transcription***
When you hear the number, read the sentence with the intonation indicated by the transcription.

1 'Is there a ⟋car ·park
2 'Meet me at the ⟍bus ·stop
3 It 'really 'isnt the ∨best
4 I⟍cycled to ·work
5 ⟋What was it ·called

## Audio Unit 17 Intonation

***Exercise 1 Repetition of tonic syllable plus tail***
Listen and repeat, taking care to continue the pitch movement of the tone over the tail:

| | | |
|---|---|---|
| ⟍Bill ·bought it | ⟍Four of them ·came | ⟍Why do you ·do it |
| ⟋Bill ·bought it | ⟋Four of them ·came | ⟋Why do you ·do it |
| ∨Bill ·bought it | ∨Four of them ·came | ∨Why do you ·do it |
| ∧Bill ·bought it | ∧Four of them ·came | ∧Why do you ·do it |

***Exercise 2 Production of tonic syllable plus tail***
The items from Exercise 1 will be used again. When you hear the number, say the item with the tone that is marked. (1–12)

***Exercise 3 High and low head***
The following tone-units will be repeated with high and low heads. Listen and repeat:

'Taxes have 'risen by 'five per ⟍cent
ˌTaxes have ˌrisen by ˌfive per ⟍cent

'Havent you 'asked the 'boss for ⟋more
ˌHavent you ˌasked the ˌboss for ⟋more

We 'dont have 'time to 'read the ⟍paper
We ˌdont have ˌtime to ˌread the ⟍paper

'Wouldnt you 'like to 'read it on the ⟋train
ˌWouldnt you ˌlike to ˌread it on the ⟋train

### *Exercise 4 Transcription of tone-units*

Each item will be pronounced as one tone-unit, and will be heard three times. You must do the following things:

a) Identify the tonic syllable and underline it.
b) Decide which tone it carries (only ╲, ╱ and ∨ are used in this exercise) and put the appropriate tone-mark before the tonic syllable.
c) Listen for stressed syllables preceding the tonic syllable and mark them high (ˈ) or low (ˌ).
d) Listen for stressed syllables in the tail and mark them (if there are any) with a raised dot (·).

You will probably need to pause the CD to complete the transcription of each item.

1 Now heres the weather forecast
2 You didnt say anything about rates
3 A few years ago they were top
4 No one could say the cinema was dead
5 Is there anything you wouldnt eat
6 Have you ever considered writing
7 That was what he claimed to be
8 We try to do our shopping in the market
9 But I never go there now
10 It wouldnt be difficult to find out

Now check your transcriptions. If there is time, you will find it useful to go back to the start of Exercise 4 and practise repeating the items while looking at the transcriptions.

## Audio Unit 18 Intonation: extracts from conversation

The following extracts are from the same recorded conversations as were used in Audio Unit 14. Each extract will be heard three times, with four or five seconds between repetitions. Mark the intonation; the instructions for how to do this are given in the text for Audio Unit 17, Exercise 4. In addition, for numbers 10–16 you will need to use the vertical line | to separate tone-units.

### *Transcription*

ONE TONE-UNIT

1 it looks like a French magazine
2 the television is plugged in
3 does your colander have a handle
4 a flap on it
5 you tell me about yours
6 well dark hair
7 more than halfway

8 but er not in the other corners
9 a sort of Daily Sketch format newspaper

TWO TONE-UNITS

10 on the top on the lid
11 well theyre on alternate steps theyre not on every step
12 what about the vent at the back
13 and a ladys handbag hanging on a nail on the wall
14 you do the left hand bit of the picture and Ill do the right hand bit
15 were being very particular but we just havent hit upon one of the differences yet

THREE TONE-UNITS

16 and what about your television two knobs in the front

Now check your intonation marking.

## Audio Unit 19 Further practice on connected speech

***Exercise 1 Dictation***

You will hear five sentences spoken rapidly. Each will be given three times. Write each sentence down in *normal spelling.* (1–5)

Compare what you have written with the correct version.

***Exercise 2 Transcription***

Now skip backwards on the CD and listen to the above sentences again; this time *transcribe* what you hear, using mainly phonemic symbols but also using raised h (ʰ) to indicate a weak voiceless vowel, as in 'potato' pʰteɪtəʊ. Do not mark intonation. (1–5)

***Exercise 3 Reading intonation***

When you hear the number, say the sentence with the intonation indicated. You will then hear the correct pronunciation, which you should repeat.

1 I ˌthought you were on ↘<u>holi</u>day this ·week
2 ∨<u>Some</u> ·day | Im ˌgoing to get ˌround to ˌmending the ↘<u>fuse</u>
3 There were a ↘<u>lot</u> | ˈnot just ˈone or ∨<u>two</u>
4 ˈDidnt ˈanyone ˈtry to ↗<u>stop</u> them
5 ˈLeave it till ˈafter youve ˈhad some ↗<u>tea</u> | ˌotherwise youll be ˌtoo ˌfull to ↘<u>eat</u>

***Exercise 4 Study passage***

The following passage will first be read as continuous speech, then each tone-unit will be heard separately, twice.

They're building wind farms all over the area where we live. We can see long lines of them along the tops of the hills, and down by the coast there are wind turbines out at sea and along the shore. They only build them where there's plenty of wind, obviously. We certainly get a lot of that near us. You could say the landscape's been completely transformed, but most people don't seem to mind.

a) Transcribe each tone-unit using phonemic symbols, but paying attention to connected-speech features such as elisions and assimilations.
b) Add intonation transcription to each tone-unit.

Check your transcription.

## Audio Unit 20 Transcription of connected speech

Listen to the recording on which this exercise is based:

it was rather frightening because there there are scores of these bicycles and er you really have to have your wits about you all the time because the you know they stop suddenly and it's awkward because the traffic regulations are more honoured in the breach than the observance I'm not in not really sure what regulations there are er for instance the er traffic lights red red lights do not apply if you're turning right erm which means that if you're coming up to a traffic light and there's erm someone stopped who wants to go straight on or turn left and you want to turn right then you pull out overtake them and then cut across in front

The above passage will now be heard divided up into 27 tone-units, each of which will be heard three times. Incomplete tone-units (those without a tonic syllable) are omitted. The main object of the exercise is to transcribe the intonation; however, for a harder exercise taking more time, you can also write a transcription using phonemic symbols plus any non-phonemic symbols you may need. The transcription given in the answers section is in this form.

it was rather frightening
because there there are scores
of these bicycles
you really have to
have your wits about you
all the time
because the you know they stop suddenly
its awkward
because the traffic regulations
are more honoured in the breach
than the observance
Im not in not really sure what
regulations there are
for instance
the er traffic lights
red red lights

do not apply
if youre turning right
which means that
if youre coming up to a traffic light
someone stopped
who wants to go straight on
or turn left
and you want to turn right
then you pull out
overtake them
and then cut across
in front

Now check your transcription.

# Answers to written exercises

## Chapter 1

1 i) BBC (BBC Pronunciation); ii) RP (Received Pronunciation); iii) GB (General British)
2 Accent is concerned only with pronunciation differences, while dialect refers to all language variation including grammatical and lexical factors.
3 stress
4 a) three (lʌv) b) three (hɑːf) c) four (rɪst)
d) five (ʃrɪŋk) e) two (ɔːt)

## Chapter 2

1 a) Soft palate or velum
b) Alveolar ridge
c) Front of tongue
d) Hard palate
e) Lower lip
2 a) Close back rounded
b) Close-mid front unrounded
c) Open front unrounded
d) Close front unrounded
e) Close-mid back rounded
3
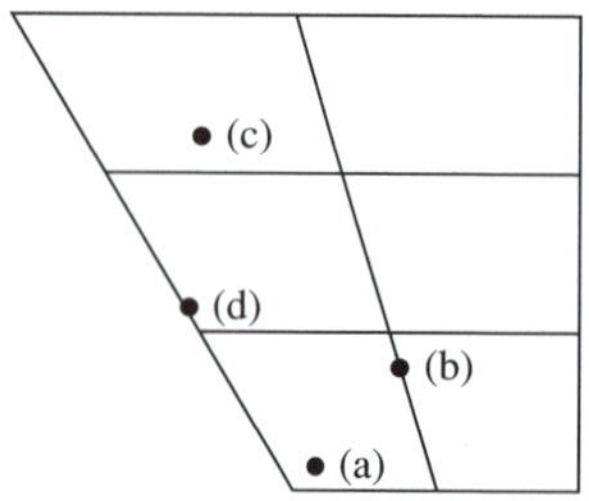

4 a) e e) ʊ
b) ʌ f) ɒ
c) ʊ g) æ
d) ɪ h) e

## Chapter 3

1

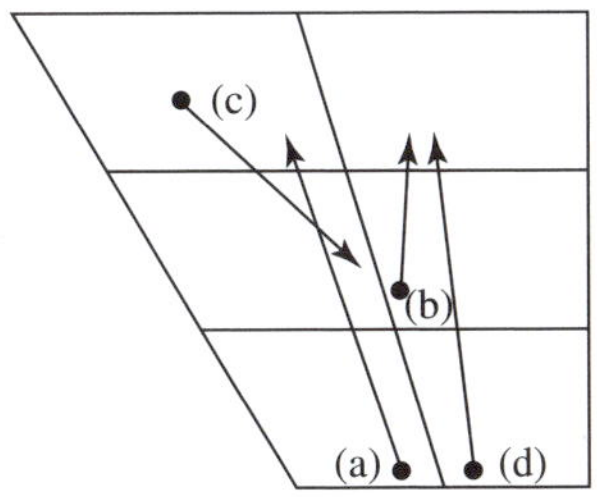


2 a) ɔː b) ɔː c) ɑː d) ɜː e) uː f) iː g) ɜː h) iː i) ɜː

3 a) əʊ b) aɪ c) aʊ d) eɪ e) ɪə f) ɔɪ g) eə h) aɪ i) eɪ

## Chapter 4

1 You will obviously not have written descriptions identical to the ones given below. The important thing is to check that the sequence of articulatory events is more or less the same.

a) goat

Starting from the position for normal breathing, the back of the tongue is raised to form a closure against the velum (soft palate). The lungs are compressed to produce higher air pressure in the vocal tract and the vocal folds are brought together in the voicing position. The vocal folds begin to vibrate, and the back of the tongue is lowered to allow the compressed air to escape. The tongue is moved to a mid-central vowel and then moves in the direction of a closer, backer vowel: the lips are moderately rounded for the second part. The tongue blade is raised to make a closure against the alveolar ridge, the vocal folds are separated and voicing ceases. Then the compressed air is released quietly and the lips return to an unrounded shape.

b) ape

The tongue is moved slightly upward and forward, and the vocal folds are brought together to begin voicing. The tongue glides to a slightly closer and more central vowel position. Then the lips are pressed together, making a closure, and at the same time the vocal folds are separated so that voicing ceases. The lips are then opened and the compressed air is released quietly, while the tongue is lowered to the position for normal breathing.

2 a) beɪk b) gəʊt c) daʊt d) bɔːt e) tɪk f) baʊ g) bɔːd h) gɑːd i) piː

## Chapter 5

| | | |
|---|---|---|
| a) speed | spiːd | [spiːd̥] |
| b) partake | pɑːteɪk | [pʰɑˑtʰeɪk] |
| c) book | bʊk | [b̥ʊ̆k] |
| d) goat | gəʊt | [g̊ə̆ʊt] |
| e) car | kɑː | [kʰɑː] |
| f) bad | bæd | [b̥æd̥] |
| g) appeared | əpɪəd | [əpʰɪəd̥] |
| h) toast | təʊst | [tʰə̆ʊst] |
| i) stalk | stɔːk | [stɔˑk] |

## Chapter 6

1 a) fɪʃɪz
b) ʃeɪvə
c) sɪksθ
d) ðiːz
e) ətʃiːv
f) ʌðəz
g) meʒə
h) əhed

2 Starting from the position for normal breathing, the lower lip is brought into contact with the upper teeth. The lungs are compressed, causing air to flow through the constriction, producing fricative noise. The tongue moves to the position for ɪ. The vocal folds are brought together, causing voicing to begin, and at the same time the lower lip is lowered. Then the tongue blade is raised to make a fairly wide constriction in the post-alveolar region and the vocal folds are separated to stop voicing; the flow of air causes fricative noise. Next, the vocal folds are brought together to begin voicing again and at the same time the tongue is lowered from the constriction position into the ɪ vowel posture. The tongue blade is then raised against the alveolar ridge, forming a constriction which results in fricative noise. This is initially accompanied by voicing, which then dies away. Finally, the tongue is lowered from the alveolar constriction, the vocal folds are separated and normal breathing is resumed.

## Chapter 7

1

| | |
|---|---|
| Plosives: | p t k b d g |
| Fricatives: | f θ s ʃ h v ð z ʒ |
| Affricates: | tʃ dʒ |
| Nasals: | m n ŋ |
| Lateral: | l |
| Approximants: | r w j |

(This course has also mentioned the possibility of ç and ʍ.)

2 a) səʊfə
b) vɜːs
c) stɪərɪŋ
d) bredkrʌm

e) skweə  g) bɔːt

f) æŋgə  h) naɪntiːn

3 a) The soft palate is raised for the b plosive and remains raised for æ. It is lowered for n, then raised again for the final ə.

b) The soft palate remains lowered during the articulation of m, and is then raised for the rest of the syllable.

c) The soft palate is raised for the æ vowel, then lowered for ŋ. It is then raised for the g plosive and remains raised for the l.

## Chapter 8

a)

| PRE-INITIAL | INITIAL | POST-INITIAL | PEAK | FINAL | POST-FINAL |
|---|---|---|---|---|---|
| s | k | w | iː | l | d |
| ONSET | | | PEAK | CODA | |

(It would be possible to treat l as pre-final and d as final, but the above analysis is slightly preferable in that d here is a suffix and we know that l occurs finally in 'squeal' skwiːl.)

b)

| | FINAL | POST-FINAL 1 | POST-FINAL 2 |
|---|---|---|---|
| eɪ | t | θ | s |
| PEAK | CODA | | |

c)

| PRE-INITIAL | INITIAL | POST-INITIAL | | FINAL |
|---|---|---|---|---|
| s | p | l | æ | ʃ |
| ONSET | | | PEAK | CODA |

d)

| INITIAL | | FINAL | POST-FINAL 1 | POST-FINAL 2 | POST-FINAL 3 |
|---|---|---|---|---|---|
| t | e | k | s | t | s |
| ONSET | PEAK | CODA | | | |

## Chapter 9

1 ə pətɪkjələ prɒbləm əv ðə bəʊt wəz ə liːk

2 əʊpn̩ɪŋ ðə bɒtl̩ prɪzentɪd nəʊ dɪfɪkl̩ti

3 ðər ɪz nəʊ ɔːltɜːnətɪv tə ðə gʌvn̩mənts prəpəʊzl̩
4 wi ɔːt tə meɪk ə kəlekʃn̩ tə kʌvə ði ɪkspensɪz
(also possible: kl̩ekʃn̩)
5 faɪnl̩i ðeɪ əraɪvd ət ə hɑːbər ət ði edʒ əv ðə maʊntɪnz
(also possible: hɑːbr̩)

## Chapter 10

| | | | |
|---|---|---|---|
| 1 a) | pro'tect | prə'tekt | |
| b) | 'clamber | 'klæmbə | |
| c) | fes'toon | fes'tuːn | |
| d) | de'test | dɪ'test | |
| e) | 'bellow | 'beləʊ | |
| f) | 'menace | 'menɪs | |
| g) | disco'nnect | ˌdɪskə'nekt | |
| h) | 'enter | 'entərɪŋ | ('entr̩ɪŋ) |
| 2 a) | 'language | 'læŋgwɪdʒ | |
| b) | 'captain | 'kæptɪn | |
| c) | ca'reer | kə'rɪə | |
| d) | 'paper | 'peɪpə | |
| e) | e'vent | ɪ'vent | |
| f) | 'jonquil | 'dʒɒŋkwɪl | |
| g) | 'injury | 'ɪndʒəri | ('ɪndʒr̩i) |
| h) | co'nnection | kə'nekʃən | (kə'nekʃn̩) |

## Chapter 11

1 and 2

| | | |
|---|---|---|
| a) | 'shopˌkeeper | 'ʃɒpˌkiːpə |
| b) | ˌopen'ended | ˌəʊpən'endɪd |
| c) | ˌJava'nese | ˌdʒɑːvə'niːz |
| d) | 'birthmark | 'bɜːθmɑːk |
| e) | ˌanti'clockwise | ˌæntɪ'klɒkwaɪz |
| g) | ˌconfir'mation | ˌkɒnfə'meɪʃn̩ |
| h) | ˌeight'sided | ˌeɪt'saɪdɪd |
| h) | 'fruitcake | 'fruːtˌkeɪk |
| i) | de'fective | dɪ'fektɪv |
| j) | 'roof ˌtimber | 'ruːfˌtɪmbə |

## Chapter 12

1 aɪ wɒnt ə tə pɑːk ðæt kɑːr əʊvə ðeə
2 əv ɔːl ðə prəpəʊzl̩z ðə wʌn ðət juː meɪd wəz ðə sɪliəst

3 dʒeɪn ən bɪl kəd əv drɪvn̩ tuː ɒn frɒm ðə pɑːti
(kʊd is also possible)
4 tə kʌm tə ðə pɔɪnt wɒt ʃl̩ wi duː fə ðə rest əv ðə wiːk
5 həz eniwʌn gɒt ən aɪdɪə weər ɪt keɪm frɒm
6 pədestriənz məst ɔːlweɪz juːz ðə krɒsɪŋz prəvaɪdɪd
7 iːtʃ wʌn wəz ə pɜːfɪkt ɪgzɑːmpl̩ əv ði ɑːt ðət əd biːn dɪveləpt ðeə

## Chapter 13

1 In this data there is no evidence of ŋ contrasting with n, since ŋ never occurs except before k and g. So all phonetic ŋ consonants are phonemic n.
a) θɪng
b) θɪnk
c) θɪnkɪng
d) fɪngə
e) sɪngə
f) sɪngɪng
2 a) saʊnd
b) æŋgə
c) kɑːnt
d) kæmpə
e) bɒnd
3 The phoneme t is realised as [t̬] when it occurs between vowels if the preceding vowel is stressed and the following vowel is unstressed.
4

| | p | d | s | m | z |
|---|---|---|---|---|---|
| Continuant | – | – | + | + | + |
| Alveolar | – | + | + | – | + |
| Voiced | – | + | – | + | + |

5 a) All the vowels are close or close-mid (or between these heights).
b) All require the tongue blade to be raised for their articulation, and all are in the alveolar or post-alveolar region.
c) None of these requires the raising of the tongue blade – all are front or back articulations.
d) All are voiceless.
e) All are rounded or end with lip-rounding.
f) All are approximants (they create very little obstruction to the airflow).

## Chapter 14

1 a) A ⁞ bird in the ⁞ hand is worth ⁞ two in the ⁞ bush ⁞
b) ⁞ Over a ⁞ quarter of a ⁞ century has e ⁞ lapsed since his ⁞ death ⁞

c) Com ¦ puters con ¦ sume a con ¦ siderable a ¦ mount of ¦ money and ¦ time ¦
d) ¦ Most of them have a ¦ rrived on the ¦ bus ¦
e) ¦ Newspaper ¦ editors are in ¦ variably ¦ under ¦ worked ¦

2 a)

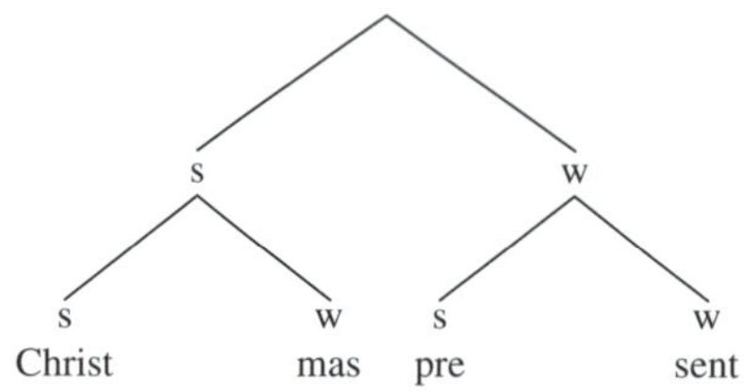


b)

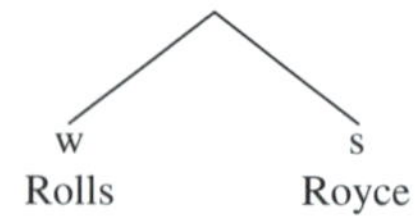


c)

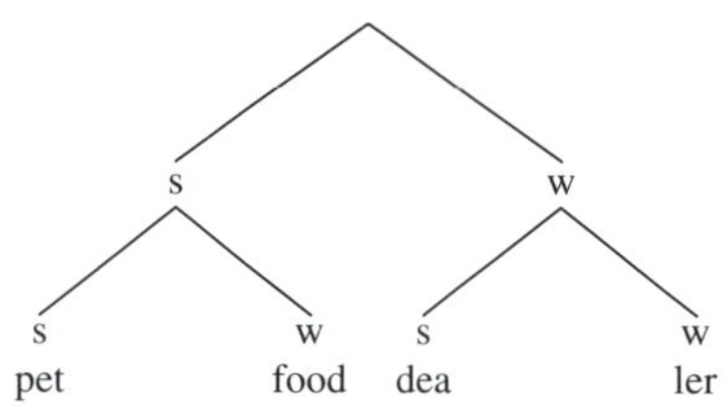


d)

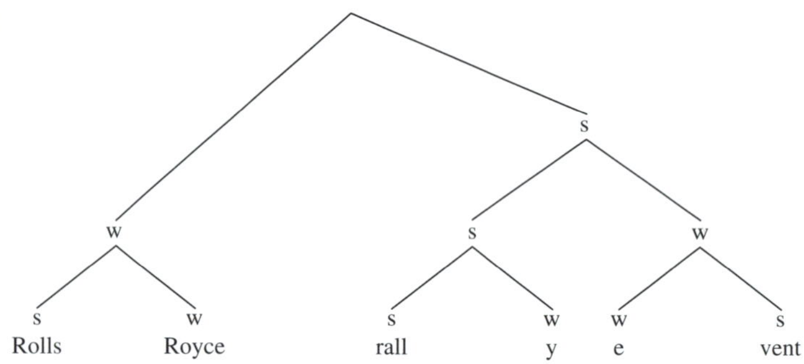


(the stress levels of 'Rolls' and 'Royce' are exchanged to avoid "stress clash" between 'Royce' and 'ra-'.)

3 a) wʌŋ kɔːz əv æsmər ɪs spəʊs tə bi ælədʒiz
b) wɒt ði ɜːbm̩ pɒpjəleɪʃn̩ kədʒuːz ɪz betə treɪnz
c) ʃi æks pətɪkjəli wel ɪn̪n̪ə fɜːs siːn
(Each of the above represents just one possible pronunciation: many others are possible.)

## Chapter 15

1 This train is for ↗Leeds ↗York and ↘Hull
2 Can you give me a ↗lift
∨Possibly Where ↘to
3 ↘No Certainly ↘not Go a↘way
4 Did you know hed been convicted of drunken ↗driving ∧No
5 If I give him ↗money he goes and ↘spends it
If I lend him the ↗bike he ↘loses it
Hes completely unre↘liable

## Chapter 16

1 (This is an exercise where there is more than one correct answer.)
   a) buy it for me
   b) hear it
   c) talk to him
2 a) 'mind the step
   b) 'this is the 'ten to 'seven train
   c) 'keep the 'food hot
3 a) 'Only when the ∨wind ·blows

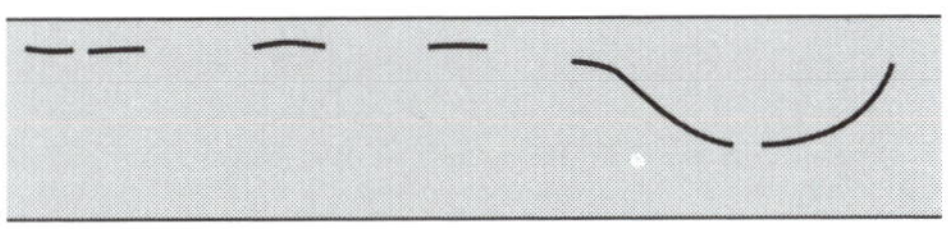

   b) ╱When did you ·say

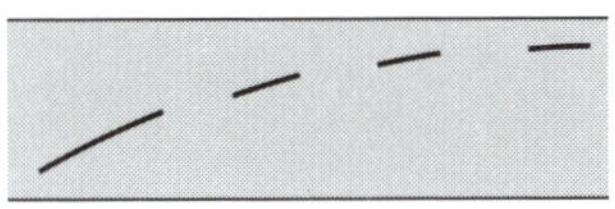

   c) 'What was the ╲name of the ·place

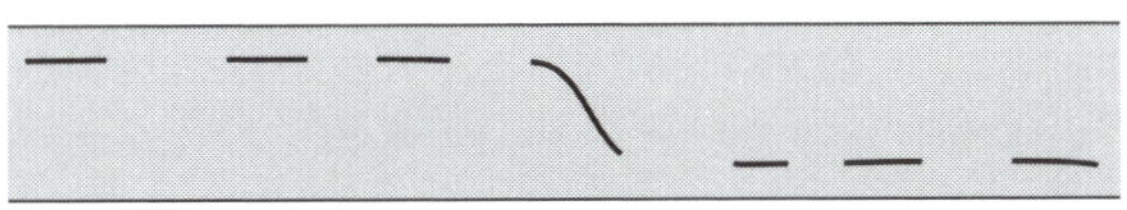

## Chapter 17

1 a) 'Which was the ╱cheap one did you ·say

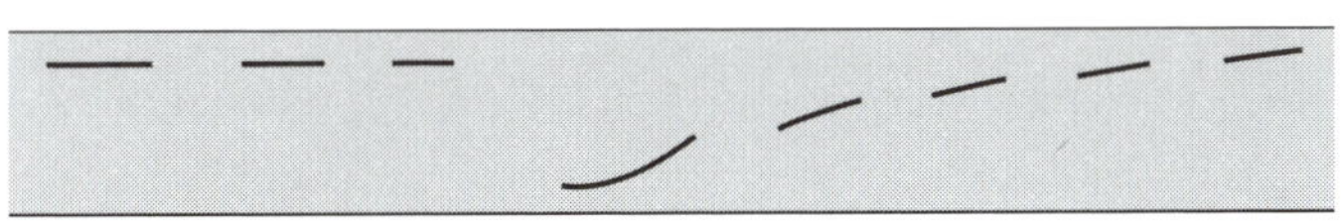

   b) I 'only 'want to ∨taste it

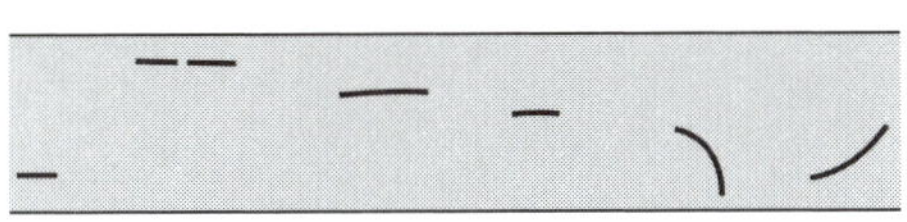

   c) ˌShe would have ˌthought it was ∧obvious

   d) There 'wasnt 'even a 'piece of ╲bread in the ·house

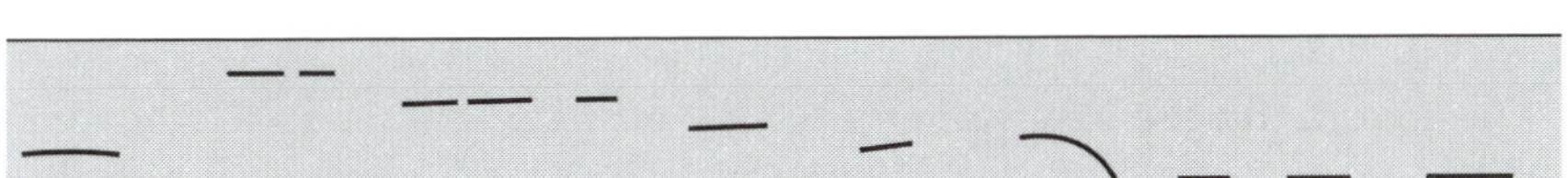

e) \Now will you be·lieve me

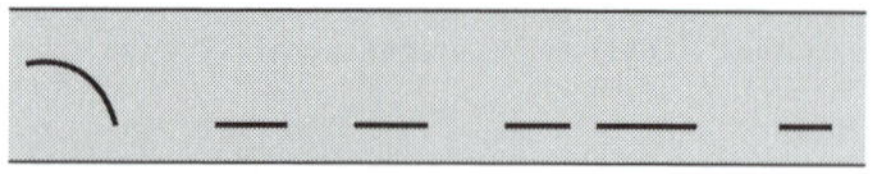

2 a) ˌopp ort /un it y

b) vac tua lly

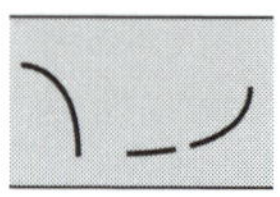

c) \con fid ent ly

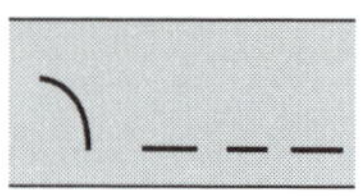

d) mag ∧ni fi cent

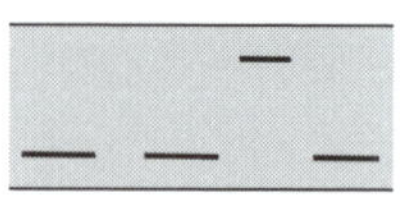

e) re /la tion ship

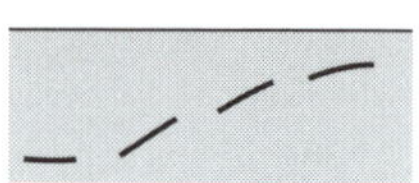

f) ˌaf ter vnoon

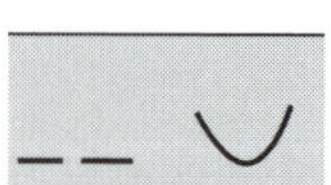

## Chapter 18

(The following are possible intonation patterns, but others could be correct.)

1 Its ˈrather vcold
2 Beˈcause I ˈcant a\fford it
3 Youre \silly then
4 Oh vplease
5 ˌSeven o/clock | ˌseven /thirty | and \eight
6 ∧Four
7 Ive ˌgot to ˌdo the /shopping
8 vSome of them ·might

## Chapter 19

1 a) right | can I do the shopping for you
   b) right | can I do the shopping for you
   c) first the professor explained her theory
   d) no | first the professor explained her theory
   e) first she explained her theory
   f) no | ten past three
   g) no | ten past three
   h) no | ten past three

2 a) he wrote the letter sadly
   b) he wrote the letter | sadly
   c) four plus six | divided by two | equals five
   d) four | plus six divided by two | equals seven
   e) we broke one thing | after another fell down
   f) we broke one thing after another | that night

## Chapter 20

1 This accent has a distribution for ŋ similar to BBC pronunciation (i.e. a case can be made for a ŋ phoneme), except that in the case of the participial '-ing' ending n is found instead of ŋ.

2 This accent has two additional long vowels (eː, oː) and, correspondingly, two fewer diphthongs (eɪ, əʊ). This situation is found in many Northern accents.

3 The fricatives θ, ð, h are missing from the phoneme inventory, and f, v are used in place of θ, ð. This accent has w where BBC pronunciation has "dark l". This is typical of a Cockney accent.

4 This data is based on the traditional working-class accent of Bristol, where words of more than one syllable do not usually end in ə. The accent is rhotic, so where there is an 'r' in the spelling (as in 'mother') an r is pronounced: where the spelling does not have 'r', an l sound is added, resulting in the loss of distinctiveness in some words (cf. 'idea', 'ideal'; 'area', 'aerial').

5 Here we appear to have three vowels where BBC pronunciation has two: the word 'cat' has the equivalent of æ, 'calm' has a vowel similar to ɑː while in the set of words that have æ in many Northern accents ('plaster', 'grass', etc.) an additional long vowel aː is used. This is found in Shropshire.

# Answers to recorded exercises

## Audio Unit 1

### *Exercise 2*

1 radical ● • •
2 emigration • • ● •
3 enormous • ● •
4 disability • • ● • •
5 alive • ●

## Audio Unit 2

### *Exercise 2*

1 æ in bæn 'ban'
2 ʌ in hʌb 'hub'
3 ɪ in fɪl 'fill'
4 ɒ in mɒs 'moss'
5 e in led 'led'
6 ʊ in pʊt 'put'
7 ʌ in kʌm 'come'
8 ɪ in mɪd 'mid'
9 ɒ in bɒm 'bomb'
10 e in sel 'sell'

## Audio Unit 3

### *Exercise 3*

1 iː in siːt 'seat'
2 ɑː in dɑːk 'dark'
3 ɜː in bɜːd 'bird'
4 ɔː in fɔːt 'fought'
5 ɑː in pɑːt 'part'
6 uː in fuːd 'food'
7 ɜː in kɜːt 'curt'
8 ɑː in pɑːk 'park'
9 iː in niːd 'need'
10 ɔː in hɔːs 'horse'

### *Exercise 5*

1 ɜː in hɜːd 'heard'
2 ɒ in sɒŋ 'song'
3 ɔː in sɔː 'saw'
4 ʌ in kʌm 'come'
5 ɑː in mɑːtʃ 'march'
6 ʊ in fʊl 'full'

7 ɑː in pɑːt 'part'
8 ɒ in dɒl 'doll'
9 ʌ in lʌv 'love'
10 ɜː in bɜːn 'burn'

*Exercise 7*

1 ɪə in fɪəs 'fierce'
2 eə in keəd 'cared'
3 ʊə in mʊəz 'moors'
4 eɪ in reɪd 'raid'
5 aɪ in taɪm 'time'
6 əʊ in kəʊt 'coat'
7 aɪ in kaɪt 'kite'
8 ɪə in bɪəd 'beard'
9 ʊə in tʊəz 'tours'
10 əʊ in bəʊn 'bone'
11 ɔɪ in bɔɪl 'boil'
12 aʊ in taʊn 'town'

## Audio Unit 4

*Exercise 3 b)*

1 p in hɑːp 'harp'
2 g in rəʊg 'rogue'
3 t in eɪt 'eight'
4 d in raɪd 'ride'
5 b in mɒb 'mob'
6 k in eɪk 'ache'
7 d in əʊd 'ode'
8 p in rɪp 'rip'
9 g in sæg 'sag'
10 t in fiːt 'feet'

*Exercise 5*

1 'debate'
2 'copied'
3 'buttercup'
4 'cuckoo'
5 'decayed'
6 'guarded'
7 'dedicated'
8 'paddock'
9 'boutique'
10 'appetite'

## Audio Unit 5

*Exercise 3*

1 geɪt 'gate'
2 kəʊt 'coat'
3 bɪt 'bit'
4 taɪəd 'tired'
5 biːt 'beat'
6 pəʊk 'poke'
7 kɑːt 'cart'
8 kɔːt 'caught'
9 paʊə 'power'
10 kɔːd 'cord'
11 gæp 'gap'
12 bɪəd 'beard'
13 kɑː 'car'
14 peɪd 'paid'
15 gʌt 'gut'
16 daʊt 'doubt'
17 təʊd 'toad'
18 duː 'do'
19 peə 'pair'
20 dek 'deck'

### *Exercise 4*

1 'keep'
2 'boat'
3 'cup'
4 'dirt'
5 'bike'
6 'cab'
7 'gate'
8 'cared'
9 'tired'
10 'bird'
11 'duck'
12 'cope'
13 'dog'
14 'coward'
15 'bake'
16 'tied'
17 'beard'
18 'put'
19 'bug'
20 'doubt'

## Audio Unit 6

### *Exercise 2*

a) initial position

1 ʃ in ʃəʊ 'show'
2 θ in θaɪ 'thigh'
3 z in zuː 'zoo'
4 f in fɑː 'far'
5 ð in ðəʊ 'though'

b) medial position

6 v in əʊvə 'over'
7 ʒ in meʒə 'measure'
8 s in aɪsɪŋ 'icing'
9 ʃ in eɪʃə 'Asia'
10 h in əhed 'ahead'

c) final position

11 ð in ləʊð 'loathe'
12 v in iːv 'Eve'
13 ʃ in æʃ 'ash'
14 f in rʌf 'rough'
15 θ in əʊθ 'oath'

## Audio Unit 7

### *Exercise 6*

1 juːʒuəl 'usual'
2 rɪmeɪn 'remain'
3 eksəsaɪz 'exercise'
4 weərɪŋ 'wearing'
5 ɜːdʒənt 'urgent'
6 mɪnɪməm 'minimum'
7 vaɪələns 'violence'
8 emfəsɪs 'emphasis'
9 dʒentli 'gently'
10 θɪŋkɪŋ 'thinking'
11 taɪpraɪtə 'typewriter'
12 jɪəli 'yearly'

## Audio Unit 8

### *Exercise 6 (spellings)*

1 'scraped'
2 'grudged'
3 'clothes'
4 'scripts'
5 'crunched'
6 'thrones'
7 'plunged'
8 'quench'

## Audio Unit 9

### *Exercise 5*

1 ˈɡɑːdn̩ə ‘gardener’
2 ˈkɒləm ‘column’
3 ˈhændl̩z ‘handles’
4 əˈlaɪv ‘alive’
5 prɪˈtend ‘pretend’
6 ˈsʌdn̩ ‘sudden’
7 ˈkæləs ‘callous’
8 ˈθretn̩ɪŋ ‘threatening’
9 pəˈlaɪt ‘polite’
10 ˈpʌzl̩ ‘puzzle’

## Audio Unit 10

### *Exercise 1*

1 ˈenəmi
2 kəˈlekt
3 ˈkæpɪtl̩
4 kɑːˈneɪʃn̩
5 ˈpærədaɪs
6 səbˈtrækt
7 ˈelɪfənt
8 əbˈzɜːvə
9 ˈprɒfɪt
10 ˌentəˈteɪn

### *Exercise 2 (spellings)*

1 Shrewsbury
2 Polperro
3 Aberdeen
4 Wolverhampton
5 Aberystwyth
6 Birmingham
7 Northampton
8 Dundee
9 Canterbury
10 Basingstoke

## Audio Unit 12

### *Exercise 3*

1 ˈliːv ðə ˈrest əv ðə ˈfuːd fə ˈlʌnʃ
2 ˈɑːnt ðə səm ˈletəz fər ə tu ˈəʊpən
3 ˈweə də ði ˈegz ˈkʌm frɒm
4 ˈriːd ɪz ˈbʊk ən ˈraɪt səm ˈnəʊts
5 ət ˈliːst wi kən ˈtraɪ ən ˈhelp

## Audio Unit 13

### *Exercise 1 (spellings)*

1 Colchester
2 Carlisle
3 Hereford
4 Scunthorpe
5 Glamorgan
6 Holyhead

7 Framlingham
8 Southend
9 Cheltenham
10 Inverness

*Exercise 2*

1 ˈlestəʃə (Leicestershire)
2 dʌnˈfɜːmlɪn (Dunfermline)
3 ˈstiːvn̩ɪdʒ (Stevenage)
4 penˈzæns (Penzance)
5 ˈɡɪlfəd (Guildford)
6 kəʊlˈreɪn (Coleraine)
7 ˈhʌdəsfiːld (Huddersfield)
8 heɪlzˈəʊɪn (Halesowen)
9 ˈwɪlmzləʊ (Wilmslow)
10 ˈbɑːnstəpl̩ (Barnstaple)

*Exercise 3*

1 ˈJames deˈcided to ˈtype the ˈletter himˈself
2 The ˈplane was aˈpproaching the ˈrunway at ˈhigh ˈspeed
3 ˈTry to ˈsee the ˈother ˈpersons ˈpoint of ˈview
4 You ˈput your ˈbrakes on when the ˈlight ˈturns to ˈred
5 In a ˈshort ˈtime the ˈhouse was ˈfull of ˈchildren

## Audio Unit 14

*Exercise 1*

1 ¦ ˈEach ¦ ˈperson in the ¦ ˈgroup was ¦ ˈtrained in sur ¦ ˈvival ¦
2 A ¦ ˈbout ¦ ˈthree ¦ ˈhundred ¦ ˈsoldiers were ¦ ˈlined ¦ ˈup ¦
3 ¦ ˈBuying a ¦ ˈnew com ¦ ˈputer is a ¦ ˈmajor ex ¦ ˈpense ¦
4 ¦ ˈAll the ¦ ˈpeople who ¦ ˈcame to the ¦ ˈwedding were from ¦ ˈEngland ¦
5 ¦ ˈTry to be as ¦ ˈtactful as you ¦ ˈcan when you ¦ ˈtalk to him ¦

*Exercise 2*

*Note:* When recordings of conversational speech are used, it is no longer possible to give definite decisions about "right" and "wrong" answers. Some problems, points of interest and alternative possibilities are mentioned.

1 ə bjuːtʰfl̩ ɡɜːl (Careful speech would have had bjuːtɪfl̩ or bjuːtɪfʊl.)
2 wi siːm tə hæv ə defnət wʌn ðeə (Careful speech would have defɪnɪt, defɪnət or defn̩ət; notice that this speaker uses a glottal stop at the end of 'definite' so that the transcription – phonetic rather than phonemic – defnəʔ would be acceptable. There is a good example of assimilation in the pronunciation of 'one there'; as often happens when n and ð are combined, the n becomes dental n̪. In addition, the ð loses its friction – which is always weak – and becomes a dental nasal, so that this could be transcribed phonetically as wʌn̪n̪eə.)
3 kʊd ɪt bi ə stuːl rɑːððn̩ə teɪbl̩ (Careful speech would have rɑːðə dən ə; the ð is long, so the symbol is written twice to indicate this.)

4 ə fɪθ ɪn (Careful speech would have fɪfθ; the transcription cannot, of course, show very fine details of articulation, but it is likely that though the sound one hears is most like θ, there is some slight constriction between upper teeth and lower lip as well.)

5 eni pʰkjuːljærətɪz əbaʊt ðæt (The main elision is of the ɪ vowel in the first syllable of 'peculiarities': a less noticeable case is that instead of having i before the æ in this word the speaker has a non-syllabic j; note the glottal stop at the end of 'about'.)

6 æn haʊ mni straɪps ɒn jɔːz (Careful speech would have meni; it is perhaps surprising that the speaker has æ rather than ə in 'and'; jɔːz is a frequently found alternative pronunciation to jʊəz.)

7 wel ɪt əpɪəz tə bʌtn̩ ʌp ɪs gɒt θriː (The elision is in 'its'; careful speech would have ɪts or, since this speaker uses glottal stops quite frequently – notice one between 'it' and 'appears', and another at the end of 'got' – ɪʔs.)

8 ɔː ðə wɒtʃəkɔːl ɪt ðə sɪl ('What do you call it' or 'what d' you call it' is used frequently when speakers cannot remember a word, and is always pronounced rapidly.)

9 baɪ kɒləm ɪntʰ kɒləmz ɔːraɪt (Careful speech would have ɪntə and ɔːl raɪt.)

10 daɪəmən ʃeɪp pætʃ (Careful speech would have daɪəmənd ʃeɪpt pætʃ.)

11 ænd aɪ ʃd θɪŋk frɒm ɪkspɪrɪəns f kɪtʃɪn naɪvz (Careful speech would have ʃʊd or ʃəd and əv.)

12 wɒt ʃ wi duː neks gəʊ daʊn (Careful speech would have ʃəl and nekst.)

13 ðiː tɒp f ðə bɒtl̩ ɪz pr̥dʒektɪŋ aʊtwədz ɪntʰ ðə ruːm (Careful speech would have əv, prədʒektɪŋ and ɪntə; the r in 'projecting' is devoiced as well as being syllabic; notice the glottal stops, one before the k in 'projecting' and another before the t in 'outwards': the strong form of 'the' at the beginning is probably a sort of slight hesitation.)

## Audio Unit 15

### *Exercise 3*

| | |
|---|---|
| 1 ˅one | 6 ˏsix |
| 2 ˎtwo | 7 ˎnow |
| 3 ˏthree | 8 ˅you |
| 4 ˄four | 9 ˄more |
| 5 ˎfive | 10 ˏus |

## Audio Unit 16

### *Exercise 1*

1 We could go by <u>bus</u>

2 Of <u>course</u> its broken

3 The car was where Id <u>left</u> it

4 How much is the <u>bigg</u>est one

5 I knew it would go wrong
6 It was too cold
7 Here it is
8 That was a loud noise
9 We could go from Manchester
10 Have you finished

*Exercise 4*

1 ˈWhat ˈtime will they ↗come
2 A ˈday reˈturn to ↘London
3 The ˈNorth ↘Pole would be warmer
4 ˈHave you deˈcided to ↗buy it
5 I reˈcorded them on ca↘ssette

## Audio Unit 17

*Exercise 4*

1 ˈNow ˈheres the ↘weather ·forecast
2 You ˌdidnt say ˌanything about ↗rates
3 A ˌfew ˌyears ago they were ↘top
4 ˈNo one could ˈsay the ˈcinema was ∨dead
5 Is there ↗anything you ·wouldnt ·eat
6 ˈHave you ˈever conˈsidered ↗writing
7 ˌThat was ˌwhat he ∨claimed to be
8 We ˈtry to ˈdo our ˈshopping in the ↘market
9 But I ↘never ·go there ·now
10 It ˌwouldnt be ˌdifficult to find ↗out

## Audio Unit 18

*Note:* Since these extracts were not spoken deliberately for illustrating intonation, it is not possible to claim that the transcription given here is the only correct version. There are several places where other transcriptions would be acceptable, and suggestions about alternative possibilities are given with some items, in addition to a few other comments.

1 it ˈlooks like a ˈFrench maga↘zine (slight hesitation between 'looks' and 'like')
2 the ˈtelevision ˈis plugged ∨in
3 ˈdoes your ˈcolander have a ↘handle ('does' possibly not stressed)
4 a ↗flap on it
5 ˈyou tell me about ↗yours (narrow pitch movement on 'yours'; 'tell' may also be stressed)
6 ˈwell ↘dark hair
7 ˌmore than ˌhalf ↗way
8 but er ˈnot in the ↘other ·corners
9 a ˌsort of ˌDaily ↘Sketch ·format ·newspaper ('sort' possibly not stressed)

10 'on the ↘top | 'on the ↘lid (both pronunciations of 'on' might be unstressed)
11 well theyre 'on al ∨ternate ·steps | theyre 'not on ∨every ·step
12 'what about the ↘vent | at the ↘back
13 and a 'ladys ↘handbag | ˌhanging on a ˌnail on the ↘wall
14 'you do the ↘left hand ·bit of the ·picture | and ˌIll do the ↘right hand ·bit
15 were being 'very par ∨ticular | but we 'just haven't 'hit upon 'one of the ↘differences ·yet (stress on 'just' is weak or absent)
16 and 'what about your tele↘vision | 'two ↗knobs | in the ↗front

## Audio Unit 19

### *Exercise 1*

1 I suppose the best thing's to try later.
2 If he's coming today there ought to be a letter around.
3 The world's greatest lawn tennis festival begins on Monday.
4 We've fixed for the repair man to come and mend it under guarantee.
5 The number's been engaged for over an hour.

### *Exercise 2*

1 aɪ spəʊz ð bes θɪŋz tʰ traɪ leɪtə
2 ɪf ɪz kʌmɪŋ tʰdeɪ ðr̩ ɔːt tʰ bi ə letr̩ r̥aʊnd
3 ðə wɜːlz greɪtṣ lɔːn tenɪs festʰvl̩ bɪgɪnz ɒm mʌndeɪ
4 wɪf fɪks fə ðə rɪpeə mæn tʰ kʌm əm mend ɪt ʌndə gærn̩tiː
5 ð nʌmbəz bɪn ɪŋgeɪdʒ fr̩ əʊvr̩ ən aʊə

### *Exercise 4*

| ðeə 'bɪldɪŋ ↘wɪn fɑːmz | 'ɔːl 'əʊvə ði ↗eəriə | ˌweə wi ↘lɪv | wi kən siː 'lɒŋ ↘laɪnz əv ðəm | əˌlɒŋ ðə ˌtɒps əv ðə ↘hɪlz | ən 'daʊn baɪ ðə ∨kəʊst | ðər ə 'wɪn 'tɜːbaɪnz 'aʊt ət ↗siː | 'ænd ə'lɒŋ ðə ↘ʃɔː | ðeɪ 'əʊnli 'bɪld ðəm 'weə ðəz 'plenti əv ∨wɪnd | ʌɒbviəsli | wi ˌsɜːtn̩li ˌget ə ˌlɒt əv ↘ðæt nɪər ·ʌs | ju ∨kʊd ·seɪ | ðə ˌlænskeɪps ˌbiːŋ kəmˌpliːtli træns↘fɔːmd | bəp 'məʊs 'piːpl̩ 'dəʊnt siːm tə ↘maɪnd |

## Audio Unit 20

*Note:* Transcription of natural speech involves making decisions that have the effect of simplifying complex phonetic events. The broad transcription given below is not claimed to be completely accurate, nor to be the only "correct" version.

ɪwəz 'rɑːðə ↘fraɪʔnɪŋ
bɪkəz ðə ðərə ↘skɔːz
ə ðiːz ↘baɪskl̩z
ju 'riːli ↘hæv tu

ˌhæv jə wɪts ə\baʊtʃu

ˈɔːl ðə \taɪm

bɪkəz ðə jə nəʊ ðə ðeɪ vstɒp ·sʌdn̩li

ɪts _ɔːkwəd

bkəz ðə \træfɪk regjə·leɪʃn̩z

ɑː ˌmɔː ˌɒnəd ɪn ðə \briːtʃ

ðən ði əb/zɜːvəns

aɪm ˈnɒt ɪn \nɒt riːli ·ʃɔː wɒt

ˌregjəleɪʃn̩z ðər \ɑː

fr̩ \ɪnstəns

ðiː ə \træfɪk ·laɪts

ˈred·\red ·laɪts

du ˌnɒt ə\plaɪ

fɔː ˌtɜːnɪŋ \raɪt

wɪtʃ \miːnz ðət

ˈɪf jə ˈkʌmɪŋ ˈʌp tu ə \træfɪk ·laɪt

ˈsʌmwʌn \stɒpt

hu ˌwɒnts tə ˌgəʊ streɪt \ɒn

ɔː ˌtɜːn \left

ən ˈjuː wɒnt tə tɜːn vraɪt

ðen ju ˈpʊl /aʊt

ˌəʊvə vteɪk ðəm

ən ðen ˈkʌt ə\krɒs

ɪn \frʌnt

# Recommendations for general reading

References to reading on specific topics are given at the end of each chapter. The following is a list of basic books and papers recommended for more general study: if you wish to go more fully into any of the areas given below you would do well to start by reading these. I would consider it very desirable that any library provided for students using this book should possess most or all of the books listed. I give full bibliographic references to the books recommended in this section.

## English phonetics and phonology

The best and most comprehensive book in this field is A. C. Gimson's book originally titled *Introduction to the Pronunciation of English*, now in its Seventh Edition edited by A. Cruttenden with the title *The Pronunciation of English* (London, Edward Arnold, 2008); the level is considerably more advanced and the content much more detailed than the present course. All writers on the pronunciation of British English owe a debt to Daniel Jones, whose book *An Outline of English Phonetics* first appeared in 1918 and was last reprinted in its Ninth Edition (Cambridge University Press, 1975), but the book, though still of interest, must be considered out of date.

Two other books that approach the subject in rather different ways are G. O. Knowles, *Patterns of Spoken English* (London: Longman, 1987) and C. W. Kreidler, *The Pronunciation of English*, Second Edition (Oxford: Blackwell, 2004). A. McMahon, *An Introduction to English Phonology* (Edinburgh: Edinburgh University Press, 2002) covers the theory of phonology in more depth than this book: it is short and clearly written. H. Giegerich, *English Phonology: An Introduction* (Cambridge: Cambridge University Press, 1992) is more advanced, and contains valuable information and ideas. I would also recommend *Practical Phonetics and Phonology* by B. Collins and I. Mees (Second Edition, London: Routledge, 2008).

## General phonetics

I have written a basic introductory book on general phonetics, called *Phonetics* in the series 'Oxford Introductions to Language Studies' (Oxford: Oxford University Press, 2002). There are many good introductory books at a more advanced level: I would recommend P. Ladefoged, *A Course in Phonetics* (Fifth Edition, Boston: Thomson, 2006), but see also the same author's *Vowels and Consonants* (Second Edition, Oxford: Blackwell, 2004) or M. Ashby and J. Maidment, *Introducing Phonetic Science* (Cambridge: Cambridge University Press, 2005). Also recommended is *Phonetics: The Science of Speech* by M. Ball and J. Rahilly (London: Edward Arnold, 1999). D. Abercrombie, *Elements of General Phonetics* (Edinburgh: Edinburgh University Press, 1967) is a well-written classic, but less suitable as basic introductory reading. J. C. Catford, *A Practical Introduction to Phonetics* (Oxford: Oxford University Press, 1988) is good for explaining the nature of practical phonetics; a simpler and more practical book is P. Ashby, *Speech Sounds* (Second Edition, London: Routledge, 2005). J. Laver, *Principles of Phonetics* (Cambridge: Cambridge University Press, 1994) is a very comprehensive and advanced textbook.

## Phonology

Several books explain the basic elements of phonological theory. F. Katamba, *An Introduction to Phonology* (London: Longman, 1989) is a good introduction. Covering both this area and the previous one in a readable and comprehensive way is J. Clark, C. Yallop and J. Fletcher, *An Introduction to Phonetics and Phonology* (Third Edition, Oxford: Blackwell, 2007). A lively and interesting course in phonology is I. Roca and W. Johnson, *A Course in Phonology* (Oxford: Blackwell, 1999). A recent addition to the literature is D. Odden's *Introducing Phonology* (Cambridge: Cambridge University Press, 2005). The classic work on the generative phonology of English is N. Chomsky and M. Halle, *The Sound Pattern of English* (New York: Harper and Row, 1968); most people find this very difficult.

## Accents of English

The major work in this area is J. C. Wells, *Accents of English,* 3 vols. (Cambridge: Cambridge University Press, 1982), which is a large and very valuable work dealing with accents of English throughout the world. A shorter and much easier introduction is A. Hughes, P. Trudgill and D. Watt, *English Accents and Dialects* (Third Edition, London: Edward Arnold, 2005). See also P. Foulkes and G. Docherty, *Urban Voices* (London: Edward Arnold, 1999) and P. Trudgill, *The Dialects of England* (Second Edition, Oxford: Blackwell, 1999).

## Teaching the pronunciation of English

I do not include here books which are mainly classroom materials. Good introductions to the principles of English pronunciation teaching are M. Celce-Murcia, D. Brinton and J. Goodwin, *Teaching Pronunciation* (Cambridge: Cambridge University Press, 1996), C. Dalton and B. Seidlhofer, *Pronunciation* (Oxford: Oxford University Press, 1994) and J. Kenworthy, *Teaching English Pronunciation* (London: Longman, 1987). M. Hewings, *Pronunciation Practice Activities* (Cambridge: Cambridge University Press, 2004) contains much practical advice. A. Cruttenden's revision of A. C. Gimson's *The Pronunciation of*

*English* (Seventh Edition, London: Edward Arnold, 2008) has a useful discussion of requirements for English pronunciation teaching in Chapter 13.

### Pronunciation dictionaries

Most modern English dictionaries now print recommended pronunciations for each word listed, so for most purposes a dictionary which gives only pronunciations and not meanings is of limited value unless it gives a lot more information than an ordinary dictionary could. A few such dictionaries are currently available for British English. One is the Seventeenth Edition of the *Cambridge English Pronouncing Dictionary,* originally by Daniel Jones, edited by P. Roach, J. Hartman and J. Setter (Cambridge: Cambridge University Press, 2006). Jones' work was the main reference work on English pronunciation for most of the twentieth century; I was the principal editor for this new edition, and have tried to keep it compatible with this book. There is a CD-ROM disk to accompany the dictionary which allows you to hear the English and American pronunciations of any word. Another dictionary is J. C. Wells, *Longman Pronunciation Dictionary* (Third Edition, London: Longman, 2008). See also C. Upton, W. Kretzschmar and R. Konopka (eds.), *Oxford Dictionary of Pronunciation* (Oxford: Oxford University Press, 2001). A useful addition to the list is L. Olausson and C. Sangster, *The Oxford BBC Guide to Pronunciation* (Oxford: Oxford University Press, 2006), which makes use of the BBC Pronunciation Research Unit's database to suggest pronunciations of difficult names, words and phrases.

### Intonation and stress

Good introductions to intonation are A. Cruttenden, *Intonation* (Second Edition, Cambridge: Cambridge University Press, 1997), J. C. Wells, *English Intonation* (Cambridge: Cambridge University Press, 2006) and E. Couper-Kuhlen, *An Introduction to English Prosody* (London: Edward Arnold, 1986). D. R. Ladd, *Intonational Phonology* (Cambridge: Cambridge University Press, 1996) is much more difficult, but covers contemporary theoretical issues in an interesting way. E. Fudge, *English Word Stress* (London: Allen and Unwin, 1984) is a useful textbook on word stress.

# Bibliography


Abercrombie, D. (1967) *Elements of General Phonetics*, Edinburgh: Edinburgh University Press.

Abercrombie, D. (1991) 'RP today: its position and prospects', in D. Abercrombie, *Fifty Years in Phonetics*, Edinburgh: Edinburgh University Press, pp. 48–53.

Adams, C. (1979) *English Speech Rhythm and the Foreign Learner*, The Hague: Mouton.

Ashby, P. (2005) *Speech Sounds*, 2nd edn., London: Routledge.

Ashby, M. and Maidment, J. (2005) *Introducing Phonetic Science*, Cambridge: Cambridge University Press.

Ball, M. and Rahilly, J. (1999) *Phonetics: The Science of Speech*, London: Arnold.

Bauer, L. (1983) *English Word-Formation*, Cambridge: Cambridge University Press.

Bolinger, D. (1972) 'Accent is predictable – if you're a mind-reader', *Language*, vol. 48, pp. 633–44.

Brazil, D. (1994) *Pronunciation for Advanced Learners of English*, Cambridge: Cambridge University Press.

Brazil, D., Coulthard, M. and Johns, C. (1980) *Discourse Intonation and Language Teaching*, London: Longman.

Brown, G. (1990) *Listening to Spoken English*, London: Longman.

Brown, G., Curry, K. and Kenworthy, J. (1980) *Questions of Intonation*, London: Croom Helm.

Brown, G. and Yule, G. (1983) *Teaching the Spoken Language*, Cambridge: Cambridge University Press.

Catford, J. C. (1977) *Fundamental Problems in Phonetics*, Edinburgh: Edinburgh University Press.

Catford, J. C. (1988) *A Practical Introduction to Phonetics*, Oxford: Oxford University Press.

Celce-Murcia, M., Brinton, D. and Goodwin, J. (1996) *Teaching Pronunciation*, Cambridge: Cambridge University Press.

Chen, M. (1970) 'Vowel length variation as a function of the voicing of the consonant environment', *Phonetica*, vol. 22, pp. 129–59.

Chomsky, N. and Halle, M. (1968) *The Sound Pattern of English*, New York: Harper and Row.

Clark, J., Yallop, C. and Fletcher, J. (2007) *An Introduction to Phonetics and Phonology*, 3rd edn., Oxford: Blackwell.

Collins, B. and Mees, I. (2008) *Practical Phonetics and Phonology*, 2nd edn., London: Routledge.

Couper-Kuhlen, E. (1986) *An Introduction to English Prosody*, London: Edward Arnold.

Cruttenden, A. (1997) *Intonation*, 2nd edn., Cambridge: Cambridge University Press.

Cruttenden, A. (ed.) (2008) *Gimson's Pronunciation of English*, 7th edn., London: Edward Arnold.

Crystal, D. (1969) *Prosodic Systems and Intonation in English*, Cambridge: Cambridge University Press.

Crystal, D. (2003) *English as a Global Language*, 2nd edn., Cambridge: Cambridge University Press.

Crystal, D. and Quirk, R. (1964) *Systems of Prosodic and Paralinguistic Features in English*, The Hague: Mouton.

Dalton, C. and Seidlhofer, B. (1994) *Pronunciation*, Oxford: Oxford University Press.

Dauer, R. (1983) 'Stress-timing and syllable-timing reanalysed', *Journal of Phonetics*, vol. 11, pp. 51–62.

Davidsen-Nielsen, N. (1969) 'English stops after initial /s/', *English Studies*, vol. 50, pp. 321–8.

Dimitrova, S. (1997) 'Bulgarian speech rhythm: stress-timed or syllable-timed?', *Journal of the International Phonetic Association*, vol. 27, pp. 27–34.

Foulkes, P. and Docherty, G. (eds.) (1999) *Urban Voices*, London: Arnold.

Fox, A. T. C. (1973) 'Tone sequences in English', *Archivum Linguisticum*, vol. 4, pp. 17–26.

Fromkin, V. A. (ed.) (1978) *Tone: A Linguistic Survey*, New York: Academic Press.

Fudge, E. (1969) 'Syllables', *Journal of Linguistics*, vol. 5, pp. 253–86.

Fudge, E. (1984) *English Word Stress*, London: Allen and Unwin.

Fudge, E. (1999) 'Words and feet', *Journal of Linguistics*, vol. 35, pp. 273–96.

Giegerich, H. (1992) *English Phonology: An Introduction*, Cambridge: Cambridge University Press.

Gimson, A. C. (1964) 'Phonetic change and the RP vowel system', in D. Abercrombie *et al.* (eds.) *In Honour of Daniel Jones*, London: Longman, pp. 131–6.

Goldsmith, J. A. (1990) *Autosegmental and Metrical Phonology*, Oxford: Blackwell.

Halliday, M. A. K. (1967) *Intonation and Grammar in British English*, The Hague: Mouton.

Harris, J. (1994) *English Sound Structure*, Oxford: Blackwell.

Hewings, M. (2004) *Pronunciation Practice Activities*, Cambridge: Cambridge University Press.

Hewings, M. (2007) *English Pronunciation in Use; Advanced*, Cambridge: Cambridge University Press.

Hirst, D. and di Cristo, A. (eds.) (1998) *Intonation Systems*, Cambridge: Cambridge University Press.

Hogg, R. and McCully, C. (1987) *Metrical Phonology: A Coursebook*, Cambridge: Cambridge University Press.

Honikman, B. (1964) 'Articulatory settings' in D. Abercrombie *et al.* (eds.) *In Honour of Daniel Jones*, London: Longman, pp. 73–84.

Hughes, A., Trudgill, P. and Watt, D. (2005) *English Accents and Dialects*, 4th edn., London: Edward Arnold.

Hyman, L. (1975) *Phonology: Theory and Analysis*, New York: Holt, Rinehart.

International Phonetic Association (1999) *Handbook of the International Phonetic Association*, Cambridge: Cambridge University Press.

Jakobson, R. and Halle, M. (1964) 'Tenseness and laxness', in D. Abercrombie *et al.* (eds.) *In Honour of Daniel Jones*, London: Longman, pp. 96–101.

James, A. R. (1988) *The Acquisition of a 2nd Language Phonology*, Tübingen: Narr.

Jenkins, J. (2000) *The Phonology of English as an International Language*, Oxford: Oxford University Press.

Jones, D. (1931) 'The word as a phonetic entity', *Le Maître Phonétique*, vol. 36, pp. 60–5.

Jones, D. (1956) *The Pronunciation of English*, 4th edn., Cambridge: Cambridge University Press (first published 1909).

Jones, D. (1975) *An Outline of English Phonetics*, 9th edn., Cambridge: Cambridge University Press (first published 1918).

Jones, D. (1976) *The Phoneme: its Nature and Use*, Cambridge: Cambridge University Press (first published 1950).

Jones, D., eds. Roach, P., Hartman, J. and Setter, J. (2006) *Cambridge English Pronouncing Dictionary*, Cambridge: Cambridge University Press (first published 1917).

Katamba, F. (1989) *An Introduction to Phonology*, London: Longman.

Kenworthy, J. (1987) *Teaching English Pronunciation*, London: Longman.

Knowles, G. (1987) *Patterns of Spoken English*, London: Longman.

Kreidler, C. (2004) *The Pronunciation of English*, 2nd edn., Oxford: Blackwell.

Ladd, D. R. (1996) *Intonational Phonology*, Cambridge: Cambridge University Press.

Ladefoged, P. (2004) *Vowels and Consonants*, 2nd edn., Oxford; Blackwell.

Ladefoged, P. (2006) *A Course in Phonetics*, 5th edn., Boston: Thomson.

Laver, J. (1980) *The Phonetic Description of Voice Quality*, Cambridge: Cambridge University Press.

Laver, J. (1994) *Principles of Phonetics*, Cambridge: Cambridge University Press.

Lee, W. R. (1958) *English Intonation: A New Approach*, Amsterdam: North Holland.

Lehiste, I. (1977) 'Isochrony reconsidered', *Journal of Phonetics*, vol. 5, pp. 253–63.

Lisker, L. (1970) 'Supraglottal air pressure in the production of English stops', *Language and Speech*, vol. 13, pp. 215–30.

MacCarthy, P. A. D. (1952) *English Pronunciation*, 4th edn., Cambridge: Heffer.

McMahon, A. (2002) *An Introduction to English Phonology*, Edinburgh: Edinburgh University Press.

Mitchell, T. F. (1969) Review of Abercrombie (1967), *Journal of Linguistics*, vol. 5, pp. 153–64.

Obendorfer, R. (1998) *Weak Forms in Present-Day English*, Oslo: Novus Press.

O'Connor, J. D. and Arnold, G. F. (1973) *The Intonation of Colloquial English*, 2nd edn., London: Longman.

O'Connor, J. D. and Tooley, O. (1964) 'The perceptibility of certain word boundaries', in D. Abercrombie *et al.* (eds.) *In Honour of Daniel Jones*, pp. 171–6, London: Longman.

O'Connor, J. D. and Trim, J. L. (1953) 'Vowel, consonant and syllable: a phonological definition', *Word*, vol. 9, pp. 103–22.

Odden, D. (2005) *Introducing Phonology*, Cambridge: Cambridge University Press.

Olausson, L. and Sangster, C. (eds.) (2006) *The Oxford BBC Guide to Pronunciation*, Oxford: Oxford University Press.

Pike, K. L. (1943) *Phonetics*, Ann Arbor: University of Michigan Press.

Pike, K. L. (1945) *The Intonation of American English*, Ann Arbor: University of Michigan Press.

Pike, K. L. (1947) *Phonemics*, Ann Arbor: University of Michigan Press.

Pike, K. L. (1948) *Tone Languages*, Ann Arbor: University of Michigan Press.

Pullum, G. K. and Ladusaw, W. (1996) *Phonetic Symbol Guide*, 2nd edn., Chicago: University of Chicago Press.

Radford, A., Atkinson, M., Britain, D., Clahsen, H. and Spencer, A. (1999) *Linguistics: An Introduction*, Cambridge: Cambridge University Press.

Raphael, L. J., Borden, G. and Harris, K. (2006) *Speech Science Primer*, London: Lippincott, Williams and Wilkins.

Roach, P. J. (1982) 'On the distinction between "stress-timed" and "syllable-timed" languages', in D. Crystal (ed.) *Linguistic Controversies*, London: Edward Arnold.

Roach, P. J. (1994) 'Conversion between prosodic transcription systems: "Standard British" and ToBI', *Speech Communication*, vol. 15, pp. 91–9.

Roach, P. J. (2002) *Phonetics*, Oxford: Oxford University Press.

Roach, P. J. (2004) 'Illustration of British English: Received Pronunciation', *Journal of the International Phonetic Association*, vol. 34.2, pp. 239–46.

Roach, P. J. (2005) 'Representing the English model', in Dzubialska-Kołaczyk, K. and Przedlacka, J. (eds.) *English Pronunciation Models: a Changing Scene*, pp. 393–9, Basel: Peter Lang.

Roca, I. and Johnson, W. (1999) *A Course in Phonology*, Oxford: Blackwell.

Sapir, E. (1925) 'Sound patterns in language', *Language*, vol. 1, pp. 37–51.

Schmerling, S. (1976) *Aspects of English Sentence Stress*, Austin: University of Texas Press.

Shockey, L. (2003) *Sound Patterns of Spoken English*, Oxford: Blackwell.

Spolsky, D. (1998) *Sociolinguistics*, Oxford: Oxford University Press.

Taylor, D. S. (1981) 'Non-native speakers and the rhythm of English', *International Review of Applied Linguistics*, vol. 19, pp. 219–26.

Tench, P. (1996) *The Intonation Systems of English*, London: Cassell.

Trager, G. and Smith, H. (1951) *An Outline of English Structure*, Washington: American Council of Learned Societies.

Trudgill, P. (1999) *The Dialects of England*, 2nd edn., Oxford: Blackwell.

Upton, C., Kretzschmar, W. and Konopka, R. (eds.) (2001) *Oxford Dictionary of Pronunciation*, Oxford: Oxford University Press.

Wells, J. C. (1982) *Accents of English*, Cambridge: Cambridge University Press.

Wells, J. C. (2006) *English Intonation*, Cambridge: Cambridge University Press.

Wells, J. C. (2008) *Longman Pronunciation Dictionary*, 3rd edn., London: Longman.

Williams, B. (1996) 'The formulation of a transcription system for British English', in Knowles, G., Wichmann, A. and Alderson, P., *Working with Speech*, London: Longman.

# Index